Sino-EU Economic Relations

René W.H. van der Linden • Piotr Łasak

Sino-EU Economic Relations

Balancing De-risking Strategy with Global Cooperation and Competition

palgrave
macmillan

René W.H. van der Linden
International Business
The Hague University of Applied Sciences
The Hague, The Netherlands

Piotr Łasak
Institute of Economics, Finance and Management; Faculty of Management and Social Communication
Jagiellonian University
Cracow, Poland

ISBN 978-3-031-71813-7 ISBN 978-3-031-71814-4 (eBook)
https://doi.org/10.1007/978-3-031-71814-4

This Palgrave Macmillan imprint is published by the registered company Springer Nature Switzerland AG.
The registered company address is: Gewerbestrasse 11, 6330 Cham, Switzerland

Contents

List of Figures

List of Tables

CHAPTER 1

Introduction

Abstract One of the most important current issues in the twenty first century is the rise of the Chinese economy and its impact on Europe and the world. The focus of this conceptual descriptive pivot provides an overview of the EU-27 (excluding UK) economic relations with China as one of the two largest economic hegemonies in the world. The EU is the world's largest trader of industrial goods and services and ranks first in both inward and outward international investments. Apart from the already extensive Sino-EU trade and investment relations, there have also recently been increasingly more connections in the areas of financial sector and ecological development. In light of increasing geopolitical tensions with China, the EU is increasingly forced to navigate between scenarios of multilateralism, transatlantic alliance, and intensifying cooperation with China, which has created an increasing balancing act. As the Sino-US trade and especially technology disputes continue, the EU can exert important global influence to bring more balance between the two power blocs. In response to a recently hardening perception of China in the West, the EU has adopted a series of defensive economic measures as part of the EU's economic security strategy. The urgent question arises as to how the EU should position itself in these areas in the competition between the US and China or US-EU-China triangle of interconnectedness with the biggest global GDP share in this decade. In this context, it is also interesting to find out to what extent curbing economic ties with

R. W.H. van der Linden, P. Łasak, *Sino-EU Economic Relations*,
https://doi.org/10.1007/978-3-031-71814-4_1

China is much more difficult for the EU than for the US. China-EU relations are increasingly focused on "de-risking" rather than "decoupling", limiting the EU's vulnerability to eventually becoming self-sufficient from a variety of China-related geopolitical tensions. In fact, a Sino-EU "de-risking" strategy means a less aggressive and comprehensive approach than the "decoupling" of economic ties that until recently was promoted by the US through the trade and tech war. Ultimately, the EU and its individual member states have always strived for dialogue on disputes with China, whether or not through WTO settlement. The EU's major challenge in this decade is to utilize the potential policy areas for Sino-EU cooperation as much as possible with a common EU strategy towards China.

Keywords US-EU-China triangle • Multilateralism • Global value chains • Transatlantic alliance • Rules-based approach • World order • "De-risking" strategy • Economic security strategy • "Decoupling" • Country-agnostic approach to economic security • State-owned enterprise (SOE) • "Made in China" brand • "Dual circulation" strategy • 14th Five Year Plan (2021–2025) • BRICS • Belt and Road Initiative • Shanghai Cooperation Organization • Paris Climate Agreement • Green Deal plan • Inflation Reduction Act • Central bank digital currencies

Since the 1957 Treaty of Rome, there have been decades of booms, emphasized by "Europhiles", and stagnation, stressed by "Eurosceptics", in the European integration process in building a united Europe.[1] One of the most important current issues here is the rise of the Chinese economy and the impact this situation has on Europe and the world. In recent years, there have been strong economic and political tensions between China and the US, resulting in a deterioration or "decoupling" of their ties. This pivot provides an overview of the European Union's (EU or EU-27 excluding UK) economic relations with China and the rest of the world amid the ongoing conflict between the US and China as the two largest hegemonies. The focus of this conceptual descriptive study is mainly on the Sino-EU relationship rather than the EU-US relations that are inextricably linked to it with the geopolitical and economic interdependence of

[1] Unless stated otherwise, in this study the term Europe is interchangeable with the abbreviations EU-27 or EU.

the US-EU-China triangle in the background. With almost 25 percent of the world's gross domestic product (GDP) and 10 percent of the world's population, Europe has deep economic ties with both China and the US, acting as a locus of geostrategic competition between the two superpowers. The current economic relationship between China and the EU is already very extensive. The EU is the world's largest trader of industrial goods and services and ranks first in both inward and outward international investments. Bilateral trade and investment flows between the EU and China have almost doubled in the last ten years, making the relationship significant for both parties. China accounted for around 9 percent of overall EU exports in 2022, behind the US (19.8 percent) and the UK (12.8 percent), according to Eurostat. In addition, China was the largest partner for EU imports of goods (20.8 percent) in 2022 (EP, 2023). The interdependence between the two is therefore significant. The EU is the most important trading partner for 80 countries, so it faces the urgent question of how to position itself in the competition between the US and China. In this context, it is also interesting to find out to what extent curbing economic ties with China is much more difficult for the EU than for the US.

From 2018 onwards, a wave of Sino-US protectionism has also affected Sino-EU trade and technology relations in various ways. Multilateralism as a trade scenario, including the proper functioning of the World Trade Organisation (WTO), has been adversely affected, resulting in possible new trade restrictions aimed at the EU as the world's largest surplus trading bloc. The trade measures taken by the US against China could lead to retaliatory measures with indirect consequences for the EU. These could be positive for some sectors, if EU exporters have gained a comparative advantage against US exporters in Chinese markets for those US goods on which import tariffs have been imposed and that the EU can produce. Conversely, EU exporters have an advantage in the US market compared with Chinese exports for the sectors targeted with tariffs by the US. However, this positive scenario will become less strong due to the complexity of global value chains (GVCs), which could lead to increases in EU production costs due to the import tariffs of third countries, as long as they are within the EU production chain. In the ongoing Sino-US trade and tech war, the EU can exert important global influence to bring more balance to both power blocs. The following three scenarios can be distinguished for this: economic multilateralism, enhancing the EU's reliance on the transatlantic alliance, and strengthening the cooperation with

China. The first scenario involves economic multilateralism amid strategic competition between the US and China. The push for multilateralism by both, the EU and the US, is partly aimed at reforming the role of the WTO concerning China, which joined it in 2001. While the US has long had complaints about China's "economic model", the EU is mainly focused on protecting "fair trading conditions" within the WTO when it comes to, for example, the pervasive role of production subsidies and the problem of the large role of state-owned enterprises with their preferential access to the market in many sectors and their special connection with the Chinese Communist Party. Both the EU and the US have been involved in several trade disputes within the WTO with China for many years. On the other hand, China's expectations of WTO reform do not seem to be in line with the EU's. China expects to enjoy a special status as an emerging economy, which should allow China to continue to keep its economic model while sustaining to enjoy the benefits of open trade.

The second scenario aims for the EU to further strengthen its transatlantic alliance with the US in order to contain the economic and technological rise of China. However, as the US has complaints about the EU's trade surpluses with the US and is dissatisfied with the current distribution of costs and benefits of the transatlantic alliance, the EU alliance with the US could become more expensive for the EU than ever before. Furthermore, too much dependence on the US means that the EU will have to adapt its current rules-based approach as a core value of its internal market and the world order. In addition, there is another practical reason that would make it very expensive for the EU to focus entirely on the transatlantic alliance with the US. The EU is not a single country, but a group of countries with different views on the relationship with both the US and China, which will make it difficult to follow a common EU course. This dilemma has become even more pronounced over the course of this decade with the trend towards a more multipolar world order in which, surrounded by all kinds of geopolitical conflicts, both the more democratic American hegemony and the more autocratic Chinese hegemony are increasingly pitted against each other with the EU as an important trading bloc in between, with both the US and China trying to attract as many allies as possible. Some EU member states have the same approach as the US, while other countries are more focused on future cooperation with China. Under such circumstances, the EU should also adopt its own strategy for cooperation with China. By taking a coordinated approach to China, the EU will bring a far greater weight to bear in negotiations than its member states individually, and can then avoid conflicts that might arise when members pursue divergent paths. Both China and the EU have extensive and growing economic relations and many EU companies continue to maintain their ties with China as an option for the EU. The challenge is to investigate what the most feasible option is for the EU in light of the new geopolitical relationships.

The third scenario is that the EU will strengthen its cooperation with China, while maintaining a neutral relationship with the US as an anchor country. The reason for such an approach is that the Chinese market is simply too large to avoid. This third scenario could be beneficial for the EU if China really opens up to the EU foreign competition including equal treatment in that market, which is not easy to be achieved given China's state-led economic model. In the event of an ongoing Sino-US trade and tech war, the EU can better develop its own internet-related sector by strengthening cooperation with China. However, the key stumbling block will continue to be China's state capitalism and the lack of market access for foreign companies (Herrero, 2019). China's continued disregard for the rules-based international order, increasingly aggressive economic actions and support for Russia in the war with Ukraine entail direct risks for the EU's economic and security interests. Meanwhile, China's military power is beginning to match its economic power. China's strategy of "military-civil fusion" is designed to integrate innovative civilian technologies into military systems. In response, the US and EU are trying to slow China's defense and security modernization by tightening export controls. Considering these challenges, the EU and most of its member states have adjusted their assessments of China to view the country not primarily as an economic partner, but increasingly as a multidimensional systemic rival. These new developments imply a shift in EU policy towards greater convergence with the US, especially as it relates to the growing economic threat from China's unfair trade practices and strategically motivated investments in sensitive infrastructure and technologies. Recently, Chinese policies have brought about a series of economic and security problems to the EU and its individual member states. In addition to providing political and economic support to Russia, trade imbalances and substantial Chinese infrastructure investments in the EU also undermine its economic security. A tricky point in the Sino-EU relationship remains that China is trying to interfere and create division in the EU and its member states through media influence, disinformation campaigns, undermining of EU institutions whether or not via cyber attacks, coercion of individual member states and policymakers, and the uneven supply of economic incentives.

Over the past decade, the global geopolitical environment has changed dramatically with China becoming more outwardly assertive and pursuing more authoritarian internal policies. Together with China's growing power and global influence and the increasing rivalry between China and the US, this has forced Europe to answer the question of how to relate to China today, its policies, actions, and behaviour, as ideas from the past no longer seem relevant. Within this context, the EU has sought a new strategy and a new approach towards China, a so-called "de-risking" strategy that better reflects current geopolitical, political, diplomatic, and economic realities. From 2019 onwards, the EU's trade and investment dependence on China has increased sharply, resulting in economic and security risks. Supply chain disruptions during the Covid-19 pandemic and the war in Ukraine have exposed the EU's vulnerability due to its dependence on China as the main supplier of key resources crucial to the EU's economic progress and green transition. China accounts for almost all of the EU's rare earth supply, accounting for 97 percent of it the import of lithium, a key input for electric vehicles batteries. The EU also imports about 80 percent of its solar panels from China. Beyond the geopolitical circumstances of the last few years, security and political issues are increasingly coming into play through China's presence in critical infrastructure and sanctions and other retaliatory measures. In addition, there are also some economic factors behind the EU's "de-risking" strategy, such as the increasingly unfavourable trade balance; China's shrinking market for European exporters; strategic dependencies on the EU for procurement; the declining EU foreign direct investment into China and generally declining outward foreign direct investment from China globally (USCC, 2023).

China has simultaneously been considered as a partner for cooperation and negotiations on major global issues such as climate change, a technological and economic competitor as well as a systemic rival with its own set of values. However, since 2019 relations between Beijing and Brussels have become increasingly tense. Besides the Covid-19 pandemic with its devastating impact in Europe and beyond, EU-China relations have also been affected in a number of ways. These include: economic issues such as fair trade practices and respect of intellectual property rights, limited market access in China; a lack of reciprocity for European companies; concerns over 5G security; general tensions and in particular Beijing's military threats towards Taiwan; human rights issues in China, especially in Xinjiang, Tibet, and Hong Kong; and China's position on Russia's invasion of Ukraine. Taken together, these events and developments have increased tensions between Brussels and Beijing and have hardened perceptions of China in the EU. In this context, as part of the Economic Security Strategy adopted by the EU in June 2023, the EU has built a set of defensive economic measures, ranging from a foreign direct investment screening mechanism to a white paper on state subsidies, a 5G "toolbox" aimed at restricting access to non-European telecommunication manufacturers (mainly Chinese) to the European market and more recently an anti-coercion instrument (EP, 2024).

With the aim of making the EU more self-sufficient in global relations, in 2021 the concept of "strategic autonomy" was initially intended to protect the EU in the areas of trade, finance, and economy from the consequences of US tariffs and extraterritorial sanctions. However, exposure to supply chain risks from the Covid-19 pandemic and Russia's invasion of Ukraine in 2022 have completely reshaped the EU's economic strategy. Instead of protecting itself from US economic policies, Brussels is now following Washington's efforts to reduce economic dependence on China even though the EU economic and security approach is different from that of the US. While the US has given up on opening new markets with China and supports protectionist measures that violate WTO multilateral rules, the EU insists that GVCs must remain open. The reduced US involvement in the WTO, in particular by blocking the Appellate Body from its dispute settlement system, has more or less forced the EU to anticipate the risks associated with offensive unilateral actions related to its security and economic policy. Actually, the EU has adopted a country-agnostic approach to economic security that is coherent with its alignment on multilateral rules based on non-discrimination. The mantra "as open as possible, as closed as necessary" remains the cornerstone of what can be considered an "open" economic security strategy for the EU, making its strategic autonomy more limited than the US when it comes to building the pillars for the promotion and protection of its trading bloc (Jacques Delors Institute, 2024).

The China-EU relations are increasingly focused on "de-risking" rather than "decoupling", limiting the EU's vulnerability to eventually becoming self-sufficient from a variety of China-related geopolitical tensions. In fact, a Sino-EU "de-risking" strategy means a less aggressive and comprehensive approach than the "decoupling" of economic ties that until recently was promoted by the US through the trade and tech war. Decoupling refers to a complete separation of ties between two or more economies. It involves dismantling existing trade and investment relationships, cutting supply chains, and establishing new economic partnerships elsewhere. It also refers to the tendency to reduce interdependencies and economic dependence on a country, such as China, for reasons of national security (Van der Linden & Łasak, 2023). De-risking, on the other hand, is a more nuanced, less confrontational, more strategic and gradual approach that focuses on mitigating specific risks associated with economic engagement with a particular country. It involves diversifying supply chains, identifying alternative sources of goods and services, and implementing measures to reduce exposure to potential disruptions. Like decoupling, de-risking is motivated by a desire to reduce reliance on a single supplier or to protect against potential economic or geopolitical events. However, unlike decoupling, de-risking seeks to continue basic trade and investment activities once the risks have been dealt with (Capri, 2023). In practice, this means efforts to reduce economic dependence on China in certain areas where trade and investment relations may pose security risks. The key to this agenda is the diversification of strategically important supply chains, both to increase resilience and to hinder the entry of hostile countries to sensitive technology such as advanced semiconductors. The EU's de-risking strategy recognizes that economic risks and security risks are interlinked. In June 2023 the European Commission presented a new economic security strategy designed to reduce the bloc's risk exposure to supply chains, critical infrastructure, and digital technologies. The strategy aims to assess the EU's vulnerabilities and strengthen existing measures such as rules on inbound Foreign Direct Investment (FDI) and export controls to protect the EU economy. It also announces a new outbound investment mechanism for key technologies with military applications, the so-called dual-use technologies, to be launched by end-2023. In response to increased Western alignment on chip export controls, China is sending out signals that it could weaponize its dominance in critical metals through licensing restrictions on exports of key rare earth metals used in the US and EU technology and renewable energy industries. China is likely to use the demands as leverage to threaten or punish specific companies or countries. These measures are likely to have a counterproductive effect: they will further encourage the EU's diversification push, which could come at the expense of China's favourable position in the supply chains of crucial metals and materials.

The US-EU-China triangle has fuelled a complex geopolitical and economic dynamic in recent years involving the world's two largest economies marked by increasing tensions and challenges between which the EU is trying to find a delicate balancing act. The US and the EU have expressed growing concerns about China's business practices, including issues related to intellectual property, forced technology transfers and trade barriers. For years it was hoped that China would continue to open up its market, liberalise and provide a level playing field for EU and US companies, but in practice they have instead been confronted with greater state and party control, increasing nationalism along with intensifying tensions between China and the West, Taiwan, as well as other Chinese neighbours (EP, 2024). This has led to the adoption of decoupling policies to protect strategic interests and national security including restrictions on Chinese investments in key sectors, restrictions on public procurement (e.g. ban of the Chinese giant Huawei Technologies), higher duties and embargoes on certain strategic products (e.g. advanced semiconductors). As for the first side of the triangle, the US-China relationship, it has been characterized by interdependence and cooperation for at least the last thirty years of globalization. However, recent geopolitical tensions such as the Russian invasion of Ukraine and Chinese assertiveness over Taiwan, strategic considerations, i.e. the rise of Beijing as a superpower and economic concerns, e.g. de-industrialization and industrial espionage, have led to the emergence of a new trend that manifests itself in three forms of decoupling. First, economic decoupling as a geopolitical tool to contain the rise of the strategic rival, for example by decreasing imports/exports from/to China or by seeking alternatives at the supply chain level (reshoring in Mexico, Vietnam, India); second, as a fundamental prerequisite for the protection of national security, for example by reducing dependence on foreign suppliers for critical sectors, such as semiconductors; and third, as a "protectionist" industrial policy course which may involve adopting policies to promote self-sufficiency and economic independence, such as increasing local production, investing in research and development of strategic sectors, and protecting domestic industries from foreign competition. The second side of the triangle, the EU-China relationship, has recently become much more complex and strategically sensitive. Although China is one of the EU's most important trading partners, de-risking has emerged in response to concerns about China's business practices, including issues of state-owned enterprise (SOE) subsidies, unfair competition, forced technology transfer, financial transparency, human rights, intellectual property, and cybersecurity. Economic relations between China and the EU focus on trade and investment, with particular attention to the automotive, energy, and green technology and agriculture sectors. Unlike the US, the EU has always tried to manage trade issues with China through dialogue and negotiations, in particular, this applies to Germany and France. In 2020, the EU and China concluded an investment deal, which aimed to improve market access and rules for bilateral investment. However, this agreement was then frozen following the sanctions passed by the European Parliament regarding the violation of human rights in the Xinjiang region. It remains a major challenge for the EU to determine a common strategy towards China. Although the third side of the triangle, the EU-US relationship, has always been economically significant, one of the main points of contention currently concerns mutual data protection. The EU has adopted a data protection law that provides strict rules on the collection, processing, and storage of personal data. This law has an impact on US companies operating in Europe, including large technology companies, the so-called Big Techs such as Google, Facebook, Amazon, and Apple, that have played a dominant role in the global digital economy. To mitigate the effects of US "protectionist" policies, the EU has taken several initiatives including the plan to achieve greater technological and digital sovereignty, which includes boosting semiconductor manufacturing capacity within the EU in order to develop a resilient and efficient semiconductor supply chain while reducing dependency on imports from other regions of the world (Rosso, 2023).[2]

[2] If we compare the economies of the EU and the US since the Covid-19 pandemic, it must be noted that the US is miles ahead of the EU in terms of prosperity. In 2023, the US economy was 13 percent larger according to OECD figures, even though there are far fewer Americans (340 million) than EU residents (449 million). However, Americans work many more working hours than Europeans (1,800 hours per employee annually compared to 1,571 in the EU). An important explanation for this transatlantic gap is the difference in productivity, expressed in GDP per hour worked, with the US performing better than the EU, especially after the pandemic. This is partly because in the US many so-called "zombie companies" simply went bankrupt during the pandemic, while in the EU they were artificially kept alive with corona support. In the US, the unemployed quickly found new jobs at other, often more productive companies, while in the EU, plagued by staff shortages, employees often stuck at zombie companies. Another explanation for the transatlantic divide is that the US has a significantly larger tech industry, with much productivity growth in recent years thanks to advances in artificial intelligence. In addition to the fact that the US invests significantly more money in (green) innovation than the EU, the US economy has been more likely to adopt new technologies than the EU. The process of "creative destruction", as the economist Joseph Schumpeter once called it, is therefore often faster in the US (Witteman, J. 2024).

The ongoing Sino-US trade and tech war from 2018 and on top of that the Russia-Ukraine war since 2022 have increasingly led to a trend of regionalization or deglobalization, which has made the US-EU-China triangle geopolitical relations considerably more complex with less and less room to manoeuvre for mutual strategic competition and cooperation. In response to this new reality, the US has initially opted for "decoupling" and the EU for a "de-risking" strategy to protect their own trading bloc and make it more self-sufficient. However, due to the increased interdependence with the Chinese economy in recent decades, the definitions of both strategies have become somewhat blurred, are partly overlapping and sometimes difficult to distinguish. In light of the intricate Sino-US trade and investment ties, the US has shifted its narrative from a decoupling to a more de-risking strategy. The Biden administration's actions remain largely consistent with de-risking and friend-shoring strategies. However, some Biden administration policies point to broader attempts to decouple certain supply chains, particularly in high-tech sectors. For example, in August 2022, the Biden administration implemented the Chips and Science Act, aligning with de-risking priorities to incentivize domestic production and reduce external dependencies on critical technologies. In October 2022, the Chips 4 Alliance united key industry players with shared views, highlighting a strategic blend of de-risking and friend-shoring strategies. Most recently, in August 2023, President Biden issued an executive order that initiated the process of establishing an outbound investment screening mechanism. To counter the US and to a lesser extent the EU "friendshoring" and "de-risking" measures, China is trying to promote their *"Made in China"* brand and thus improve quality and innovation, for example, to modernize the industrial system and accelerate the development of the so-called "new productive forces" as discussed in the National People's Congress of March 2024. Also, the "*dual circulation*" strategy as part of the 14th Five Year Plan (2021–2025) aims to stimulate domestic consumption and reduce dependence on international markets. In addition, Beijing is expanding its semiconductor production and accelerating technological progress, turning to the Middle East to secure capital. Similarly, China has prioritized its relationships within the Indo-Pacific region and increasingly focused on groups of which the US is not a member, such as the BRICS, the Belt and Road Initiative (BRI), and the Shanghai Cooperation Organization (Benson & Sicilia, 2023).

Although the three largest trading blocs are responsible for about 40 percent of global greenhouse gas emissions (GHG) and consume almost 50 percent of the world's energy, all three have taken drastic steps in recent years to best meet the goals of the Paris Climate Agreements (2015).

As part of the 14th Five Year Plan, China has announced that it intends to bring forward, to before 2030, the date by which its GHG emissions will peak and to achieve carbon neutrality by 2060. The EU has announced plans to increase the scale of their nationally determined contributions through an ambitious Green Deal plan (2019) which has recently been criticized by the rise of populist parties. At the same time, US Biden administration has outlined the most ambitious climate agenda, viewed with some scepticism by Republicans, including the Inflation Reduction Act (2022) providing funds, tax credits, grants, and loans towards the decarbonization of the economy. The decisions made in the US-EU-China triangle will increasingly have significant consequences for the world's climate and energy security. Possible Sino-EU cooperation in this regard will be further described in Chap. 5.

Although Sino-EU trade flows will continue in the coming years, this is less likely for EU-China investment ties due to China-EU capital controls screening or scrutiny of incoming investments and regulation of foreign subsidies. Meanwhile, EU investment in China in sensitive sectors will be constrained by the likely introduction of a new EU outbound investment screening regime. The scope for EU-China co-operation is narrowing as China shifts towards greater prioritization of security and ideology over economic goals. At the same time, European companies are facing calls from consumers within Europe to reduce their supply-chain exposure to China, given concerns around human rights, and environmental and social governance. As part of China's own response to "de-risking", China is also pivoting away from European markets towards "friendlier" governments and international organisations for them (EIU, 2023).

Apart from Sino-EU relations oriented on the development of relations in the real economy, there is also an important aspect of their financial relations. This has several dimensions. Firstly, some of the scenarios about the Chinese financial situation are pessimistic. The current Chinese debt is at the level of around 280 percent of GDP, with a very big part of the private debt (40 percent) rooted in the shadow banking sector. Recently, the Chinese financial crisis scenario has become more and more common.

The financial problems in China pose a danger to the Sino-EU financial relations and generate concerns about possible contagion. Secondly, Chinese banks have built an extensive network of branches and subsidiaries across the EU. It is particularly significant in the context of the Chinese striving to enter into the global financial market. On the other hand, the EU financial system is based on banks. The similarity with the nature of the Chinese financial system gives the EU a natural advantage to enter the Chinese, still underdeveloped financial market which still cannot offer the same range of services like the financial markets in developed countries. It raises the question to what extent the Chinese decision-makers will be able to exercise their geo-economic power over the European financial market, and to what extent the EU banks will be able to benefit from the cooperation. Thirdly, both sides, China and the EU are very much involved in the creation of central bank digital currencies (CBDCs). For the Chinese economy, it is a great vehicle for internationalization of its currency. However, there is a threat that the EU, with a relatively much lower level of progress in financial technology, creates the risk of Europe becoming wedged between two poles through the more advanced digitalization of financial markets in China and the US.

In more general terms, the study on recent developments in Sino-EU relations raises the following generic research questions:

- *How can the EU's sudden change in strategy towards a much more complex relationship with China from 2019 be explained?*
- *To what extent is the EU able to diversify from China in critical sectors in the coming years as a consequence of de-risking strategy?*
- *How is the EU trying to reduce its dependence on China?*
- *In which EU policy areas is there more potential for more coordination or more competition with China in this decade?*
- *What's the most effective EU's China strategy taking into account the trend towards a more multipolar world order?*
- *What are the possible EU policy options for a more coordinated trade, investment, and sustainability relationship with China?*

This pivot consists of eight chapters, of which the introduction provides a general overview of three trade scenarios with which the EU can determine its relationship with China. This first chapter also compares the "de-risking" strategy introduced by the European Commission in 2023 with the "decoupling" more applicable to the US-China relationship from

2018 onwards. The second chapter further describes the three scenarios in a historical context including the challenges of the EU's "de-risking" strategy. The third chapter discusses trade relations between the EU and China and their interdependence including the impact of the ongoing Sino-US trade war on the Sino-EU relationship. The mutual investment relations between China and the EU and their interdependencies are elaborated in Chap. 4, which also describes industries with business potential and the EU's Global Gateway Strategy. Chapter 5 discussed the cooperation and competition of sustainability, digitalization, and associated green technology policies of the EU and China and their interdependence. The Sino-EU financial cooperation and the prospects for reforming global financial markets are further examined in Chap. 6, which also discusses the quest of both trading blocs for digitalization of their currencies and the consequences for their monetary policy. The possible future policy areas for Sino-US cooperation or competition and the complications of a coordinated joint EU-China policy are explained in Chap. 7. Finally, Chap. 8 focuses on some concluding remarks and recommendations describing the EU's de-risking strategy and a possible common EU industry policy in the context of the transition from a unipolar to a multipolar world order during this decade.

References

Benson, E., & Sicilia, G. (2023, December 20). *A closer look at de-risking*. Center for Strategic & International Studies. https://www.csis.org/analysis/closer-look-de-risking

Capri, A. (2023, December 12). *China decoupling versus de-risking: What's the difference?* Hinrich Foundation. https://www.hinrichfoundation.com/research/article/trade-and-geopolitics/china-decoupling-vs-de-risking/

EIU Economist Intelligent Unit. (2023). *What does "de-risking" from China mean for Europe? Understand how the EU's economic security approach will shape future relations*. https://www.eiu.com/n/campaigns/eu-de-risking-from-china/

EP European Parliament. (2023, October). *EU-China trade relations*. https://www.europarl.europa.eu/RegData/etudes/ATAG/2023/753952/EPRS_ATA(2023)753952_EN.pdf

EP European Parliament. (2024, March). *EU-China relations: De-risking or de-coupling – The future of the EU-strategy towards China*. https://www.europarl.europa.eu/RegData/etudes/STUD/2024/754446/EXPO_STU(2024)754446_EN.pdf

Herrero, A. G. (2019, October). Europe in the midst of China–US strategic economic competition: What are the European Union's options? *Journal of Chinese Economic and Business Studies.* Routledge Taylor & Francis Group.

Jacques Delors Institute. (2024, February). *Shield up: How China, Europe, Japan and the United States shape the world through economic security.* Policy paper number 298. https://institutdelors.eu/wp-content/uploads/2024/02/PP298_Comparing-_Economic_Security_Strategies_Fabry_Kohler-Suzuk_Lamy_Sibona_EN.pdf

Rosso, S. del. (2023, August 01). *The USA-EU-China Triangle: between decoupling and de-risking, medium.* https://simonedelrosso.medium.com/the-usa-eu-china-triangle-between-decoupling-and-de-risking-9f9f7eea303e

USCC US-China Economic and Security Review commission, gov. (2023, November 11). *Europe-China relations; Convergence and divergence in transatlantic cooperation, chapter 5, section 1.* https://www.uscc.gov/sites/default/files/2023-11/Chapter_5_Section_1%2D%2DEurope-China_Relations.pdf

Van der Linden, R. W. H., & Łasak, P. (2023). *Financial interdependence, digitalization and technological rivalries: Perspectives on future cooperation and integration in Sino-American financial systems.* Springer Nature.

Witteman, J. (2024, July, 20). America is miles ahead of Europe in terms of prosperity. *de Volkskrant* (Dutch newspaper).

CHAPTER 2

The New Challenges for Sino–EU Relations

Abstract In a recent historical context, the Sino–EU relationship is initially seen as a "strategic partnership" from which both markets' businesses have benefited greatly. But due to all kinds of geopolitical disputes, their relations have gradually changed into a 'systemic rivalry' which can differ hugely per EU member state. With the rise of China and other emerging market countries in the 1990s, the share of China's GDP in global GDP has grown significantly, while the share of the US's and EU's GDP has become relatively smaller. The post-war rules-based US-led world order of multilateralism based on globalization and liberalization of goods, services, and factors of production has significantly stimulated trade and investment opportunities from which initially the US in particular, but later also the EU and China, were able to fully benefit. Although China has been participating in Western multilateral international institutions, such as the WTO, for a number of decades, it has recently become increasingly evident that their interpretation of multilateralism is based more on bilateral agreements rather than universally binding rules. With the advent of a more authoritative and assertive state-led, China-oriented regional governance system under Xi Jinping, a much more powerful China is increasingly rejecting the principles of the multilateral unipolar world order in favour of a less emphatic multipolar world order on democratic norms and values. Particularly because of China's partnership with Russia and other recent geopolitical disputes with the West, it has become

R. W.H. van der Linden, P. Łasak, *Sino-EU Economic Relations*,
https://doi.org/10.1007/978-3-031-71814-4_2

increasingly difficult for the EU to maintain an equidistant and bridging role between democratic Washington and autocratic Beijing. The response to the changed mutual relations with China as a partner, competitor, or systemic rival is the new EU 'de-risking' strategy introduced since 2023 and the interconnected EU Economic Security Strategy. The key to this agenda is the diversification of strategic key supply chains, both to increase resilience and to hinder enemy countries' access to sensitive technology such as advanced semiconductors.

Keywords World order • Covid-19 pandemic • "Strategic partnership" • "Systemic rivalry" • Central and Eastern European (CEE) countries • "Open Door Policy" • Global Security Initiative (GSI) • Group 17+1 • Three-pronged approach • Rules-based economic order • Foreign Direct Investment Screening • Cybersecurity

2.1 The Current China–EU Relationship in a Recent Historical Context

The post-war world order is based on the development of economic globalization and far-reaching liberalization of economic processes associated with the emergence of GVCs. They were the consequences of the globalization of trade and production. In the meantime, many accompanying processes occurred including far-reaching financialization of the international economy, European monetary integration, and the rapid growth of the Chinese economy. All of these developments were supported by the activity of international institutions and far-reaching multilateralism. At the moment, two important features accompanying the current process of multilateralism can be distinguished. The first one is that the cooperation and international flows in such areas as trade, capital, people, technology, ideas, and information is greater than in any previous era, and seems to be irreversible. The second one is that the economic power is shifting. Some rich countries are losing their global position, while others are gaining in importance. An example is the rise of the most important emerging market countries, abbreviated as BRICS (Brazil, Russia, India, China, and South Africa) and their growing power internationally (Bouchard et al., 2013). It creates a greater need to manage the tectonic shifts in the geopolitical and international economic scene that can cause economic obstacles in different parts of the world, whether or not through disruptions in the GVCs. In addition to developments that are important in the long term, also such particular aspects as the Covid-19 pandemic, the war in Ukraine, and the wave of refugees in 2015 have had a significant impact on the world order.

One of the most important current issues here is the rise of the Chinese economy and its impact on Europe and the world. Since the beginning of the twenty-first century, the share of Chinese GDP in global GDP has been growing, while the share of the US's and the EU's GDP is shrinking. Before the Covid-19 pandemic it was more than 10 per cent while two decades ago it was only 2–3 per cent (Fig. 2.1). Such rapid growth of the Chinese economy is causing important changes for the global economy and is not being met with an enthusiastic reception from other global partners. In recent years, there have been strong economic and political tensions between China and the US, resulting in a deterioration or "decoupling" of their ties (Van der Linden & Łasak, 2023). While initially the trade rivalry between China and the US became increasingly intense, this now also applies to their bilateral financial and technological rivalry. Despite the decoupling processes between China and the US, their markets are very attractive to each other, and in addition to decoupling,

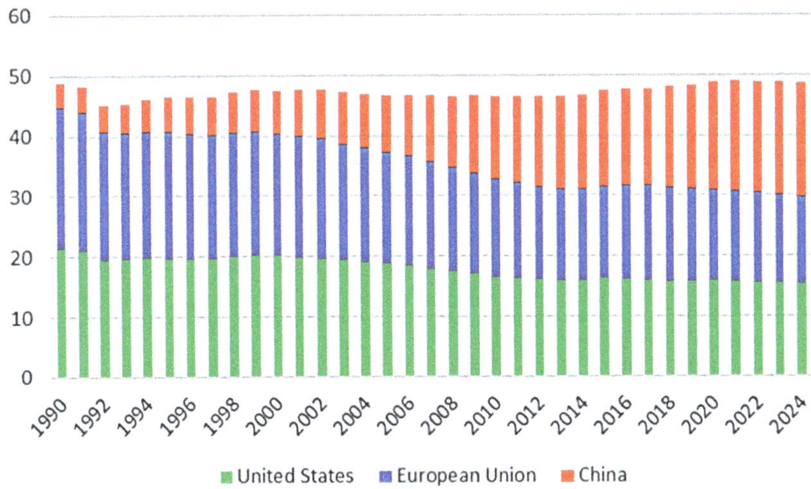

Fig. 2.1 GDP based on purchasing power parity (PPP) of China, the EU, and the US as percentage of world GDP in the period 1990–2024. Source: own elaboration based on IMF database

Sino–US cooperation initiatives are also observed in some areas such as military dialogue, renewable energy, and science and technology. As China seeks to strengthen its global influence and its impact on the current world order and the US seeks to contain China, it is argued that the future of multilateralism is bleak. The lack of trust between the two superpowers will inevitably involve a shift from the post-globalized world (Gaillard et al., 2023; Woods, 2023). An additional danger arises from the current geopolitical tensions where the Western unipolar democratic world order that has set the tone for economic developments in recent decades is increasingly being questioned by emerging economies such as China with its 'no limits partnership' with Russia and other developing countries that strive for a more multipolar world order where there is more room for different forms of authoritarianism (see Chap. 8).

For most of the 1990s and 2000s, both the EU and its member states viewed China primarily as an economic opportunity. This view of China was reinforced by China's accession to the WTO in 2001. Although political differences persisted, the EU's main hope was that continued economic exchanges with Beijing and unprecedented economic progress in China would eventually lead to political change. Since 2003, the EU–China relationship has been called a "strategic partnership", and business between Chinese and Western companies has only increased in subsequent years. However, EU–China relations soon started to cool. China grew dissatisfied that the EU had neither lifted its military embargo as a result of the 1989 massacre in Tiananmen Square nor granted the country market economy status. This was interpreted not only as the EU's inability to break free from the US influence but also as a failure to honour its WTO obligations and hence a disrespectful political gesture. For its part, the EU grew dissatisfied not only with economic results from relations that did not meet its expectations but also with China's unwillingness to open its market to European firms, while access to the European market for Chinese firms became significantly easier. In addition, some aspects of human rights problems in China have emerged in connection with the 2008 Beijing Olympics and, in particular, the protests in Tibet.

When Xi Jinping became China's leader in 2012, there were initial hopes that he would further deepen the reform process in China, but relations continued to deteriorate as China's economic policies became more statist, its political system became increasingly centralized and authoritarian, and its foreign policy displayed greater assertion. The BRI introduced in 2013 was initially seen as an economic opportunity. At this time, a diplomatic initiative between China and sixteen Central and Eastern European (CEE) countries (eleven of which were EU members) was developing quickly, raising hopes for economic benefits in the CEE region, but fuelling worries elsewhere in the EU that China was dividing the continent. The shift towards a more critical EU position towards China began in 2017, which also coincided with the election of Donald Trump and a deterioration of US–China relations. The EU was becoming increasingly dissatisfied and worried about domestic developments in China and some Chinese foreign policy actions, such as those in the South China Sea and the Taiwan Strait. In March 2019, the European Commission (EC) released an "EU-China: A strategic outlook" document introducing a "partner, competitor, systemic rival" triptych that would become an influential framework through which the EU would strategically approach China. An important change in the EU–China strategy compared to the period before March 2019 is that economic opportunities in China are no longer emphasized, but China is regarded as an economic competitor. The label "partner", in turn, is mainly applied to areas of global governance (such as climate change, global health, and piracy), where the EU views China as a necessary actor to negotiate with, despite sharing different perspectives. Naturally, the twenty-seven27 individual EU member states differ in their relations with China, whether or not because of their involvement in the BRI. For example, countries like Lithuania and the Czech Republic have focused more on "systemic rivalry" with China, often leading them to outright question their obligations to the country. The Hungarian government, on the other hand, sees China solely as an economic opportunity and has largely abandoned the triptych (EP, 2024).

2.2 The Strategy Based on Multilateralism

The term "multilateralism" has a universal meaning, which is a way of operating in the international system according to which three or more states coordinate their behaviours based on generalized principles of conduct (Scott, 2013). Adam Smith attempted to identify multilateralism based on three key characteristics: the generation of and adherence to rules and norms, the promotion of reciprocity and inclusiveness, and the construction of institutions that embody these rules (norms) and guarantee the principles of reciprocity and inclusiveness (Erdoğan, 2023). In the current time, however, multilateralism has different meanings, and it is important to highlight that different countries have different understandings of and approaches to multilateralism. In this context also the positions of the EU and China on multilateralism are different.

Europe has a long history of confrontation and conflicts and knows well all their negative aspects. For this reason, currently, it strongly supports international integration and cooperation. The best option for the achievement of this goal is the pursuit of multilateralism. Multilateralism is, however, a part of EU values and principles, and the concept of multilateralism is engrained in the European DNA. Moreover, Europe not only bases the process of its integration on multilateralism but also belongs to the winners of the development of multilateralism. Europeans are highly dependent on global markets, international finance, innovation, and cooperation between countries and regions. The whole process of European integration runs by the rules of multilateralism. In the European dimension, multilateralism means primarily cooperation through collective actions. Europe also attaches great importance to international organizations in the international political system, especially when it comes to providing a stable framework for dialogue between states (Erdoğan, 2023).

China has been an active participant in many international institutions in recent decades. It played a crucial role, especially since 1978 when the "Open Door Policy" was announced by Deng Xiaoping. Since that time China has perceived the peaceful international environment and international rules as vital for the realization of its national interests, especially for the continuation of its economic development. From the Chinese perspective, however, multilateralism is not a given international order, which should be obeyed, but rather a means by which states can achieve their own goals in an environment of dialogue that reduces the risk of violent conflict between states (Erdoğan, 2023). According to this approach, China applies policy which is described by the statement "Dialogue without confrontation, partnership without alliance". The statement presents an approach according to which multilateralism is treated as "Multilateralism with Chinese characteristics", sometimes called multibilateralism. It means that Chinese interactions with other countries are based not on universally binding rules but on bilateral agreements.

The current economic cooperation between China and the EU is mainly based on trade and investments. In this context, in order to shape Sino–EU relations based on multilateralism it is sufficient to keep the rules of the WTO (Herrero, 2019). It means imposing market practices and protecting fair trade and building the relations between the EU, China, and the rest of the world according to these rules. A big challenge, however, is the unique economic model of China. China's integration into the global trading system has been propelling its economic growth. At the same time, however, its rise has led to increasing frictions with other trade partners, due to the inherent conflicts between its "socialist market economy", the relative economic decline of the West, and the inability of the WTO to upgrade its rules and the resulting "regulatory stalemate".[1] These clashes led to a plethora of complaints against China, with those against SOEs and forced technology transfer as two prime examples (Mavroidis & Sapir, 2021). These features are part of the new Chinese policy, which stems from the growing role of the country in the multilateral trading system. The main elements of the new Chinese foreign policy embrace: (1) a shift in foreign economic strategy from convergence to divergence (i.e. the transition from accepting the multilateral world order to rejecting the principles of that order); (2) selective de-coupling from the WTO, including the creation of new rules and new spaces; and (3) the development of a new China-centric regional governance system, characterized by state-led infrastructure development (Pantekoek et al., 2022).

Despite the current situation and the growing role of China at the international level, there are some scenarios for the EU. The EU could leverage its respected social values and experiences to influence China's international strategies towards peace, sustainability, and inclusiveness. Chinese leaders would like to gain greater international recognition, which offers some opportunities for the EU. There is potential for China's convergence to some extent with policies advocated by Europeans. In the meantime, the EU could continue its role as a bridge between China and the US by working with them and other members of the WTO on the agenda of reforming this institution. The EU institutions are familiar with the challenges connected with such a strategy. The vice-president of the EU Commission and High Representative of the EU for Foreign Affairs and Security Policy, Joseph Borell, during his visit to China in October 2023 referred to the current crisis with multilateralism. He highlighted that currently "multipolarity has increased, but multilateralism has decreased". He also said that "multilateralism cannot be based on cherry-picking" (EEAS, 2023), which expresses the current EU interpretation of multilateralism.

[1] It is a situation in which the process of creation or implementation of regulations is halted or slowed down due to the lack of agreement between the parties.

2.3 The EU's Reliance on the Partnership with the US

The EU actively considers different economic and geopolitical relations with external partners, as the consequence of the current situation and the rapidly changing world order. Currently, the most natural for the EU is the strategy oriented on enhancing the strategic partnership with the US. The EU cannot be equidistant between democratic Washington and authoritarian Beijing. Its values are bound to be closer to those of the US. The EU and the US positions on China have converged especially for the last few years, due to growing Chinese assertiveness and partnership with Russia since the invasion of Ukraine. Even apart from the war in Ukraine, the EU largely agrees with the US that the authoritarian regime in Beijing opposes democratic values and universal human rights, relies on unfair competition and subsidies to gain advantage and achieve technological leadership, propagates selective multilateralism to promote its interests, reacts with massive pressure to criticism, and aggressively pursues its territorial claims. They also confirm that the Chinese approach constitutes a challenge to liberal democracies and Europe's interests in the Asia-Pacific region (Schweisgut, 2021). In such a complicated geopolitical environment, when continuing the economic approach with close relations with the US in the long run, the EU should follow the US strategy oriented on limiting China's influence in investment and technology. But the EU needs to be autonomous enough to push back against ill-considered US policies. Moreover, the strategy of closer economic relations between the EU and the US is not obvious as the US already had some disputes with the EU and Washington wants to dominate the EU economically. The most symbolic slogan describing such policy, which treated allies as foes rather than friends, is Trump's "America First". It also would be very costly for the EU to become dependent on the US and to completely limit economic cooperation with China. It means that for the success of the transatlantic partnership between the US and the EU, there is a need for a genuine strategic partnership which will serve both sides equally well. An important argument is that the US is also undecided about what policy it wants to pursue towards China. The options are between an ongoing trade and tech war on the one hand, and de-escalation and partial detente on the other (*The Economist*, 2023). Additionally, the US does not present consistent policy towards the EU. After an unprecedented degree of alignment on Russia in the first half of 2022, including the quick and efficient rollout of a series of groundbreaking sanctions packages, the US and Europe stepped back into dispute territory with the fallout from measures taken by Washington. Recent US actions have amplified the divide between "Atlanticists" and "strategic autonomists" and made it harder for Europe to follow in Washington's footsteps on, for example, export controls or outbound investment screening.

For the EU the strategy oriented on closer cooperation with the US serves economically in such a way that Europe is attempting to reduce its reliance on China in areas ranging from rare earth minerals to 5G infrastructure. Another argument for such a strategy is that US President Joe Biden uses the term "America is back". It is a signal that the US is returning to multilateralism and close cooperation with its allies against global challenges and threats. The EU is aware that more coordination with the US is needed not only to meet the challenges presented by China but also to prevent lasting damage to the multilateral system, particularly the role of the WTO. Even if it will not be possible in the long term to keep the same role of the EU as currently, during Biden's presidency, it is in Europe's interest to create a stronger but more equal alliance with the US, which increases its leverage against China. Such a strategy is possible as the US takes seriously the Chinese position as a big rival and threat and is interested in closer cooperation and economic partnership with Europe against China (Schweisgut, 2021). It is also important for the EU to diversify its policy and to strengthen relations with other partners and increase its presence in the Indo-Pacific region. The Covid-19 pandemic showed that overreliance on China-based supply chains can also be harmful to the EU economies, and greater balance and diversification in supply chains, manufacturing, and trade is needed. This broadens the EU orientation towards other countries and is consistent with the strategy supported by the US. Firms from the EU are looking to other developing countries than China, like India, Mexico, Morocco, Norway, and Turkey (*The Economist*, 2023).

China is interested in neutralizing the EU strategy for closer cooperation with the US. The approach proposed by Xi Jinping was manifested in February 2023. The initiative is a Global Security Initiative (GSI) and proposes an alternative system of international affairs to the current "rules-based" order led by the US and its partners in Europe and the Indo-Pacific. There are presented core principles of diplomacy, oriented on highlighting the importance of state sovereignty and territorial integrity, noninterference in the international affairs of states, and opposition to "unilateral" sanctions and "bloc confrontation" (Schuman et al., 2023). It is a comprehensive vision of a new world order which formulates the ideological backbone for a global governance system that elevates Chinese influence at the expense of American power. Even though this is a unilateral approach proposed by the Chinese side, Europe cannot remain completely indifferent to such far-reaching initiatives.

2.4 Strengthening the Cooperation Between China and the EU

Another scenario of future relations between China and the EU is the strategy based on Sino–EU cooperation. It means strengthening the bilateral relations between China and the EU instead of the other two scenarios: (1) strengthening the multilateral cooperation or (2) confrontation between Western countries and China. From the EU perspective, the Chinese market becomes too large to be avoided, and from this point of view, the cost of keeping a neutral position (between China and the US) is too high. It is also important that Europe is more economically exposed to China than America (*The Economist*, 2023). It is assessed that in the medium term the business opportunities will be greater in China than in the US. If China decides to open its market to foreign companies, the costs for Europe of remaining neutral between China and the US become much greater. For this reason, the best option for the EU is to cooperate not only with the US but also with China. It is notable that the current EU policy towards China presents a dual approach: cooperation and economic interdependence on the one hand and competition and conflicts on the other hand. While European leaders are aware of the necessity of strengthening the economic bonds between the EU and China, Europe is dealing with lingering apprehensions over Chinese dominance of vital resources, market access barriers, and trade imbalances. It becomes necessary for the EU to rebalance its economic partnership with China (Herrero, 2019). In this context, it is crucial to understand and address the priorities that the EU has set for its relations with China, and also the Chinese priorities for its relations with the EU. In the EU a crucial aspect is economic security. It becomes clear that the best option for the EU, apart from creating many strong ties with China and fostering a strategy oriented on building closer economic relationships, is the "de-risking" strategy aimed at hazard mitigation, partnership diversification, trade interaction reconfiguration, and relocating operations to tackle dependencies in critical sectors.

Currently, both China and the EU are promoting structural reforms oriented on enhancing economic and social development. In this context a very important link connecting China with the EU is the Chinese BRI. It gives great opportunities to promote Sino–EU relations based on win-win cooperation. The cooperation between China and the EU embraces trade and investment, but also peace, security, and people-to-people exchange. Besides these aspects, there are also some other areas with great potential for cooperation, like the environment, finance, and technology (Łasak & van der Linden, 2019). The BRI is oriented towards trade and investments in many fields. In a broader sense, it also embraces cultural aspects.

In this context for the EU, apart from strengthening trade relations, another important factor is the policy-oriented screening of the FDI to identify, evaluate, and mitigate the potential risks arising from FDI and also regulations of foreign subsidies (Politi, 2023). Over the past decade, Chinese companies have invested heavily in key sectors of the EU, including banks, carmakers, robotics, power grids and utilities, high-tech manufacturing, solar farms, roads, and railways. The involvement of Chinese capital in Europe was growing and, especially before the Covid-19 pandemic (2016–2017), it reached the highest value. Europe was the second market for Chinese brownfield FDI, when a company purchases or leases an existing facility, after the US. It should be emphasized that in recent years the share of investments by SOEs has been decreasing and the share of investments by private enterprises in total Chinese direct investments in Europe has been increasing (Table 2.1). It means that business relations have a greater chance to be based more on economic principles than political ones.

It is significant, however, that when compared to other regions, the cooperation between China and the EU is one of the most complicated. The main problem here is the lack of comprehensive uniform strategy presented by the entire EU. Some countries (here might be included the members of group 17+1) are stronger supporters of BRI and closer cooperation with China while others (mostly the Western EU countries) are more toned down (Łasak & van der Linden, 2019). The Western countries build greater cooperation with China via bilateral relations and processes. It results in a very large share and value of Chinese investments in some countries, such as Germany and the UK (Fig. 2.2). The economic

Table 2.1 The annual value of Chinese FDI in Europe (EU-27) and the UK in the period 2012–2021

	2012	*2013*	*2014*	*2015*	*2016*	*2017*	*2018*	*2019*	*2020*	*2021*
Total value (bln EUR)	12	7.7	15.4	26.9	47.4	40	20.3	15.1	7.9	10.6
Investments of private sector (bln EUR)	3.9	4.7	5	10.2	34	13	11	10.8	6.6	9.3
Share of investments of private sector in total investments	33	61	33	38	72	32	54	71	82	88
Investments of public sector (bln EUR)	8.1	3	10.4	16.7	13.5	27	9.2	4.3	1.4	1.3
Share of investments of public sector in total investments	67	39	67	62	28	68	46	29	18	12

Source: own elaboration based on Radomska 2023

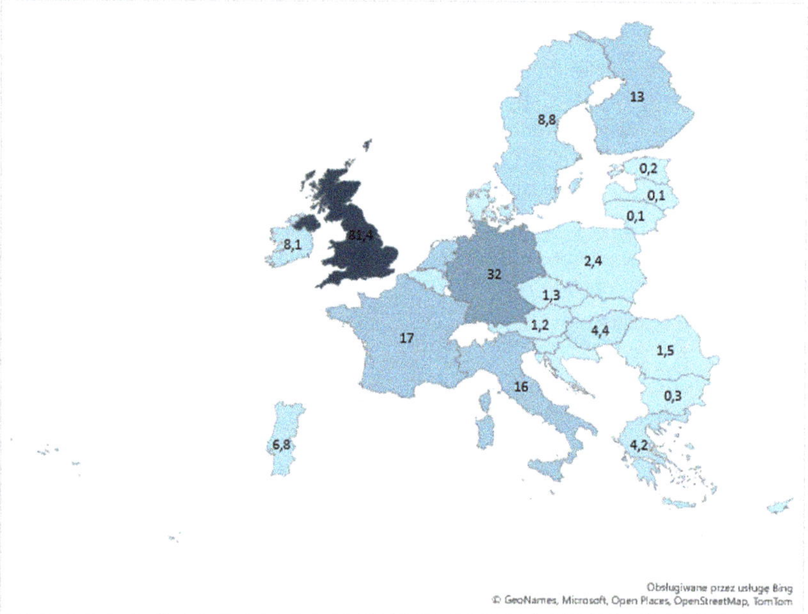

Fig. 2.2 Cumulative value of Chinese FDI inflow to European countries in the period 2000–2022 (in billion EUR). Source: own elaboration based on Rhodium Group, the Mercator Institute for China Studies, 2022

relations are much stronger between Western EU countries than Central and Eastern Europe.

When comparing the Chinese inward FDI stocks by partner country, countries like Germany, France, and Luxemburg definitely dominate (Fig. 2.3). As a result, when considering the European FDI in China by source country during the last decade, Germany, the UK (even though it is currently not an EU member state), France, and the Netherlands dominate (Fig. 2.4). The same situation is related to the Chinese FDI host countries. Among the biggest recipients of Chinese FDI during the last decade were Germany, France, and the Netherlands (Fig. 2.5).

When considering Sino–EU economic cooperation, it is important to focus not only on the value of transactions but also on the structure of the industry. There are some branches where closer cooperation with China is needed as the Chinese market offers a lot of investment opportunities (see Sect. 4.4). Here could be included such sectors as automotive and end consumer-oriented investments. Automotive investments have become the core driver of Chinese investments in Europe. Among the most important might be electric vehicles and batteries. These are followed by such consumer-oriented investments as: (1) consumer products and services and (2) entertainment, media, and education. Also, infrastructure, real

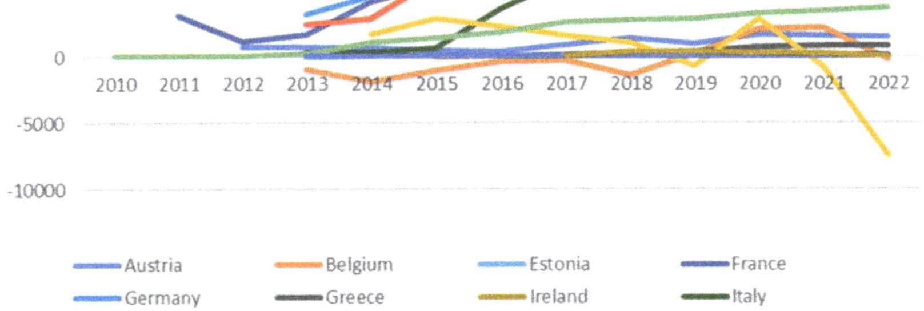

Fig. 2.3 Chinese inward FDI stocks by partner country in the period 2010–2022 (million USD). Source: own elaboration based on OECD database

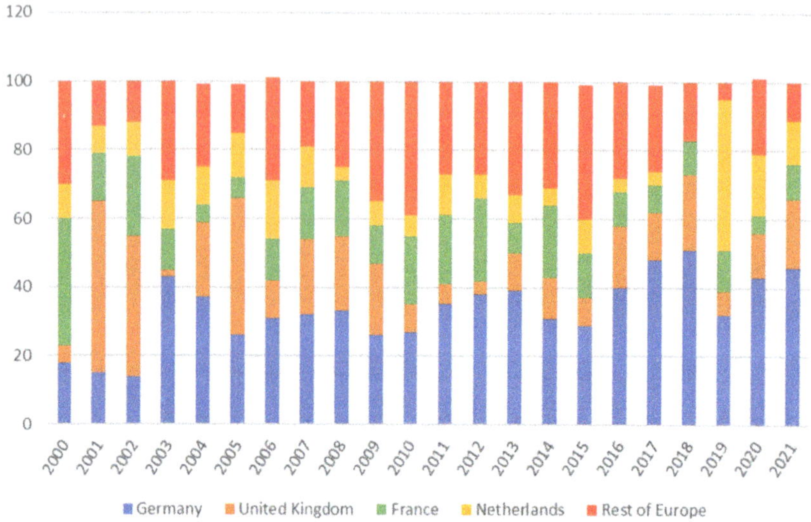

Fig. 2.4 European FDI in China by source country in the period 2000–2021 (percentage of annual FDI transaction value). Source: own elaboration based on Kratz et al., 2022

estate, finance and energy, machinery, health, pharma and biotech, and energy sectors are important. When considering European investments in China, five sectors play a crucial role, as shown in the last column of Table 2.2: automotive, food processing, pharmaceuticals and biotechnology, chemicals, and consumer products manufacturing (Huld, 2023).

Some of the enumerated branches should be protected in the EU countries. The ongoing EU policies were based on the assumption that China would gradually move towards a liberal open market economy. As China is not converging towards this kind of economic model and instead consolidates its own economic, social, and political model, the EU needs to adapt its means of engagement to this new reality. They embrace a European legal framework to improve information on and control of inbound FDI from China, a bilateral investment agreement, a reform of export controls regarding exports with dual-use potential, and guidelines for securing critical infrastructure (e.g. 5G networks). Additionally, policymakers started to address the challenge of economic coercion based on trade interdependence. Finally, industrial policy in high-tech sectors experienced a revival at the European level, the Chips Act tabled by the

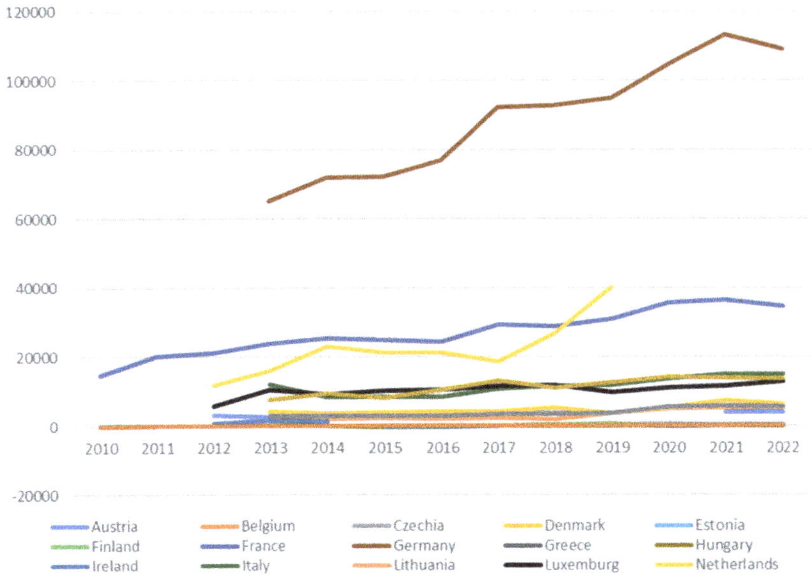

Fig. 2.5 Chinese outward FDI stocks by partner country (million USD) in the period 2010–2022. Source: own elaboration based on OECD database

Commission in February 2022 providing the latest example in kind. All of these initiatives are part of the EU's search for responses to the economic and strategic challenges inherent in its relations with China (Schild & Schmidt, 2023). More information about Sino–EU investments is given in Chap. 4.

2.5 The New Sino-EU "De-risking" Strategy

The year 2023 marks the 20th anniversary of the establishment of the comprehensive strategic partnership between China and the EU. It brought, however, a radical change in the EU approach to the Sino–EU relationship. In June 2023, the European Commission announced a new strategy called "European economic security strategy". Despite officially being aimed to reduce security risks across supply chains, critical infrastructure, and digital technology, in practice it is related to Sino–EU economic cooperation. According to the strategy, the EU is opting for strategic autonomy and economic security. It leads to a reduction of

Table 2.2 Top sectors for European FDI in China, 2000–2021 (top five sectors; percentage of total FDI transaction value over the period)

	2000–2007	*2008–2012*	*2013–2017*	*2018–2021*
1	Plastic, rubber, and other materials (14 per cent)	Automotive equipment and components (24 per cent)	Automotive equipment and components (32 per cent)	Automotive equipment and components (31 per cent)
2	Financial services (13 per cent)	Financial services (9 per cent)	Chemicals (10 per cent)	Food processing and distribution (14 per cent)
3	Automotive, equipment and components (11 per cent)	Consumer products—manufacturing (8 per cent)	Food processing and distribution (10 per cent)	Pharmaceuticals and biotechnology (10 per cent)
4	Chemicals (11 per cent)	Chemicals (8 per cent)	Plastic, rubber, and other materials (6 per cent)	Chemicals (9 per cent)
5	Coal, oil, and gas (9 per cent)	Industrial machinery (7 per cent)	Consumer products—manufacturing (5 per cent)	Consumer products – manufacturing (5 per cent)

Source: own elaboration based on Kratz et al. (2022)

dependence on "systemic rivals" like China. This EU China strategy is not only initiated by the European Commission led by Ursula von der Leyen, but is also supported by the European Council.

Compared to the US approach to Chinese policy, China–EU relations are increasingly focused on "de-risking" rather than "decoupling", limiting the EU's vulnerability to eventually becoming more self-sufficient from China. The de-risking strategy reflects a form of "trade protectionism" that contradicts the principles of market economy and free trade rules. It focuses on three aspects, enhancing Europe's independence in critical technological areas and raw material supply, as well as autonomy in production chains. They are treated as crucial for European economic security. The strategy sets out a three-pronged approach: (1) Promoting EU competitiveness by strengthening the single market, supporting a strong and resilient economy; (2) Protecting the EU's economic security through a range of existing policies and tools, and considering new ones to address possible gaps; and (3) Partnering with the broadest possible range of partners to strengthen economic security, including through furthering and finalizing trade agreements, reinforcing other partnerships, and strengthening the international rules-based economic order and multilateral institutions (EC, 2024; EP, 2024). This new approach is leading to the reduction of the role of strategic competitors like China, but at the same time maintains the cooperation in the majority of goods and services trade between China and Europe. In fact, a Sino-EU "de-risking" strategy means a less aggressive and comprehensive approach than the "decoupling" of economic ties that until recently was promoted by the US through the trade and tech war. It is, however, also a strategy with limited cooperation with China. In practice, this means efforts to reduce the economic dependence of the EU on China in certain areas where trade and investment relations may pose security risks. The key to this agenda is the diversification of strategically important supply chains, both to increase resilience and to hinder the entry of hostile countries to sensitive technology such as advanced semiconductors. The EU's de-risking strategy recognizes that economic risks and security risks are interlinked.

The strategy proposes a new assessment of vulnerabilities, strengthened rules on key areas like FDI and export controls, and new rules on outbound investment. Going into detail, four pillars for the EU economic de-risking strategy from China can be enumerated:

1. Increase competitiveness and resilience: making the EU economy and selected branches of industry more competitive and resilient (health, digital and clean-tech sectors, resilience on cyber, maritime space and digital markets).
2. Better use of existing trade instruments: activities aimed at better using the EU's existing toolbox and trade instruments.
3. Develop new defensive tools: this activity should focus on some critical sectors, and define the features of the Sino-EU relationship in sensitive areas such as microelectronics, quantum computing, robotics, artificial intelligence, and biotech. It is crucial to ensure that companies' capital, expertise, and knowledge are not used to enhance the military and intelligence capabilities of those who are also systemic rivals. The gaps must be closed which allow the leakage of emerging and sensitive technologies.
4. Align with other partners: the EU needs to better strengthen its economic security and alignment with other partners: New Zealand, Australia, India, ASEAN, and Mercosur. It is crucial to create a Global Gateway strategy.

EU's supply chain resilience and diversity of its trade must be a central element of EU economic de-risking strategy. This means that supply chains should be diversified by removing the reliance upon a single corporation or country. These aims and needed actions were strengthened at the beginning of 2024. On January 24, 2024, the European Commission adopted a comprehensive trade, investment, and research package as part of the roll-out of the European Economic Security Strategy of June 20, 2023. There were five elements of this package (EC, 2024):

1. A legislative proposal for the revision of the EU Foreign Direct Investment Screening Regulation to improve its effectiveness and efficiency.
2. A White Paper launching a process to identify potential security risks linked to EU investment in third countries (outbound investment).
3. A White Paper on how to make EU controls more effective for export of goods with civilian and military use (dual-use goods), in the interest of upholding international security and safeguarding EU security interests in the context of growing geopolitical tensions.
4. A White Paper on enhancing support for research and development involving technologies with dual-use potential.
5. A proposal for a Council Recommendation on enhancing research security.

The strategy of June 2023 identified four risk categories to be addressed as a matter of priority: supply chains; physical and cybersecurity of critical infrastructure; technology security and technology leakage; and weaponization of economic dependencies or economic coercion. The comprehensive trade, investment, and research package is aimed to address these issues. The plans do not name any country, but the EU contrasts "reliable partners" with "countries of concern" and highlights "de-risking", the bloc's policy of reducing economic reliance on China, which the bloc regards with more suspicion due to its close ties to Russia (Reuters, 2024). However, it is significant that some actions are difficult to accomplish. For this reason, the EU has scaled back its plans for tighter controls on outbound investment and sensitive technology exports to avoid a "turf war", i.e. a confrontation between EU member states for access to resources or capital (Bounds, 2024). The last initiative highlights that de-risking is crucial for the EU, but also actively managed cooperation (on both internal and external level) is important for shaping proper relations between the EU and its economic partners, especially for Sino–EU relations.

References

Bouchard, C., Peterson, J., & Tocci, N. (Eds.). (2013). *Multilateralism in the 21st century: Europe's quest for effectiveness*. Routledge.

Bounds, A. (2024, January 24). EU scales back China investment screening plans to avoid 'turf war'. *Financial Times*. https://www.ft.com/content/5baeab2d-6ef6-4882-80b7-9c2e4e186f35

EC European Commission. (2024, January 24). *Memo on European Economic Security*. https://ec.europa.eu/commission/presscorner/detail/en/qanda_24_364

EEAS. (2023, October 13). *China: Speech by high representative/vice-president Josep Borrell at Peking University*. https://www.eeas.europa.eu/eeas/china-speech-high-representativevice-president-josep-borrell-peking-university_en

EP European Parliament. (2024, March). *EU-China relations: De-risking or de-coupling – The future of the EU-strategy towards China*. https://www.europarl.europa.eu/RegData/etudes/STUD/2024/754446/EXPO_STU(2024)754446_EN.pdf

Erdoğan, S. (2023). The European Union and Chinese approaches to multilateralism: Converging or diverging? *Bölgesel Araştırmalar Dergisi, 7*(2), 414–433.

Gaillard, N., Gotoh, F., & Michalek, R. (2023). Globalization and the liberal international order threatened by the US–China rivalry. In *The future of multilateralism and globalization in the age of the US–China rivalry* (pp. 1–12). Routledge.

Herrero, A. G. (2019). Europe in the midst of China–US strategic economic competition: What are the European Union's options? *Journal of Chinese Economics and Business Studies, 17*(4), 403–423. https://doi.org/10.1080/14765284.2019.1706292

Huld, A. (2023, January 25). *Prospects for European companies in China in 2023*. China Briefing.

Kratz, A., Barkin, N., & Dudley, L. (2022, September 14). *The chosen few: A fresh look at European FDI in China*. Rhodium Group Report.

Łasak, P., & Van der Linden, R. W. H. (2019). *The financial implications of China's belt and road initiative*. Springer International Publishing.

Mavroidis, P. C., & Sapir, A. (2021). *China and the WTO: Why multilateralism still matters*. Princeton University Press.

Pantekoek, S., Bartmann, I., & Lanz, H. (2022). *China's role in the multilateral trade system. Emerging trends, driving forces, and implications for Germany and European Union*. Fredrich Ebert Stiftung.

Politi, A. (2023). The paradigm shift in EU-China relations and the limits of the EU's current strategy towards China: A relational perspective. *Asian Affairs*, 1–24.

Reuters. (2024). https://www.reuters.com/markets/europe/eu-draws-up-economic-security-plans-with-mind-china-2024-01-24/

Schild, J., & Schmidt, D. (2023). *EU and US foreign economic policy responses to China: The end of naivety*. Taylor & Francis.

Schuman, M., Fulton, J., & Gering, T. (2023, June 21). *How Beijing's newest global initiatives seek to remake the world order*. Atlantic Council Issue Brief.

Schweisgut, H. D. (2021). The European Union: Caught between the United States and China. *Politique etrangere*, (3), 25–37.

Scott, D. A. (2013). Multipolarity, multilateralism and beyond…? EU–China understandings of the international system. *International Relations, 27*(1), 30–51.

The Economist. (2023, May 15). *Europe can't decide how to unplug from China*. https://www.economist.com/international/2023/05/15/europe-cant-decide-how-to-unplug-from-china

Van der Linden, R. W. H., & Łasak, P. (2023). *Financial interdependence, digitalization and technological rivalries: Perspectives on future cooperation and integration in Sino-American financial systems*. Springer Nature.

Woods, N. (2023). Multilateralism in the twenty-first century. *Global Perspectives, 4*(1). https://doi.org/10.1525/gp.2023.68310

CHAPTER 3

Sino–EU Trade Relations and Their Interdependencies

Abstract The ongoing Sino-US trade and tech war has indirectly led to the EU playing an even greater role as one of China's most important trading partners. Conversely, the Chinese market is also very important for the EU, as China is the third largest destination for EU exports. Since the Second World War, the EU has played a central role in developing the rules-based international trading system, allowing its companies to enjoy fairer market access abroad. The EU's Common Commercial or Trade Policy operates as a single player within the WTO and is represented by the European Commission rather than individual member states. In recent decades, the WTO has been expanded to include many transition and developing countries with their own wishes to reform the WTO such as gaining better access to global value chains. The EU is looking for opportunities to modernize the WTO through, among other aspects, state interventions as an approach to climate transition and more inclusiveness of developing countries. However, recently there has been little motivation from the US and China to reform the WTO, endangering the EU as a defender of the WTO. Another more current issue concerns the changing European industrial landscape, as China has been trying to export its overcapacity for a long time and has opened many more firms and factories than the markets need. In response, both the US and EU express some concerns about fair competition with Chinese state-owned enterprises and call for reciprocity on trade and market access. Although China is further

R. W.H. van der Linden, P. Łasak, *Sino-EU Economic Relations*,
https://doi.org/10.1007/978-3-031-71814-4_3

opening its market to foreign firms, it is still denied the "market economy" status at the WTO by both the US and the EU. All these developments have led to the EU being increasingly forced to manoeuvre between the desire to protect a cleaner environment with dependence on China's cheap electric cars, solar panels, and rare earths and, on the other hand, the desire for a common EU industrial policy, which forces the EU, like the US, to resort to protectionism in the hope of becoming less import dependent on China.

Keywords Bretton Woods Conference • WTO Dispute Settlement Body • Carbon Border Adjustment Mechanism • Non-market economy status • US Inflation Reduction Act • US Chips Act • EU-Asia connectivity strategy (2018)

3.1 The Current Trade Pattern Between the EU, China, and the US

For more than a decade, the EU has had a trade deficit in goods with China, while running a surplus in trade in services. This trade deficit in goods has increased sharply from 2020 with a more or less stable smaller surplus in services trade. Over the same period, the EU has had a trade surplus in goods with the US, which has stagnated somewhat since 2020 with a deficit in services trade. Significant impacts on Sino-EU trade had such geopolitical tensions as the Covid-19 pandemic and later the war in Ukraine. The EU trade balance has significantly deteriorated since the beginning of the pandemic. This change was unilateral, and unfavourable for the EU. The total value of EU-China trade has grown, accelerating from just 4.6 per cent year-on-year growth in 2020 to over 20 per cent year-on-year growth in 2021 and 2022. Despite such acceleration, it has been driven mainly by China's exports to the EU and is in line with China's overall strong trade numbers over this period. The growth in China's exports is in part thanks to the sharp increase in demand in Western countries for Chinese-made goods during the pandemic (Fig. 3.1).

The EU had a trade deficit of EUR 395.7 billion in 2022, expanding further from EUR 250.3 billion in 2021. Only one EU member state, Ireland, recorded a trade surplus with China in 2022. China remains the EU's largest source of imports, with total imports reaching EUR 626

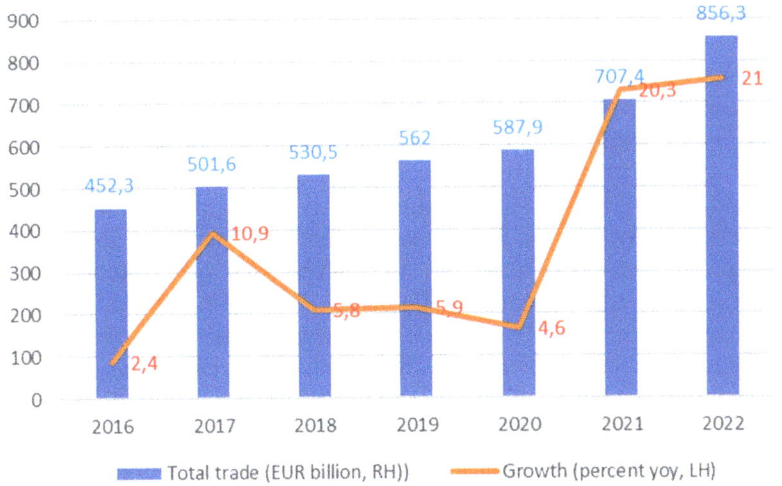

Fig. 3.1 Growth in EU-China trade. Source: own elaboration based on Eurostat

billion, accounting for 20.8 per cent of all EU imports in 2022. The deficit improved in 2023, and it achieved the level of EUR 291 billion.

China is the third largest destination for EU exports, after the US and the UK, with exports to China reaching EUR 230 billion in 2022, accounting for 9 per cent of the EU's total exports.

China's largest trade partner within the EU in 2022 was Germany, with total trade reaching EUR 236.9 billion, according to Eurostat data. Germany was also the largest exporter of goods to China, with total exports reaching EUR 106.9 billion in 2022. However, the Netherlands was the largest importer of Chinese goods, with total imports reaching EUR 130 billion (EC Eurostat, 2024).

Although China has been Germany's most important trading partner for many years, over the period 2023–2024, US trade potential with Germany has increased at the expense of China's, especially in the automotive industry. Relatively strong growth in the US has boosted demand for German products, while China's weaker domestic demand and ability to produce goods it previously imported from Germany (especially cars) has reduced exports to China. Although Germany has long approached China as a strategic trading partner, it has recently urged its companies, partly due to geopolitical conflicts, to reduce risks from China in accordance with the new EU and German China strategy. In addition, the

Chinese economy has been stagnating for a number of years and the German business community is experiencing increasing competition from subsidized Chinese companies (Kiderlin, 2024).

The top-traded goods between the EU and China are machinery and vehicles, other manufactured goods, and chemicals. China's top export goods to the EU in 2022 were telecommunications equipment, followed by automatic data processing machines, and electrical machinery and equipment. Meanwhile, the EU's top exported goods to China are motor cars and vehicles, electronic tubes and valves, and auto components. Leading services exports from the US to the EU are in the professional and management services, intellectual property, and financial services sectors. Leading services exports from China to the EU are business services, transportation, computer and information services, construction services, and travel. While machinery and vehicles dominate two-way trade, there are many other important trade industries. For instance, Europe remains highly reliant on China for light manufactured goods, such as toys, furniture, textiles, apparel, and footwear, while several EU countries also export significant numbers of food and agricultural products to China, as well as niche speciality products, such as leather goods and alcohol.

Given the current geopolitical environment, it is unlikely that the EU will return to a more balanced trade situation with China. It is mostly the result of the high dependence of the EU on Chinese imports for its green energy transition, which has only accelerated since Russia invaded Ukraine in February 2022 (Huld, 2023).

3.2 The Current Role of the WTO in the Three Blocs' Relationships

So far, the EU has played a central role in developing the international trading system since the Second World War. As a result of the Bretton Woods Conference (July 1–23, 1944), aimed at shaping the post-war international trade order, the General Agreement on Trade and Tariffs (GATT) was signed in 1947, which gradually reduced tariffs on manufactured goods in particular. The main aim of the agreement was to promote international trade by reducing or eliminating trade barriers and support international cooperation in this area. In January 1, 1995, GATT was replaced by the WTO, which is an intergovernmental organization that regulates and facilitates international trade and pursues a broader goal of liberalizing not only goods, but also services and intellectual property rights. The functioning of the WTO is organized under the United Nations system and focuses on enforcement from member states of several principles related to the world trading system. The WTO is also responsible for a dispute settlement system related to international trade, development of international agreements related to trade policy, and the accession process of new WTO members, as well as for ensuring their compliance with international trade rules.

Currently, the EU is exploring the possibility of modernizing or reforming the WTO. Like the GATT (and later the WTO), the EU was itself originally designed to remove customs barriers and promote trade between its member states. The EU single market was partly inspired by GATT principles and practices. The EU has always been among the main promoters of effective international trade based on the rule of law. Such a system helps ensure that its businesses enjoy fair market access abroad, and thus supports economic growth, both domestically and in third countries, particularly less developed ones. Nowadays intra-EU trade liberalization is much greater than the solution implemented via the WTO.

The EU's common commercial policy is one of the areas in which the EU as such has full and exclusive competency. In other words, the EU operates as a single actor at the WTO and is represented by the Commission rather than by the member states. The Commission negotiates trade agreements and defends the EU's interests before the WTO Dispute Settlement Body on behalf of all twenty-seven member states. The Commission regularly consults and reports to the Council and Parliament on the content and strategy for the multilateral discussions. Under the Lisbon Treaty, the Council and Parliament are co-legislators with an equal say on international trade matters.

Through the WTO, the EU has also sought to promote a multilateral framework for trade negotiations, intended to complement bilateral negotiations. However, the stalemate in the Doha Round and the fact that other trading partners have turned to bilateral agreements have compelled the EU to partly reconsider its long-standing strategy and return to regional and bilateral negotiations.

The current impasses at the WTO are also a sign that the international trading system has changed dramatically in the past twenty years. The system has evolved, with new actors—essentially transition and developing countries—playing a central role. The liberalization of the international trading system has benefited some developing countries, which have experienced an unprecedented phase of sustained economic growth. The EU is well aware of these new dynamics. It has pointed to the need to move beyond the negotiation approach of the past years and try innovative approaches to address the increased importance of regulatory issues, as compared to tariffs. In 2023, the EU identified the following three areas as key for WTO deliberative engagement:

- Trade policy and state intervention in support of industrial sectors. State interventions, such as subsidies, can be an important part of addressing policy challenges like the climate transition, but can also have impacts on trade and investment.
- Trade and global environmental challenges. As WTO members step up their efforts on the climate transition, there is a need to look at how measures are designed and their impact on trade.
- Trade and inclusiveness. How to share the benefits of trade more widely, how to better link poorer developing countries into global supply chains, and how to better integrate stakeholders in the trade policymaking process are all issues which need discussion.

The EU continues to play a leading role in the WTO's ongoing reform, process with a fully functioning WTO dispute settlement system by 2024 remaining the EU's top priority. Other priorities concern the negotiation function and that the WTO builds on recent multilateral and plurilateral progress and reaches ambitious outcomes in ongoing work (EP, 2023).

The EU is highly dependent on a functioning multilateral trading system for its growth, prosperity, and economic stability. Since 1995, the WTO has embodied that system. But the EU, the US, and many non-Western actors now recognize that the organization is in crisis. Some areas are indicated as those which should be submitted to deep reforms (Table 3.1). Europeans are among the prominent defenders of the existing system and key supporters of WTO reform. But at the same time, the EU is increasingly using trade policy to serve its climate change agenda in ways that risk undermining the trading bloc's multilateral credibility. If the EU wants to achieve both its trade and climate change goals, it must reconcile these two agendas.

The European Commission understands the WTO crisis as comprising four main elements. Firstly, the organization's rules have not kept up with the changing patterns of global trade, which has diminished its negotiating function. Secondly, the WTO fails to ensure that all members comply

Table 3.1 The main areas where WTO reforms are needed

Problem	*Current situation*	*Suggested changes*
Further trade liberalization and greater role of developing countries	The Doha Round is the last one and it ended up with stagnation in trade liberalization. Developed countries focus more on intellectual property rights whereas developing countries are oriented on liberalization of agricultural products, removal of trade concessions, etc.	Development of mechanisms aimed at considering to the same extent the interests of all member states
Dispute resolution system	Changes in the length of the processes, asymmetry of power between different countries	The reforms of the principles related to the dispute resolution system: shorter time frames, establishment of permanent panel body, special treatment of developing countries
The status of WTO member countries	Two-thirds of the WTO's 164 member states continue to claim "developing country" status, a designation that allows them to take advantage of certain benefits and exemptions to obligations not granted to advanced economies	The implementation of the status of a developing or developed country
Implementation of market mechanisms	The lack of a level playing field between member states by creating stronger rules and definitions governing state-owned enterprises and "market-distorting subsidies"	Improvement of transparency and subsidy notifications from member states, removing investment barriers in service industries, and adopting specific rules to discourage forced technology transfers

Source: own elaboration

with their obligation to report their trade measures. Thirdly, the organization's dispute settlement system has been paralyzed since 2019, when the US began to block the appointment of appellate judges. These judicial vetoes stem from Washington's own perception of the crisis, that is, its assessment that the WTO tends to hand down rulings that are either reflective of judicial overreach or just outright wrong. Finally, the WTO's rules and principles are straining under the weight of the geopolitical rivalry between the US and China (which are each other's largest trade partners). The US has, for example, introduced major subsidies for a green economy and semiconductors that include stipulations for a minimum level of domestic production or "local content requirements" whose use the WTO restricts. It has also unilaterally applied export controls to limit China's access to advanced semiconductor technologies. US policymakers, in turn, maintain that the WTO has allowed Beijing to "hack" the rules to its benefit. The Biden administration does not differ markedly from its predecessors in these assessments and its response, despite its declarative support for multilateralism. Middle-income countries have their own set of concerns. In India and South Africa especially, leaders object to the WTO's inability to incorporate their development interests into its agenda. They also tend to oppose a move from multilateral to plurilateral formats, which the EU and others have privileged in the face of the organization's broader negotiating deadlock. Despite all the opposition the WTO has encountered in recent years, the WTO continues to play a crucial role as the pole of stability in world trade. Forty-seven members (including the EU) have created a functioning interim mechanism, which has already proven its usefulness in hearing dozens of disputes. At least two-thirds of world trade is still based on the WTO, and informal discussions on WTO reform began in 2022.

However, the US may not be willing to make a serious effort to make the WTO reasonably functional again. It should unblock the appellate body and refrain from openly violating WTO rules, for example through further export controls. It appears that the US is currently putting its great power competition with China ahead of the stability of the international trading system. This risks the marginalization of the WTO and the increasing fragmentation of world trade. In contrast, China has no interest in further decline within the WTO, but it is also unlikely that the country will push for reforms. China is the world's largest exporter and benefits enormously from the stability provided by the current WTO system. China also appears to have met the letter of its WTO obligations, although critics doubt this. China therefore has little incentive to accept additional concessions that could accompany reforms. On the contrary, China is taking advantage of the US withdrawal from the WTO by gradually strengthening its position in the organization's secretariat in Geneva. Moreover, the US trade war against China provides alibi for Beijing to maintain its various trade restrictions and industrial subsidies.

The EU and its member states are thus key defenders and reformers of the WTO system. But the bloc's trade policy seems to be pulling it in opposite directions. On the one hand, the EU is positioning itself as a leader in efforts to preserve and reform the WTO by addressing the elements of the crisis as the European Commission understands them. The EU relies for this on its like-minded partners from the Ottawa Group, who share a belief in the urgency of modernizing WTO rules. But the EU also aims to reach a "high degree of convergence in the reform agenda" with the US, and is planning a major round of diplomacy with African countries to build consensus on WTO reform. On the other hand, the EU is increasingly using trade policy in support of its efforts to combat climate change. This approach could be effective in addressing the bloc's climate priorities. But it could also undermine the existing multilateral trading system. The most prominent of the EU's initiatives in the trade-and-climate area is its Carbon Border Adjustment Mechanism (CBAM), which will apply higher tariffs on carbon-intensive goods entering the bloc. This initiative is proving highly controversial, as are recent directives on deforestation and corporate sustainability due diligence, mainly due to their unilateral character. India, for instance, has recently protested that the CBAM could amount to behind-the-border protectionism and has raised those concerns at the WTO Committee on Trade and Investment. Governments in Southern Africa fear the CBAM's economic consequences—since their exports to the EU are frequently based on carbon-intensive production.

The EU needs to engage in three types of actions to reconcile its trade and climate agendas. Firstly, it should build stronger and more diverse coalitions. It has already begun to do this through its co-leadership of the Coalition of Trade Ministers on Climate, which Ecuador, the EU, Kenya, and New Zealand announced at the World Economic Forum in Davos earlier this year. The coalition involves more than fifty countries (including all EU member states) and aims to boost international cooperation on climate, trade, and sustainable development through discussions at a high, ministerial level. Notably, its membership goes beyond the usual suspects of the Ottawa Group and includes eight African members as well as the US. But it needs to prove its usefulness: the coalition still does not have an agreed agenda, and China and India are not on board. The EU and member states need to help build a broader coalition, with a critical mass, if the initiative is to exert pressure on the latter two who are among the world's largest CO^2 emitters. Secondly, the EU needs to defend its trade-and-climate measures. It should show readiness to engage in a two-way exchange with other WTO members on the design of its instruments and their implementation, and it holds strong cards to make its case. Even if the CBAM is a unilateral measure, the EU can still justify it under the rules of the WTO whose jurisprudence has already overcome the alleged conflict between trade commitments and climate action. Moreover, trade experts underline that the true challenge is not in justifying the permissibility of CBAMs in principle, but in "ensuring that their design does not undermine their stated objectives". Finally, the EU should respond with care to the US Inflation Reduction Act (IRA). The bloc's recent actions and statements suggest that it has opted for a non-confrontational approach to the US's set of green subsidies. The EU's response involves loosening state aid rules to extend its own subsidies and trying to include European firms as far as possible in American supply chains and tax credit regimes. This approach poses a risk for the EU's reputation as a defender of a rules-based international trading system. However, leaders in Brussels seem to have concluded that they cannot afford (economically and strategically) to confront the US and China if these countries are pursuing a different line. Still, the EU should at least try to show that it can make industrial policy without resorting to local content requirements like the US. It should also aim to boost European competitiveness more broadly in ways that do not clash with WTO rules and principles. Ultimately, the EU needs to promote a multilateral or plurilateral agreement on permissible environmental subsidies and this should engage all of the world's largest CO^2 emitters (Zerka, 2023).

3.3 The Need for Greater Trade Liberalization Versus Trade Protectionism in Sino–EU Relations

Since mutual import tariffs were gradually reduced in 1994 and China joined the WTO in 2001, trade between China and the EU has grown enormously. The EU increased imports of goods from China and, to a lesser extent, exports to China. European consumers and producers benefit from increased trade with China in several ways. For European consumers, this means a greater diversity of products available at significantly lower prices. The prices of electrical appliances, electronics, plastics, and textiles in particular are lower than they would have been without this trade cooperation. This benefits both consumers and producers who use these products as input. EU producers benefit from easier access to a large market and therefore export larger volumes to China. Among the EU member states, it is mainly the Eastern European countries, Finland, Sweden, and the Netherlands that are most closely intertwined with Chinese production chains. As European producers are able to import cheaper resources (i.e. parts and materials) from China, their level of competitiveness on the global market has also increased. Economic integration with China has a geopolitical dimension, too. It reduces the potential tensions, as the costs related to a trade conflict are higher when there is greater economic interdependence. As a result, countries may use economic sanctions, such as imposing import tariffs, to achieve certain political goals. However, this knife cuts both ways. There is a concern that China has gained too much geopolitical power due to a growing mutual dependence. Europe is importing a large number of products from China, some of which have few alternatives (i.e. rare earth metals). This makes Europe vulnerable to Chinese sanctions of a geopolitical nature. For example, Lithuania was punished with a trade boycott by China for increasing its ties with Taiwan. One of the solutions to counter such dependence is a decoupling from China, which would mean fewer or even no related imports or exports (CPB, 2022).

China's non-market economy (NME) status had a major impact on China's successes in the WTO. It means that when entering the WTO, China has been subject to a special presumption that Chinese producers cannot prove market economy conditions exist in their industries. For this reason foreign investigating authorities were forced to use Chinese prices and costs on products subject to anti-dumping measures. The special status was granted to the Chinese economy for fifteen years. Under Article 15 of China's Protocol of Accession, NME status would no longer apply if China could establish under the national law of the importing WTO member that it is a market economy; otherwise, the NME provision would expire on December 11, 2016. This date has passed, but the US continues to label China an NME. In response to the continued NME treatment, China issued a complaint with the WTO against the EU on December 12, 2016. A similar case has been made against the US; however, the US case is not progressing. This is one of the reasons for the tensions between China, the US, and the EU (Griswold & Parks, 2019).

When China joined the WTO in 2001, the country agreed to reform and liberalize important parts of its economy. Although it has made progress and continues to liberalize several non-sensitive industries, issues remain regarding a lack of transparency; industrial policies and non-tariff measures that discriminate against foreign companies; strong government intervention in the economy which means that state-owned enterprises are in a dominant position with unequal access to subsidies and cheap financing; and poor enforcement of intellectual property rights. In its relationship with China, the EU is primarily focused on promoting reciprocity, a level playing field, and fair competition in the field of trade. The strategy includes a strong focus on improving market access opportunities. Reference is also made to the problems of overcapacity. It calls for an ambitious commitment from China at the multilateral level (EU, 2023).

Over the years, Europe's industrial landscape has been reshaped several times by China opening far more firms and factories than markets need. Whereas in the past the threat involved basic commodities such as steel, lately China has achieved dominance in advanced sectors that European firms once led, like wind turbines and solar energy. Another such sector is cars, an industry with a powerful grip on public hearts and minds. China has focused on battery-powered electric vehicles. Even after consolidation in the sector, over one hundred firms still produce such cars. A few brands are world-class. Most are cheaper than Western rivals. Chinese firms became dominant through a mixture of subsidies and coercive transfers of foreign technologies, but also hard work and foresight, as they leapfrogged slow-to-change foreign firms. They make far more cars than China's market demands.

Some European governments are ready to resort to crude protectionism. In October 2023 the European Commission launched an investigation into Chinese electric vehicles and whether their makers receive subsidies that break international trade laws and harm EU firms. The probe could see punitive tariffs imposed. It has already angered China. German carmakers—whose Chinese operations remain huge, though less profitable than before—are anxious about retaliation. In a recent speech, Ursula von der Leyen retorted to German politicians that Europe faces unsustainable competition. "There is clear overcapacity in China, and this overcapacity will be exported. Especially if overcapacity is driven by direct and indirect subsidies", she said. "This will worsen as China's economy slows down, and its domestic demand does not pick up" (*The Economist*, 2023)

If we consider the Sino–EU trade relationship from a European perspective, the EU's policy objectives can be depicted as three sides of a triangle (Fig. 3.2). On the one hand, there is the EU's determination, like the US and China, to embrace green, low-carbon technologies. For example, the EU could choose to impose no or minimal tariffs on imports of

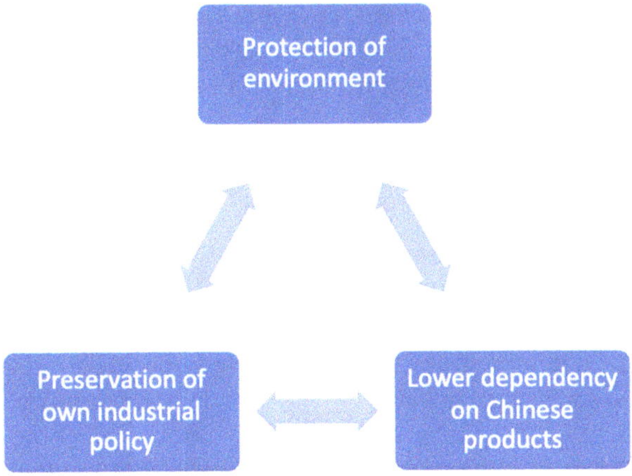

Fig. 3.2 The EU's policy objectives triangle. Source: own elaboration

relatively cheap Chinese electric cars, because that is good for the environment. However, the downside of this is that this might lead to de-industrialization and loss of technological knowledge in strategic industrial sectors, with all the dire social consequences that entails. On another side of the triangle is its desire to end damaging dependencies on Chinese products and inputs. In recent years, China has explicitly sought to make the West dependent on itself by controlling all parts of the global supply chains in green and high technologies and securing access to necessary resources. The third side of the triangle is aimed at maintaining or creating an EU industrial policy to retain or create new industrial jobs as much as possible. In the US, the Congress under President Biden has approved the Inflation Reduction Act (IRA) (2022), which provides hundreds of billions of dollars in investments in, and subsidies for, domestic production of electric cars, wind turbines, and hydrogen. In addition, thanks to the Chips Act of 2022, more investment in the construction of electronics factories is being made than ever. Currently, the EU cannot achieve all three sides of its triangle at the same time, but the urgent question that increasingly arises within the EU in the current geopolitical playing field between the US and China is whether the EU needs a proactive common industrial policy or should leave this to the individual member states (see Chap. 8). Not only can the potential negative consequences of overcapacity from China be better controlled through a common EU industrial policy, it is also likely that the EU member states will then compete less with each other for tax benefits and low labor costs in sectors where the EU countries have common interests, such as defence and energy (Mees, 2024).

The EU could prioritize the first goal, focusing on the environment by importing Chinese-made electric vehicles and other clean tech, but that would ignore fears about lost businesses and jobs. European officials worry that millions of subsidized Chinese cars could be dumped on its markets each year, especially as tariffs and other rules close US markets to batteries from China. Of course, guarding European jobs and businesses by blocking Chinese vehicles would raise the opposite problem: the EU would be less green than it wants to be and such protectionism would also harm drivers.

A bigger challenge pertains to the second side of the triangle. China is determined to keep the EU reliant on its supply chains. Indeed, in 2020 Xi Jinping called such dependencies a "powerful counter-measure" for controlling foreigners. Since then China has imposed export controls on critical minerals, including a form of man-made graphite that European firms need to make advanced batteries. The EU could work to avoid dependencies on Chinese technologies while trying to keep factories humming at home. But without Chinese minerals, for instance, those same factories cannot produce electric cars or batteries at scale, forcing Europe to forgo or delay its low-carbon revolution. For years to come, then, Europe must choose between the planet, independence from China, and shielding industry at home.

China, for its part, continues to invest heavily in manufacturing. Chinese officials appear to believe that their country's market power and control of clean technologies will force Europe to back down. They hope that von der Leyen's commission will lack support from key EU governments. Perhaps they are right. If they are wrong, this could end with a trade war (*The Economist*, 2023).

3.4 The Consequences of the Sino-US Trade War for Sino–EU Relations

Since 2018, the trade war between the US and China has had economic consequences for these largest trading blocs, but this certainly also applies to the EU through trade diversion to European markets. So far, the

Sino-US trade war has created both new opportunities for the EU member states to expand their trade with China, and threats since the EU was also the target of US trade barriers, sanctions, or threats of sanctions. Among the EU member states, Germany and France could benefit the most from this Sino-US trade dispute. European companies can gain market share in China; thanks to trade substitution caused by tariffs, this may particularly apply to the European automotive industry. On the other hand, tariffs that increase in the US-China trade war have led to a slowdown in the Chinese economy, resulting in rising labour costs in China that offer fewer opportunities for European companies present in China. The US and the EU share some concerns about China's trade policy. Both the US and the EU have a large trade deficit with China (USD 382.3 billion for the US and EUR 395.7 billion for the EU in 2022). However, within the EU the situation varies from member state to member state. Germany has a trade surplus with China, while France, Italy, and Spain have trade deficits. This difference makes it difficult for the EU to formulate a common Sino-EU trade policy.

Both the US and the EU express some concerns about China's state-owned companies and fair competition in this country and are asking for reciprocity in trade and market access. This needs to be guaranteed by the Chinese authorities since the EU continues to have a greater volume of business and investments with the US, so the Chinese offer should be highly attractive to European producers considering directing products to China instead of the US. Although China is further opening its market to foreign companies, it is still assigned "market economy" status at the WTO by both the US and the EU. Washington and Brussels have also complained about possible breaches of intellectual property rights by Chinese companies. Furthermore, the US and the EU feel challenged by the world's growing interest in China's BRI. Whereas Washington has rejected this programme, the EU has mixed perceptions about the BRI, as several EU members chose to join China's initiative. Moreover, the EU-Asia connectivity strategy (2018) to enhance connectivity in a rules-based and sustainable manner by means of infrastructure upgrading, developed together with Japan, is not an alternative to the BRI, but a complementary project. Although the European Commission described China as a systemic rival, the EU is looking to develop cooperation with China. As China and the EU are both the targets of US trade sanctions, more coordination is required between the two trading blocs to promote free trade. Beijing and Brussels have repeatedly claimed their willingness to fight against protectionism and support multilateralism (Goulard, 2020). However, the US dramatically increased protectionist measures against China in May 2024 to protect their own market by increasing tariffs on electric vehicles (EVs) from 25 to 100 per cent due to extensive Chinese state subsidies and non-market practices that could lead to substantial risks of overcapacity. Partly in response to this with a similar argument, the EU has recently also considered taking protectionist measures at a more limited level. Given the huge volume of trade between China and the EU in the automotive industry, Chinese authorities have repeatedly urged Brussels to avoid protectionist actions against Chinese EVs, warning that such actions could lead to trade frictions spiralling out of control and this could lead to countermeasures, for example with the export of pork from the EU to China (Wang & Tao, 2024).

References

CPB. (2022, June). *Economic interwovenness with China through trade: Two sides of the same coin*. Netherlands Bureau for Economic Policy Analysis. https://www.cpb.nl/sites/default/files/omnidownload/CPB-Publication-Economic-interwovenness-with-China-through-trade.pdf

EC Eurostat. (2024, March 04). *China-EU – International trade in goods statistics*. https://ec.europa.eu/eurostat/statistics-explained/index.php?title=China-EU_-_international_trade_in_goods_statistics

EP European Parliament. (2023, February 22). *The European Union and the World Trade Organization*. https://www.europarl.europa.eu/factsheets/en/sheet/161/the-european-union-and-the-world-trade-organization

EU European Union. (2023). *Trade*. https://policy.trade.ec.europa.eu/eu-trade-relationships-country-and-region/countries-and-regions/china_en

Goulard, S. (2020). The impact of the US–China trade war on the European Union. *Global Journal of Emerging Market Economies, 12*(1), 56–68.

Griswold, D., & Parks, D. (2019). *Is China a non-market economy?* https://www.mercatus.org/economic-insights/expert-commentary/china-non-market-economy

Huld, A. (2023, April 04). *EU-China relations – Trade, investment, and recent developments*. China Briefing. https://www.china-briefing.com/news/eu-china-relations-trade-investment-and-recent-developments

Kiderlin, S. (2024, May). The U.S. is now Germany's biggest trading partner — Taking over from China. *CNBC*. https://www.cnbc.com/2024/05/10/the-us-is-now-germanys-biggest-trading-partner-ahead-of-china.html

Mees, H. (2024, June 04). Europe needs its own industrial policy. *Volkskrant* (Dutch newspaper).

The Economist. (2023, December 07). *China and the EU risk a trade war.* https://www.economist.com/china/2023/12/07/china-and-the-eu-risk-a-trade-war?

Wang, C., & Tao, M. (2024, June 03). Chinese officials urge EU to avoid protectionist actions. *Global Times.* https://www.globaltimes.cn/page/202406/1313556.shtml

Zerka, P. (2023, May 15). *Multilateral trade: The green European genie at the WTO.* European Council on Foreign Relations (ecfr.eu). https://ecfr.eu/article/multilateral-trade-the-green-european-genie-at-the-wto/

CHAPTER 4

Sino-EU Investment Relations and Their Interdependencies

Abstract Since the outbreak of the Covid-19 pandemic, the EU's foreign direct investments in China have declined somewhat compared to the previous decade, with a greater concentration of investments in certain sectors coming from a more limited number of European countries. This is partly the result of tensions with the US over semiconductor technology, concerns about increased anti-espionage activities and a more general stagnation of the Chinese economy with declining interest rates compared to those in the US and the EU. Conversely, China's global foreign investment has recently fallen due to geopolitical tensions, the ongoing Sino-US trade and tech war, tighter outward capital controls, the Chinese government's crackdown on its technology sector (e.g. Alibaba), and stricter screening of investments in the EU. The overall decline in Chinese investment in the EU has been accompanied by a recent surge of Chinese greenfield investment including electric vehicles above those of mergers and acquisitions at a much lower level than a few years ago. Before 2019, Sino-EU investment opportunities were discussed through a Comprehensive Investment Agreement (CAI) to strengthen cross-border economic ties between the two strategic markets in terms of market access, a level playing field, sustainable development, and a mechanism for the settlement of disputes between states. However, the more recent deterioration in EU–China relations has led to the suspension of ratification of the CAI. Since 2019 the European Commission has launched and adopted

R. W.H. van der Linden, P. Łasak, *Sino-EU Economic Relations*,
https://doi.org/10.1007/978-3-031-71814-4_4

several instruments and regulations as part of the EU's "de-risking" and Economic Security Strategy. They were aimed at improving capacities to deal with the increasing economic and geopolitical influence of China, whose government is increasingly prioritizing politics and national security over much-needed structural economic reforms. In contrast to the EU's more defensive "de-risking" strategy, the more offensive Global Gateway Initiative (GGI), as a response to China's Belt and Road Initiative, is more focused on leveraging specific EU infrastructure and connectivity programmes and diversifying supply chains to strengthen influence in the Global South at the expense of China.

Keywords Renminbi • Electric vehicle • Bilateral investment treaties • Free trade agreements • Comprehensive Agreement on Investment • Cross-border economic ties • General Agreement on Trade in Services • International Labour Organization • International procurement instrument • Global Gateway Initiative • EU Chips Act • European Economic Security Strategy • "middle income trap" • 13th (2015–2020) and 14th (2021–2025) Five Year Plans • Organisation for Economic Co-operation and Development • Greenfield investment • Mergers and acquisitions • EU Single Market • EU Foreign Subsidy Regulation • EU Anti-Coercive Instrument • Battery electric vehicles • Digital transformation • Big Tech companies • Belt and Road Initiative • CEEC-China cooperation • Global South

4.1 The European and Chinese Environment for Investment

EU's Investments in China

Although in recent years China has been the second largest recipient of foreign direct investments (FDI) worldwide, Fig. 4.1 shows that EU countries' investments in China fell sharply between 2019 and 2021, from USD 7.3 billion in 2019 to USD 5.7 billion in 2020, an annualized decline of 11.8 per cent. This fell further to USD 5.1 billion in 2021, a year-on-year decline of 10.4 per cent. The fact that the decline in EU investment in China began even before the pandemic suggests that the issue may be more systemic, with EU companies blaming the difficulties faced by EU countries in entering the Chinese market. As a result, many

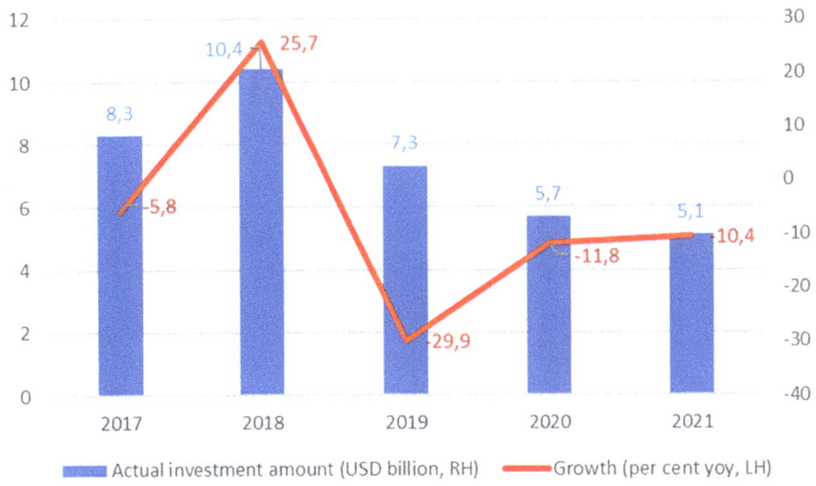

Fig. 4.1 EU investment in China from 2017 to 2021. Source: own elaboration based on Statistical Bulletin of FDI in China, Ministry of Commerce

European companies, although not yet leaving China, were considering diversifying from China as a result of the restrictions. The decline in foreign direct investment has been partly attributed to China's strained ties with the West and higher interest rates elsewhere. The US and other Western countries have raised interest rates from 2021 to control inflation, while China has cut rates to pump up the slowing economy. Although growth data recovered somewhat in 2022, it is possible that this sudden turnaround is the result of a few very large projects that took place in 2022, such as large investments from German companies Volkswagen and BASF, rather than being a sign of an improving trend (Huld, 2023a).

Figure 4.2 shows that compared to the past decade, foreign investors have recently become more hesitant to invest in China (Hale et al., 2023). A more general trend in European (EU + UK) FDI investments in China is that compared to a decade ago, there is a greater concentration of investments in certain sectors (e.g. automotive, food processing, pharmaceutical and biotechnology, chemicals and production of consumer products) and these FDIs come from a more limited number of European countries (Germany, the Netherlands, Great Britain, and France). While larger companies still invest in China, such as the German car manufacturer BMW, which acquired a controlling stake in its Chinese joint venture, BMW

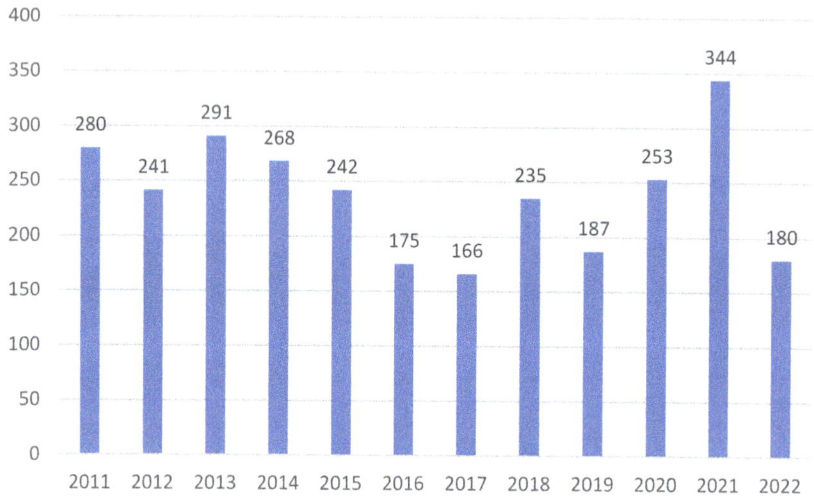

Fig. 4.2 Foreign direct investment in China in 2011–2022 (million USD). Source: own elaboration based on Statista

Brilliance, in February 2022, it is less attractive for smaller European companies, which are more risk averse, to enter the Chinese market. Since the outbreak of the Covid-19 pandemic, virtually no new European investors have entered the Chinese market (Huld, 2023b).

In 2023, the net flow of FDI into China was increasingly negative, while a decade ago, by contrast, China was attracting net inflows of FDI. One of the reasons why the total outflows of foreign direct investment exceeds the inflows are tensions with the US over semiconductor technology, and concerns about increased anti-spying activities have increased risks. Also, China's slowing economy, low interest rates, and a geopolitical battle with the US have cast doubt on the country's economic potential. The changing preference to continue foreign direct investment in China is also reflected in 2023 as international investors have withdrawn some USD 25 billion from the market for Chinese "A" shares, namely those denominated in renminbi (RMB) and listed in Shanghai or Shenzhen. Until the end of 2022, China had implemented one of the strictest pandemic lockdowns in the world through its "zero-Covid" policy. This has caused disruptions in the supply chains of many companies, such as tech giant Apple, which makes most of its iPhones in China. The company has since diversified its supply chain by moving some production to India. In 2023, there is a trend that more companies have gradually shifted to a diversification strategy as tensions between China and the US have increased with new export restrictions on raw materials and technology needed to make advanced chips. Although the large multinational companies that have been present in the Chinese market for decades are not prepared to give up the market share they have built up over all these years, there is a reassessment and reorientation, especially in the area of possible new investments in China. Many companies also consider the impact of interest rates. While many Western countries have raised interest rates from the end of 2021, China bucked this trend. Many major central banks, including the Federal Reserve System (Fed) and the European Central Bank (ECB), have raised interest rates to tackle inflation. The higher borrowing costs, which promise higher returns, also attract foreign capital. Meanwhile, policymakers in China have lowered borrowing costs to support the Chinese economy and the struggling real estate sector. The RMB fell in value by more than 5 per cent against the USD and EUR in 2023. Foreign investors in China with excess cash and income in China have increasingly transferred these funds, including their holdings of government bonds, abroad, where they will earn higher investment returns compared to investments in China (Liang, 2023).

China's Investments in the EU

China's global outbound investments continued to fall in 2022 due to geopolitical tensions, e.g. the ongoing Sino-US trade and tech war and the Russian invasion of Ukraine, plus ongoing domestic constraints on outbound capital flows, economic uncertainty caused by the tech rectification campaign, i.e. Chinese government's crackdown on the tech sector, and China's adherence to a zero-Covid strategy for most of 2022. In addition, companies increasingly had to cope with stricter screening of investments in the EU. Chinese investments in the EU have undergone profound changes over the past decade. Compared to 2016, China's capital controls were much looser, economic and regulatory conditions were more favourable, and supervision of Chinese investments in Europe was much more limited. After years of strong expansion of Chinese greenfield investments in the EU and a decline in M&A transactions, the former have outpaced the latter for the first time in twenty years, which is mainly due to the electric vehicle (EV) sector (Fig. 4.3). Greenfield investments are preferred by

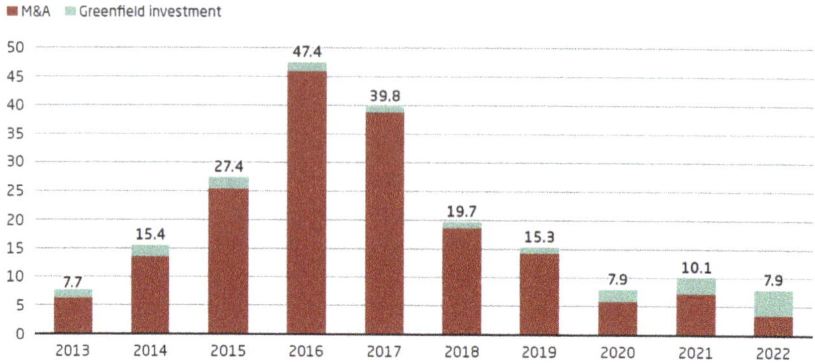

Fig. 4.3 Chinese greenfield investment in Europe overtakes M&A volume (EUR billion)

Chinese companies as they can enable them to set up and develop new local companies rather than attempt buyouts. The increase in greenfield investment was driven mainly by a few large-scale projects, almost exclusively concentrated in the automotive sector and to a lesser degree in data centres as Chinese battery giants including CATL, Envision AESC, and SVOLT invested in building battery plants in Germany, Hungary, the UK, and France. The concentration of Chinese investment in Europe is even greater than in the past decade, with the "Big Three" economies Germany, France, and the UK responsible for 68 per cent of Chinese FDI in the region (Merics, 2023).

China's increasing interest in the EU, the world's second-largest EV market after China, is understandable as the EU is characterized by a relatively good charging infrastructure and generous government subsidies, developed within a broader green agenda to decarbonize road transport. The investments in battery factories are part of a global push by Chinese companies into the EV value chain. It is also a reflection of the competitiveness of Chinese companies and their ambition to gain more market share abroad, with Europe being the largest EV market after China. As part of the EU's efforts to decarbonize the economy, the sale of cars with combustion engines will be banned by 2035. The car market is undergoing major shifts, while at the same time Europe does not have any major battery players of its own. Chinese companies are trying to position themselves in the market and have announced a total of USD 17.5 billion since

2018. It is likely that by 2030, 30 per cent of European battery capacity will be supplied by Chinese companies. This approach helps them save on tariffs and transport costs while mitigating the risks of political opposition. Chinese manufacturers can benefit from producing in Europe instead of exporting to it (Kuo, 2023).

Although Chinese investment has remained relatively stable in its geographical spread, there have been big changes in its sectoral distribution with a sharp downturn in energy, infrastructure, real estate and finance, the sectors that dominated Chinese investment in Europe until 2017. This stems from a greater focus on reducing financial risks from highly indebted companies in these sectors in China, stricter capital controls, and now tighter investment screening measures in Europe, particularly in critical infrastructure because of deteriorating EU–China relations and Russia's invasion of Ukraine. The fall in Chinese investment in these SOE-dominated sectors is also linked with the fall in Chinese SOE investment in Europe. Chinese capital now flows towards sectors where Chinese private firms are highly competitive, like automotive and consumer-oriented sectors like video gaming or household products. The EU has become an increasingly important region in China's global expansion of electric vehicles, which shows both China's strength in the EV supply chain and growing need to be close to the market to gain a foothold in Europe's auto industry. Another new development in Chinese investment in the EU is that it is increasingly concentrated in a limited number of companies, including CATL and Tencent. Moreover, the investors were mainly large SOEs acquiring European companies, while now it consists mainly of private companies building greenfield assets in Europe. It makes sense for China to expand its investments in batteries in Europe, the second largest EV market in the world after China. Furthermore, unlike other major automotive hubs such as Japan or South Korea, Europe has few major battery firms of its own and is still very open to Chinese investment in the industry. The Sino-EU battery expansion could also lay the foundation for a broader manufacturing base in Europe if it proves successful for Chinese EV makers. Currently, this export impulse is dominated by imports from Tesla's production site in Shanghai, but by producing in Europe, rather than exporting to it, Chinese EV manufacturers could save on tariffs and transport costs and temper the increasing geopolitical risks. The EU approach is in stark contrast to the American pursuit of a "China-free" battery supply chain. For example, the US IRA ties EV tax credits to batteries that are free from minerals or components from entities of concern including from China. The incentives offered by the IRA, combined with rising energy costs in Europe, have prompted some companies, including Tesla and Northvolt, to postpone energy-intensive battery projects and focus on the US. On the other hand, Chinese companies are more likely to complete projects in Europe because they have fewer opportunities to expand in the US, bringing Sino-EU battery investments closer together again.

In its relationship with China, the EU is not introducing hard investment restrictions, but is introducing an investment monitoring system. While most of the decline in Chinese investments in Europe is due to domestic investment factors, also the implementation by member states of European investment screening or review regulations has contributed to this trend. The EU established its framework for coordinating FDI screening through Regulation 2019/452, adopted in March 2019, a policy which has been enforced since October 2020. This regulation grants the European Commission powers to review private transactions related to FDI. This applies in particular to sensitive sectors relating to critical infrastructure and strategic dual-use technologies, for example, planned acquisitions of semiconductor firms, a sector that both the Chinese and European governments regard as highly strategic (Gehringer, 2023). Chinese investments in strategic sectors may face stricter review processes and limitations. It is also worth noting that European screening mechanisms have been reviewing investments by Chinese-owned European firms, such as Syngenta. Although the EU's FDI screening mechanism potentially reduces China's investments in the EU, the recent US export controls on semiconductor equipment are more likely to prompt China to invest more in European technology suppliers as a substitute for the US, given the opportunity (Merics, 2023). The diversity of the European market also allows Chinese companies to explore various types of investment opportunities across sectors such as technology, manufacturing, finance, and energy. While the EU boasts significant advantages in areas like technological innovation and talent development, Chinese companies can establish research and development centres or collaborate on joint labs in Europe to engage with high-level research institutions and universities. This fosters technological exchange and innovation, enhancing the competitiveness of both parties (GT, 2023).

4.2 Bilateral Sino-EU Investment Policy and Cooperation in Enhancing Their Market Access

China currently has active bilateral investment treaties (BITs) with all EU countries except Ireland. These BITs are international agreements establishing the terms and conditions for private investment by one contracting country to another contracting country, as codified by the most-favoured-nation (MFN) or non-discrimination clause. They also usually include clauses on dispute mechanisms in the event, including arbitration in a neutral international court. There are currently no free trade agreements or investment treaties between China and the EU as a bloc (Huld, 2023a, b).

On December 30, 2020, the EU and China concluded in-principle negotiations on a Comprehensive Agreement on Investment (CAI), the first round of which started in 2014. The CAI is a landmark agreement, in which China committed to improving market access and ensuring equal treatment for EU companies. This includes commitments to implementing "terms of disciplines for state-owned enterprises, transparency of subsidies and rules against the forced transfer of technologies". The more comprehensive CAI can replace the BITs that regulate how host states treat foreign investors from the treaty partner that most EU member states have with China to secure greater access and more predictable conditions for European firms and rectify the low levels of European investment in China. The CAI's aims are to create significant opportunities for investors from the EU and China and to strengthen cross-border economic ties between the two strategic markets. China also wants to use the CAI to boost its outbound investment activities. Once the CAI comes into force, it is expected to provide a uniform legal framework for EU members, replacing the current bilateral treaties between China and individual EU member states. In principle, the intention of the EU-China CAI is to strengthen cooperation on both sides, build an open economic order, and promote globalization. In June 2021 it was reported that it was still possible to ratify the investment deal after 2023. So far, the CAI has not yet been ratified due to the recent deterioration in the EU–China relationship, mainly due to geopolitical disputes between the two regions (see Sect. 2.1). Nevertheless, it is important to summarize the main highlights of the CAI in case new initiatives are introduced to improve the EU–China relationship. This concerns the following points:

1. Market access
2. Level playing field
3. Sustainable development
4. State-to-state dispute settlement mechanism

Market access: Currently, EU investors have been entering the Chinese market by primarily relying on (a) China's commitments in the General Agreement on Trade in Services (GATS) under the WTO framework, (b) China's regulatory regime under the Foreign Investment Industry Catalogue which was replaced by the "negative lists" issued by the Chinese government from time to time and applicable to foreign investors generally, and (c) other international/bilateral treaties/agreements entered into by China to the extent applicable. In principle, the CAI follows a "positive list" approach, specifying areas of the Chinese economy that are open to European investment. For the most part, this is a confirmation of previous openings by China, either under the auspices of the WTO or through the successive issuance of various "negative lists" for foreign investment, while new market openings were limited. On the other hand, the EU market is already largely open to Chinese investment. Chinese investors may still rely on the EU's commitments in GATS. The CAI binds the EU to open some additional markets (notably, in the manufacturing sector) whereas EU-sensitive sectors (such as energy, agriculture, fisheries, audio-visual, and public services) are all preserved in the CAI (Hong, 2021). The CAI agreement is expected to provide more investment opportunities in the following sectors: manufacturing, automotive, financial and business services, health (private hospitals), research and development, telecom/cloud services, computer services, international maritime transport, air transport-related services, environmental services, and construction services (KPMG, 2021).

Level playing field: This part of CAI mainly concerns the role of SOEs, forced technology transfer and transparency in subsidies, and granting EU firms access to China's standards-setting bodies. The CAI aims at improving the level playing field between Chinese SOEs and EU businesses by requiring the SOEs to act in accordance with commercial considerations and not to discriminate against foreign-invested market players in their procurement and sales of goods and services. The CAI will also include provisions that will oblige China to provide, upon request, information to allow for the assessment of whether a specific SOE has complied with the agreed rules set forth in the CAI. The CAI will contain rules against forced transfer of technology. The provisions will prohibit certain types of investment requirements that compel transfer of technology and interference in contractual freedom in technology licensing. Notably, China has been making efforts to address technology transfer issues in the past few years. The Foreign Investment Law emphasizes contractual freedom and prohibits forced technology transfer by administrative agencies and their working staff (Hong, 2021). The CAI will impose transparency obligations on subsidies related to services. Both the EU and China will be obliged to engage in consultations with each other to provide additional information on subsidies which may hurt the investment interests of the other side and to seek to address that negative impact. As part of the CAI, the EU and China established rules against forced technology transfer. The provisions prohibit investment requirements that force technology transfer, and protect confidential business information by improving the R&D environment.

In addition to the promotion of a fair level playing field, it is likely that the CAI will also stimulate cross-border mergers and acquisitions (M&A). The EU has comparative advantages in advanced manufacturing technology and production: the removal of investment barriers will facilitate Chinese companies to expand investment in high-tech fields and deepen cooperation with EU enterprises. Potential disposals of high-quality assets also present an opportunity for Chinese companies to expand their international operations (KPMG, 2021).

Sustainable development: The CAI will contain provisions reflecting the EU approach to sustainable development, obliging suitable decision-makers to make commitments in particular areas such as the environment, climate change, and labour protection. More specifically, the commitments will be to effectively implement the 2015 Paris Agreement on climate change; not to lower the standards of labour and environmental protection to attract investment; and work towards the ratification of the outstanding International Labour Organization (ILO) fundamental conventions and a specifically tailored implementation mechanism to address differences related to the implementation of sustainable development commitments (including government consultations, recourse to an independent panel of experts etc.).

State-to-state dispute settlement mechanism: The CAI will provide for a two-step approach to settle disputes between the EU and China about complaints related to violation: (a) consultations (possibly, mediation) and (b) if consultation fails, arbitration panel procedures. This approach is similar to that adopted in the existing bilateral treaties between China and individual EU members. An institutional framework will also be established to monitor the effective implementation of the CAI: this will include setting up an Investment Committee (for institutional oversight) at a political level as well as a specific working group concerning sustainable development (Hong, 2021). In principle, this means, first, that China reserves the right to require that senior executives of foreign non-profit organizations in China be Chinese and, second, that the rights of European law firms in China are limited. Chinese law firms should be entrusted to deal with Chinese legal matters on behalf of foreign clients. As there is increasingly strict screening of investments in Europe, the Chinese authorities remain interested in the CAI. The most immediate obstacles to the agreement are Chinese sanctions and the implementation of the ILO conventions, as attention in Europe to China's human rights practices has increased significantly in recent years. These hurdles for the CAI will be difficult to overcome as promise fatigue increases in the EU and UK. China's commitments to uphold international economic standards or respect European values and interests are increasingly viewed with scepticism. This trend is further reinforced by Beijing's tacit support for Russia during the war in Ukraine, despite its outspoken support for sovereignty and territorial integrity. From the perspective of the EU, worrisome trends include but are not limited to the following: China's tacit support for Russia in the war in Ukraine; expanding influence in international organizations, including those intended to protect and preserve human rights; military assertiveness across the Taiwan Strait, a key maritime trading route; economic coercion against both European states and its neighbours in the Indo-Pacific; efforts to export Chinese policing and security practices to authoritarian regimes; and influence over operations in Europe, all of which overlap with US concerns about China's rise. The number of substantive venues for regular dialogue on China has increased under the Biden administration. The overall stability of transatlantic relations will be crucial for coordination with China. The EU will therefore need to pay attention to anticipating and addressing the spillover effects of the US "invest-align-compete" approach to China. However, recent US export controls on China and the Inflation Reduction Act have caused friction with the EU, not only because they affect the economic prospects of European companies, but also because they have reportedly been implemented without sufficient consultation and communication about the consequences. By setting aside the merits of individual policies and regularly addressing the implications for broader transatlantic ties in US economic and technological policymaking, especially as this becomes a more important part of the US-China strategic competition, this will preserve the goodwill necessary for further coordination with China (McElwee, 2023).

In a nutshell, in the CAI, China commits to ensuring fairer treatment for EU companies in China, allowing them to compete on a more level playing field. These commitments cover state-owned enterprises, transparency of subsidies, and rules against forced technology transfer. The rules negotiated in the CAI set a high benchmark in terms of transparency, a level playing field, market access commitments, and sustainable development. The EU's work on planned autonomous measures in areas such as subsidies and due diligence continues as a matter of priority (European Union, 2023). More recently, the circumstances surrounding the EU-China CAI can in retrospect be seen as a symbolic end to the previous era, say before 2019, when China was still mainly seen as a strategic economic "partner" rather than a "competitor", and the EU-China strategy is still mainly focused on economic opportunities in China. The political agreement for the CAI announced in 2020 was quickly followed by counter-sanctions imposed by Beijing on members of the European Parliament in retaliation for the EU's sanctions against four Chinese officials and one entity linked to human rights abuses in Xinjiang. This led to the suspension of ratification of the CAI, and therefore this agreement is now regarded as no longer functioning (EP, 2024).

4.3 The Challenges in the Sino-EU Investment Policy Approach

Under Xi Jinping, China has changed and become more centralized, authoritarian, and assertive abroad, and its goals are often in contradiction with European interests and values. In 2019, the European Commission (EC) acknowledged this shift by introducing the tripartite definition of China as a partner for cooperation and negotiation, an economic competitor, and a systemic rival (see Sect. 2.1). Although China can be considered a partner, in recent years China has increasingly become a competitor and systemic rival. It is necessary to limit trade and investment flows in order to strengthen the EU's strategic autonomy and make it less dependent on the global value chains that pass through China. Importantly, the EU must do more to limit Chinese control over the EU's critical infrastructure and combat cyberattacks and disinformation campaigns. Since then, Xi and the Chinese Communist Party (CCP) have continued their path: China has become more confrontational in the Taiwan Strait and more repressive in Xinjiang, tightened control over Hong Kong, and promoted visions of an alternative world order. Increasing geopolitical and economic tensions between China and the US have put pressure on the EU to position itself in a complex triangle. The apparent "no limits" friendship with Russia, irrespective of Moscow's war against Ukraine, has changed many European countries' formerly favourable views of China, particularly in Central and Eastern Europe. On the EU level, a range of mechanisms have been created to counter the increasingly geopolitical nature of Chinese influence and competitive distortions of markets, industries, and technologies. These include investment screening, an anti-coercion instrument, an international procurement instrument (IPI), the Global Gateway Initiative (2021), and a planned law package aimed at monitoring and combatting foreign interference (including from China), as well as industrial policy initiatives such as the EU Chips Act (2023).

Since Xi Jinping came to power more than ten years ago, most European countries have gradually developed a specific China policy strategy, whether or not embedded in their policy frameworks. Increasingly, political parties, both at the national and EU level, have adopted a China policy as a topic in their programmes. This involves increasing coordination of China policy between various EU member states, which will become more challenging as one wants to connect this knowledge about China at supranational, national, and subnational level. The EU has, in recent years, launched and established several instruments and regulations that are (not only, but also) aimed at improving capabilities to deal with China's increasing economic and geopolitical clout. Among these are the following:

- International Procurement Instrument (April, 2022)
- Anti-Foreign Subsidy legislation (July, 2023)
- Foreign Direct Investment Screening (January 2024, revision)
- Anti-Coercion Instrument (December 2023)
- Anti-Forced Labour Instrument (April, 2024)
- Chips Act (September, 2023)
- Critical Raw Materials Act (May 23, 2024)
- Economic Security Strategy (June, 2023)

Taking the screening mechanism for foreign direct investment (FDI screening) as an example, sixteen EU member states have made national provisions, and four countries are preparing for implementation. In the context of China's growing strength and ambitions in science, technology, and innovation, the EU put forward in 2021 a strategy on cooperation in research and innovation: "Strategic, open, and reciprocal" (EC, 2021). It suggests measures to protect research security and integrity in member states. The EU and some member states have started developing tools to better protect their interests, but the process proves to be cumbersome. Following the Russian invasion of Ukraine in 2022 and the resulting economic fallout for European countries dependent on energy supplies from Russia, the issue of dependence on China has been fiercely discussed in Europe. The Commission's "de-risking" agenda and the June 2023 framework on a European Economic Security Strategy are aimed at minimizing risks arising from economic exchanges in geopolitically challenging times (ETNC, 2023).

4.4 China's Current Structural Reforms for a More Sustainable Growth Path and Their Impact on the EU's Industries' Potential

Since China began its economic reforms in 1978 and has had annual GDP growth rates of more than 9 per cent for decades, lifting many millions of people out of poverty, there have also been gradual significant improvements in access to healthcare, education, and other services. Although China is an upper-middle-income country and has eradicated extreme poverty, a significant number of people remain vulnerable, with incomes below a threshold commonly used to define poverty in upper-middle-income countries. China's unprecedented growth rates of the past, based on fixed investment, cheap production, and export-led growth, have largely reached their limits and led to economic, social, and environmental imbalances that characterize emerging market countries facing a "middle income trap". Reducing these imbalances requires a shift in the structure of the economy: from production to high-value services, from investment to consumption, and from high to low carbon intensity. In recent years, the high growth of the past has inevitably diminished in the face of structural constraints including declining labour force growth, adverse demographics including the ageing population, diminishing returns on investment, rising constraints to a debt-fuelled, investment-driven growth model, and slowing productivity growth. The challenge going forward is to find new drivers of sustainable growth while addressing the social and environmental legacies of China's previous development path. Structural reforms are needed to reinvigorate the shift to more balanced high-quality growth. The rapid economic growth of recent decades has outpaced the rate of institutional developments. To ensure a high-quality and sustainable growth path, major structural reforms are needed, which have become an explicit part of the 13th (2015–2020) and 14th (2021–2025) Five Year Plans. Examples of structural reforms introduced by the Chinese authorities include the lifting of restrictions on the system of residence permits, or "hukou", to spur consumption, and removing market entry barriers for private firms at the cost of state giants. The role of the state must evolve and focus on providing a clear, fair, and stable business environment, strengthening the regulatory system and the rule of law to further support the market system, and ensuring equal access to public services for all citizens. Due to its size, China is increasingly playing a central role in many regional and global development issues. Although not the leading source of historical cumulative emissions, today China is responsible for 27 per cent of annual global carbon dioxide emissions and a third of global greenhouse gas emissions, with per capita emissions now exceeding those of the EU, although slightly below the OECD average and well below US levels. Air and water pollution affects other countries, and global environmental problems cannot be solved without China's engagement. Many of the complex development challenges that China faces are relevant to other countries, including transitioning to a new growth model, rapid ageing, building a cost-effective health system, and promoting a lower-carbon energy path. Pro-market structural reforms aimed at boosting productivity, supporting rebalancing, and decarbonization would help support new engines of growth and foster a more balanced, inclusive, and green growth (World Bank, 2023).

Although the Chinese authorities' goals towards a more sustainable growth path in the last Five Year plans have focused on more structural reforms, in recent years national security has been given almost as much weight as reforms, amid investor concerns that policymakers focus more on geopolitics than on much-needed structural changes. The growing importance of national security shows that the government feels uncertain about both the domestic and international environment. This is partly explained by the fact that the structural reforms that have taken place so far are increasingly difficult to implement and that the measures that have been tried, such as partial privatization of state-owned enterprises and redistribution of revenues between central and local governments, have not been very effective. The focus on national security and downplaying reforms sends a negative signal to investors as the government prioritizes security and deems structural reforms less important recently.

The Covid-19 pandemic has brought additional challenges for the economy. China's economic recovery from the pandemic has faced increasing difficulties from a liquidity crisis in the property market that has weighed on consumer and investor confidence. Foreign investors are also concerned about Beijing's increasing focus on national security with the launch of data laws they complain are too vague and new espionage regulations. The authorities have also raided foreign consultancies and suppressed data releases, making it harder for investors to navigate the market. Structural reforms are needed to stimulate domestic consumer demand, but government loans are increasingly channelled into the manufacturing sector, especially high-tech segments, which Beijing considers as strategic in its competitive battle with the US.

To reverse China's economic slowdown in 2023, a proactive fiscal policy inclusive of tax breaks for strategic industries is expected to remain expansionary in 2024 to spur domestic demand with incentives for purchases of home appliances, electric vehicles, and consumer electronics, with a focus on "high-quality development" instead of "foreign capital". Monetary policy is likely to be relatively accommodative, and policy easing in the real estate sector is likely to continue in 2024. The Chinese central bank is limited in its ability to ease monetary policy, as there are fears that a wider interest rate differential with the US could lead to capital flight and a weakening of the RMB (Leahy & Lin, 2023).

Sino-EU economic ties hit a milestone, emerging as each other's second-largest trading partners, with daily trade in 2022 surpassing EUR 2 billion. Traditionally dominated by electronics and automobiles, bilateral trade now sees a notable surge in high-tech and green products like solar panels and electric vehicles. For Chinese businesses, the European market is pivotal, serving as a key investment destination. Their establishment of R&D and data centres, cybersecurity hubs, and battery plants in countries such as Germany and Hungary contributes to local economies, job creation, and innovation for sustainable growth. Greenfield investment has overtaken mergers and acquisitions (M&A) and has become the major form of Chinese investment in the EU (Fig. 3.3). In recent years, as the EU tightens M&A investment policies and more EU member states adopt FDI screening mechanisms, Chinese enterprises seeking M&A face amplified time, compliance costs, uncertainties, and political barriers. Despite Sino-EU economic ties, many fundamental challenges remain in their uneasy relationship. Recent ideology-led political decisions in China, such as growing restrictions against the private sector through regulatory crackdowns that benefit SOEs, neglect economic considerations and make the business environment increasingly less predictable, reliable, and efficient. China's state-led system, including direct government control over major parts of its economy, produces discriminatory outcomes and market distortions.

Many EU and US companies experience an asymmetrical business relationship and an unlevel playing field in China. In particular, businesses are affected by a disparity in market access between Chinese and foreign firms, financing advantages for Chinese firms in strategic sectors, and preferential support for selected Chinese industries. These disadvantages are accompanied by hostile policies like burdensome restrictions on foreign ownership, forced technology transfer rules, and export restrictions on raw materials, and the increasing number of counterfeit products being imported into the EU Single Market from China also remains a matter of concern. To address these many challenges, the EU must equip itself with the necessary autonomous regulatory tools to address the distortion created by China in its internal market and ensure a level playing field with Chinese companies. Instruments such as the EU Foreign Subsidy Regulation and the EU Anti-Coercive Instrument are emblematic examples. However, these autonomous measures should only be used as a last resort to limit negative externalities for the industry. Instead, the EU should prioritize strengthening engagement with China.

The EU's "de-risking" approach means more uncertainty in economic and trade cooperation and in bilateral relations. For a number of years, there has been a decline in the business opportunities of Chinese companies in the EU despite the challenges they face in the EU. When de-risking, the EU should also avoid taking unilateral trade-distorting actions and adopting restrictive measures, like barriers to trade and investment, in the name of national security. In particular, the European Commission and member states should carefully assess the need for and application of inbound and outbound investment screening instruments to prevent unintended negative consequences for businesses. At the same time, the EU must prioritize strengthening the resilience of supply chains in its de-risking strategy. An essential tool to achieve this resilience is diversification through free trade agreements, as well as sectoral partnerships such as on raw materials. China is and will remain an essential actor in geopolitics and economics. It is in the EU's shared interest to manage the relationship in a strategic way that allows businesses to reap the benefits of the Chinese market while mitigating the risks posed by its policies and geopolitical challenges and addressing level playing field distortions (AmCham EU, 2023).

In a recent report by Mario Draghi (September 2024) ten sectors are distinguished in which EU policies are needed to level up European competitiveness including energy, critical raw materials, digitalization, energy-intensive industry, clean technology, automotive-, weapons- and pharmaceutical industries, aerospace and transportation. Possible measures to make the EU more competitive include, among others, joint purchasing of gas and defense equipment; long-term contract for green and nuclear energy; more extraction, processing and recycling of raw materials within the EU; more investments in efficient EU communication networks and in its own chip industry. In addition to more intensive and better coordination in energy-intensive industries, more and more EU technology must be implemented in large sustainable projects, with additional EU funding for companies that use this kind of technology development. Ultimately, many of these European sectors such as automotive, weapons, space, pharmaceuticals and transport require a more pan-EU industrial policy with associated joint R&D and EU funding (EC, 2024). Although this EC report identifies the dangers of future competition for the EU, the overview below provides a brief description of some of the industries that still show high growth potential in 2023–2024 and most likely beyond and are open to foreign investors whether or not in China and/or in the EU.

Automotive Industry

The EU is decarbonizing its car industry at a record pace. The shift to battery-electric vehicles is bringing major changes to the European car industry. Sales of alternative energy vehicles reached a record 4.4 million units in 2022, representing 47 per cent of all new vehicle registrations in Europe. Battery electric vehicles (BEVs) led the way, with turnover increases of 28 per cent, which amounts to 12 per cent of all new vehicle registrations. With the phasing out of internal combustion engines (ICE) in sight, the automotive sector will face a complete upheaval with a transformation of the supplier base, changing customer needs, competition of newcomers, and the reality of a less car-centric society. However, for the EU, China is the biggest risk factor. Having recognized the potential of electric vehicles fifteen years ago, China has since invested vast resources in building a competitive electric vehicle ecosystem. As a result, it now leads the global EV landscape, selling more than double the number of BEVs in 2022 compared to Europe and the US combined, while also holding a competitive edge in nearly all aspects of the BEV value chain. Because they account for more than 80 per cent of EV sales in their country, Chinese brands have seen their market shares climb from less than 40 per cent in 2020 to close to 50 per cent in 2022, while the country's automotive trade balance went from a USD 31 bn deficit to a USD 7 bn surplus over the same period. At the same time, already in 2022, three of Europe's best-selling BEVs were Chinese imports. As BEVs eventually grow to account for all new car sales in Europe, Europe-made cars are likely to be substituted by those made in China – irrespective of whether they are manufactured by a Chinese, American, or European company.

Given the strategic importance of the automotive sector for the European economy, policymakers could seek reciprocal trade terms with China and the US, as well as promote BEV adoption through improved charging infrastructure. Moreover, allowing Chinese investment in local car assembly could generate more value-added in the region, while increasing self-sufficiency in raw materials critical for battery manufacturing and investing in next-generation battery technologies will further help Europe's automotive sector prepare for tomorrow's challenges (Duthoit, 2023)

Aviation Industry

With the lifting of Covid-19 restrictions, both domestic and international air travel are set to rebound in China in 2023. The increase in demand for air travel will in turn put more pressure on the industry to develop and expand. Beyond the short-term increase in demand, China has had long-standing plans to expand and upgrade its aviation sector, which will include both the building of new airports and upgrading of existing airport and fleet technology. There are several areas in the aviation industry in which foreign investment is encouraged, including the design and manufacture of civil aircraft, civil helicopters and helicopter parts, ground-effect vehicles, and unmanned aerial vehicles, among many others. There are thus ample opportunities for European companies within China's growing aviation sector. In January 2022, the European aerospace company Airbus announced that it had signed a *Memorandum of Understanding* with the city of Chengdu to establish the first sustainable aircraft "life cycle" service centre in China, which will "cover a range of activities from aircraft parking and storage, to maintenance, upgrades, conversions, dismantling and recycling services for various aircraft types".

Healthcare Industry

China's rapidly ageing population and rising standards of living are placing an ever higher demand on the country's healthcare system. As such, revenue in China's healthcare market is expected to grow at a compound annual growth rate of 5.8 per cent from 2023 to 2027 to reach a market volume of USD 22.9 billion. However, China's healthcare market remains relatively undeveloped, with total expenditure accounting for only 7.12 per cent of the total GDP in 2020. By comparison, the US's expenditure reached 18 per cent in the same year. This means that there is significant potential for market growth as China seeks to improve its health outcomes over the next decade. Sectors with significant growth potential include medical devices, online healthcare services, and biopharmaceuticals.

Renewable Energy Industry

China's renewable energy industry continues to show huge growth potential as China seeks to rapidly decarbonize its economy and reach its climate targets. In many ways, China and Europe have mutually beneficial energy goals, as both regions seek to reduce reliance on fossil fuels, in particular following the wake of the Russia-Ukraine war in the European case. Certain sectors of China's renewable energy industry, such as solar and hydropower, are already extremely saturated and would be difficult for foreign companies to penetrate. However, there are still several areas in which European companies can compete and supplement the Chinese clean energy market. These include the energy storage market, smart grids, energy-efficient technologies, and hydrogen energy.

High-End Manufacturing Industry

High-end manufacturing remains a lucrative industry in China. Having held the position as the "world's factory" for decades, China is now investing heavily in moving the manufacturing sector up the industrial value chain. This is not simply a means of increasing the value of production, but also a necessary step to future-proof the sector, as rising labour costs and an ageing labour pool will make it increasingly difficult for China to compete with cheaper high-growth markets. Automation and digital transformation will play huge roles in this process, providing many opportunities for European companies in China's robotics, automation, manufacturing solutions, and high-end machinery industries. Europe is home to a large number of companies with advanced manufacturing capabilities, particularly in the automotive sector (another industry with high growth potential in China). It is also home to a range of industry automation, machinery, and robotics companies with technological capabilities that are in demand in China's manufacturing industry (Huld, 2023b).

Information and Communication Technology (ICT)

The ICT sector has emerged in recent years as one of the core battlegrounds in the economic struggle among countries that focus their growth processes on the development of advanced technologies. Currently, the core competencies in the ITC belong to the US and China, but this sector also creates serious implications for the EU and European businesses. According to Statista, in 2023 the global market share of the European ICT sector (11.8 per cent) was equal to the market share of the Chinese ICT sector (11.7 per cent). Only the US share was higher (35.7 per cent). ICT is the crucial engine for the creation of a digital economy. However, the impacts of this sector go beyond the boundaries of the economy. It is a struggle for hegemony over geopolitical principles and values. For this reason, the scope of the ICT sector is greater than single country economies. The scope of this sector is determined by such actors as Big Tech companies (Facebook, Google, ByteDance, Alibaba, Baidu) which are providers of digital products, services, and information flow. The second group of companies is responsible for ICT infrastructure (Ericsson, Nokia, Xiaomi, and semiconductor producers) (Kawamata, 2023). All of them play for their global dominance. In such an environment the ICT sector in China and EU is developing. According to *Global Data*, the Chinese ICT market was valued at USD 544.22 billion in 2022. It was predicted that this market will reach USD 964 billion by 2027. It is also significant that the Chinese ICT market has the largest number of Internet users globally, surpassing 900 million users. This market embraces also over 1.6 billion mobile phone users, and the rapidly growing e-commerce sales amounted to over USD 2.3 trillion. According to data from the European Commission, the value of the ICT market in the EU in January 2022 was around EUR 684 billion. The EU has a significant number of Internet users, with over 400 million people having access to the Internet. There is a similar number of mobile phone users in the EU. In 2020 e-commerce sales in the EU reached over EUR 700 billion. According to the EC (https://ec.europa.eu/commission/presscorner/detail/en/ip_23_4619), currently, fibre networks, which are critical for delivering gigabit connectivity, only reach 56 per cent of households, while 5G coverage stands at 81 per cent of the population, dropping to 51 per cent in rural areas.

Sino–EU relations in the ICT sector during the last several years have been marked by both cooperation and tension. Bilateral cooperation embracing ICT trade and investment has increased. The obstacles are related to intellectual property rights and data security.

The ICT sector is as important for China as for the EU. It has two orientations, internal and global. Regarding the internal approach, it is responsible for the rapid growth of the Chinese economy, especially during the last decade. When it comes to the international level, the Chinese ICT sector plays a significant role in driving Chinese media's global outreach, providing stimulus for soft power and shaping its national image. There is also an important role for ICT in the future when the ICT infrastructure created as a part of the Belt and Road Initiative (BRI) in Global South countries will play a more important role.

Both markets, China and the EU, have their strategies related to Information and Communication Technology (ICT). In the Chinese case, apart from various national strategies aimed at advancing its ICT sector, the strategic goals are incorporated into the *Made in China 2025* which embraces all of them. The strategy is multifaceted and reflects the country's ambition to become a global leader in technology and innovation. The most significant aspects related to the Chinese approach are: (1) to promote digital connectivity and cooperation (fibre-optic cables, data centres, satellite networks) between China and countries participating in the BRI; (2) to develop the world's largest 5G technology network; (3) to implement cybersecurity laws and regulations aimed at safeguarding national security and protecting critical ICT infrastructure; (4) to continue investments in R&D boosting innovations in the ICT sector (AI, semiconductors, advanced manufacturing); (5) to promote digital economy, including e-commerce, digital payments (e-RMB), and sharing economy; and (6) to enhance international cooperation in the ICT sector through conferences, collaborations with other countries and regions, and participation in standard-setting bodies. It is significant that on the one hand, China is aiming its self-sufficiency in the ITC sector, promoting innovation-driven development, and enhancing its global competitiveness, but on the other hand the country's ICT strategy may evolve in response to domestic and international challenges.

The EU's ICT strategy is rooted in the European Commission's Digital Single Market strategy. It aims to create a harmonized environment across EU member states to foster innovation, economic growth, and job creation in the digital sector. The EU's approach aims to create such a digital ecosystem within the EU which enables trust, fairness, and inclusivity. It embraces: (1) ensuring high-speed broadband and 5G connectivity across the EU; (2) promoting digital literacy and skills development to empower citizens and businesses to fully participate in the digital economy; (3) encouraging research and innovation in ICT; (4) supporting digital transformation of business; (5) facilitating the free flow of data within the EU and promoting data-driven innovation while ensuring the protection of personal data through regulations as the General Data Protection Regulation (GDPR); (6) strengthening cybersecurity measures to protect critical infrastructure, businesses, and citizens from cyber threats and attacks; and (7) promoting fair competition and preventing fragmentation in the digital sector through such regulations as the Digital Markets Act (DM) and the Digital Services Act (DSA). The EU is strongly oriented on creation of a digital society and many activities are dedicated to this. In September 2023, the first report was published on the State of the Digital Decade. It provides a comprehensive look at progress towards achieving the digital transformation to empower a more digitally sovereign, resilient, and competitive EU (EC, 2023).

EU–China Relations and the EU's Diversification Strategy in the Mining and Processing Industry

Over the last few years, there have been increasing points of conflict between the EU and China regarding China's restrictive economic policies, serious domestic human rights violations, and claims to global leadership and the resulting geopolitical tensions. These disputes are reflected in the new version of Europe's China strategy, which sees Xi's China solely as a competitor and rival to the EU. Within this context, the EU aims to maintain economic relations with China in areas of interest to the EU, in particular raw materials trade. To reduce dependency on China, and as part of its Critical Raw Materials Act launched in the early 2020s and formally adopted by the European Commission in March 2024, the EU has invested large sums in the European mining and processing sector, for example by subsidizing European mining companies. The aim is for important raw materials such as lithium and rare earth to soon be partially mined in the EU while an increasing number of raw materials are recycled. Additionally, more raw materials processing and refining now takes place either within the EU or in countries other than China, and therefore the value chain of certain raw materials becomes increasingly detached from China. Since the geopolitical crises of the early 2020s, the EU has also pursued its strategy of "friend shoring", i.e. cooperating with "like-minded" and low-risk countries. In this way, it has revitalized raw material partnerships and built a global network of strategic partners. Even so, the EU's demand for certain critical raw materials, such as rare earths, has grown so much over the years that it continues to be dependent on supplies from China. In response to domestic repression by the Chinese authorities, the EU, in coordination with international partners, is imposing sanctions on China, which is responding with trade restrictions and an export ban on rare earth metals, in part because the Chinese military is now prioritizing national supplies. While China is increasingly hostile to Western industrialized countries, it is strengthening its alliances with autocracies and dictatorships around the world and openly proclaiming China's immanent reunification with Taiwan at any cost. The tense relations with China and the ongoing economic slowdown at home cause the EU to fear for its security of supply of raw materials. Consequently, it strengthens raw material partnerships with strategic and trustworthy actors such as Australia, Canada, and selected countries in Latin America and Africa. At the same time, the EU pushes ahead with mining and raw materials processing operations in its own member states. Massive financial resources are made available in order to diversify supply chains whereby the EU's Global Gateway Initiative is expanded into the European Infrastructure Resilience Initiative (Carry et al., 2023).

4.5 EU's Global Gateway Strategy in Response to China's Belt and Road Initiative

As described in Sect. 2.1, the EU's relations with China changed fundamentally in 2019. Before 2019, this Sino–EU relationship was more economic than geostrategic in nature, focusing on economic multilateralism and support for China's aim of reforming the WTO. The EU apparently applied Germany's soft "Change through Trade" approach to China. The idea behind this concept is that authoritarian regimes will open up economically and eventually even politically as a result of increased economic exchange. However, with regard to China (but also Russia), this approach failed. Even bilateral economic relations became tense, symbolized by the non-ratification of the Comprehensive Agreement on Investment (CAI) by the European Parliament (see Sect. 4.2). Even though Brussels' three-pronged approach towards China as a partner, competitor, and systemic rival continues to define the EU's China strategy, the focus has increasingly turned to China as a powerful adversary and means to respond to this challenge. Accordingly, the EU's stance and policies towards China have further hardened, culminating in the promotion of a de-risking strategy. Moreover, already in December 2021, the EU launched the Global Gateway Initiative (GGI), its ambitious infrastructure and connectivity scheme. The GGI is an important geo-economic project according to which until 2027, the EU plans to spend up to EUR 300 billion in quality infrastructure around the globe, ranging from the transport to the digital and health sector (Gerstl, 2023). The GGI was set up in part to improve the poor visibility of EU investments entailing a focus on high-profile, hard infrastructure projects and collecting EU investments under a single brand name. Compared to the BRI, which is often financed through loans for projects, the GGI involves providing grants. However, it is China and the BRI rather than the GGI's EU-funded training programmes that are more in the spotlight. On the one hand, the GGI promises to do things differently than the BRI in terms of sustainability and promotion of EU values. On the other hand, it also seems to move closer to the BRI in terms of pursuing strategic investments and EU interests (Mardell, 2023).

It is good to recall the Chinese project. The Belt and Road Initiative (BRI), launched by Xi Jinping in 2013, is the best-known among China's initiatives to grow global and create markets and investment opportunities for its companies but also increase political influence in the participating countries. The BRI initiates massive investments in infrastructure such as roads, bridges, and ports to restore the ancient Silk Road trade routes that connect Europe, Asia, and Africa. By investing in infrastructure, the Chinese authorities want to create new markets for Chinese companies, such as high-speed rail firms, and to export some of the country's vast excess capacity in cement, steel, and other metals (Łasak & van der Linden, 2019). The BRI seeks to turn Eurasia (dominated by China) into an economic and trade area that can rival the transatlantic region (dominated by the US). The big question in the West is to what extent China's BRI will strengthen the development of the international economic order or China's autocratic democracy-free model of development. In many ways, the BRI's first decade has been a startling success. More than 150 countries have signed up to the scheme, including 18 of the EU's 27 members. That helped make China the developing world's largest creditor, boosting its diplomatic and geopolitical influence. It has also brought concrete benefits to many developing countries, where roads and railways would otherwise have gone unbuilt. Now that the BRI has been in existence for more than a decade, the drawbacks, especially in terms of the debt traps, are increasingly recognized by ordinary citizens in particular, and the authorities have slowed down their progress. The emphasis is now increasingly on relatively "small but beautiful" investments that contribute more to the prosperity of local citizens. Current BRI projects will be less focused on new, large investments with only long-term returns. Domestic disillusion partly explains the shift: China's faltering economy has made lavish spending abroad less popular among ordinary citizens. Other countries have also become more reluctant to collaborate with China on BRI projects as global rivalry with the US increases. The EU has tightened rules around foreign investments in critical infrastructure, citing national security concerns. Although initially many Eastern and Southern European countries were involved in this (such as Bulgaria, the Czech Republic, Greece, Hungary, Italy, Latvia, Lithuania, Poland, Portugal, and Slovakia), interest in this BRI has decreased in recent years because its drawbacks have also become clearer. Comparatively, the EU or Europe as a whole has limited involvement in the BRI. In 2023, the distribution of China's BRI investment and construction engagement, by region, was 3.1 and 2.8 per cent respectively. While the BRI has created new infrastructure and made meaningful contributions to development in some countries, it has also led to over-indebtedness and unfinished or unused projects in others. Moreover, as economic ties deepen due to BRI investments, participating countries have begun to pay closer attention to China's growing political influence over them through "soft power". For example, in 2019, Italy became the only G7 country to sign up for the BRI, but it has since become a point of controversy among Italian leaders. Prime Minister Meloni called for leaving the pact in 2024 as it has no clear benefits for Italy (ETNC, 2023; *The Economist*, 2023).

The EU thus offers developing nations at least in some areas an alternative to China's BRI and the China-led Cooperation between China and Central and Eastern European Countries (China-CEEC cooperation), also known as the 14+1 (formerly 17+1 from 2019 to 2021 and 16+1 from 2021 to 2022).[1] The China-CEEC cooperation is not limited to economic efforts related to infrastructure and connectivity, and also includes initiatives related to culture, education, and tourism. Despite the existence of some multilateral elements in 14 + 1, China-CEEC cooperation is in fact an umbrella for China's bilateral approach, as Beijing negotiates key BRI projects with each individual member separately. Especially in recent years, the 14 +1 cooperation has become a bone of contention in the Sino–EU relationship. One of the main reasons for the EU's critical view of China–CEEC cooperation is that twelve of the seventeen European participants are also EU members. Thus, there were fears that China, due to its close relations with certain members (e.g. Hungary and Greece), would indirectly influence EU policy as in July 2016 when Greece and Hungary watered down an EU statement on the South China Sea. Some other major points of contention between the EU and CEEC-China cooperation concern the delayed and economically dubious Budapest-Piraeus high-speed line, a costly and oversized highway project in Montenegro and the 24.9 per cent share in a container terminal of the port of Hamburg by the Chinese state-owned firm COSCO. Another sensitive aspect here is that the Taiwan-friendly governments of CEEC, including the Baltic states, the Czech Republic, and Poland, are dissatisfied with the cooperation between China and the CEEC. These nations are leading the way in fostering closer EU–Taiwan relations, emphasizing Taiwan's democratic and human rights credentials. Since China still mainly invests in the more developed "old" Europe, especially Germany, France, the UK, and Hungary as a hub for construction of a new gigafactory for electric vehicle batteries, and the total investments in Europe, both mergers and acquisitions and greenfield investments, have decreased since 2013 (Fig. 4.3), future expectations about China-CEEC cooperation are not very positive.

[1] In the past decade, China has systematically established its own institutional frameworks to increase geopolitical and economic influence. One of these frameworks is the 16+1 initiative established in 2012 to engage with Central and Eastern European countries. It was a format that was sometimes criticized in the EU as undermining its unity. Partly due to disappointment with China's involvement in this region, Chinese support for Russia, and coercive measures to deepen relations with Taiwan, a number of countries have withdrawn from the 16 + 1 initiative, which has now become 14 + 1.

While the EU's "de-risking" strategy in response to China's increasing geopolitical influence is a defensive strategy, promoting a specific EU infrastructure and connectivity programme in the form of the GGI is an offensive strategy fueled by the BRI. Leveraging infrastructure investments and loans is a suitable means for Brussels to strengthen its economic and subsequently political influence in the Global South. However, unlike China, the EU's initiative places more emphasis on democratic values and transparency. In principle, the EU, the US, Japan, and the G7, thanks to their cooperation on infrastructure and connectivity, could rival the BRI, although their high democratic, social, environmental, and governance standards could be a deterrent for governments in the South. This will be an important geopolitical competition in the coming years between more autocratic countries such as China, Iran, and Russia, on the one hand, and the more democratic Western countries, on the other hand. Especially after 2019, it has become increasingly clear that the China-CEEC mechanism has failed to improve China's political and economic relations with the EU and the majority of its members. This also applies to the BRI, whose drawbacks have become increasingly clear in the form of "sovereign debt traps", etc. Both initiatives have led to a much more critical EU view of China's geostrategic objectives and policies (Gerstl, 2023).

References

Carry, I., Godehardt, N., & Muller, M. (2023, May 16). *The future of European-Chinese raw material supply chains: Three scenarios for 2030 and their implications.* Stiftung Wissenshaft und Politik (SWP). https://www.swp-berlin.org/en/publication/the-future-of-european-chinese-raw-material-supply-chains

Duthoit, A. (2023, May 09). *The Chinese challenge to the European automotive industry.* Allianz Research. https://www.allianz.com/en/economic_research/publications/specials_fmo/european-automotive-industry.html

EC. (2023). https://ec.europa.eu/commission/presscorner/detail/en/ip_23_4619

EC. (2024, September). *The Future of European Competitiveness, part B: in-depth analysis and recommendations.*

EC European Commission. (2021, March 18). *Europe's global approach to cooperation in research and innovation: Strategic, open, and reciprocal.* https://ec.europa.eu/commission/presscorner/detail/en/ip_21_2465

EP European Parliament. (2024, March). *EU-China relations: De-risking or de-coupling – The future of the EU-strategy towards China.* https://www.europarl.europa.eu/RegData/etudes/STUD/2024/754446/EXPO_STU(2024)754446_EN.pdf

ETNC. (2023, July). *From a China strategy to no strategy at all: Exploring the diversity of European approaches.* A report by the European Think-tank Network on China (ETNC). https://www.clingendael.org/sites/default/files/2023-07/ETNC_Report_2023_final_0.pdf

European Union. (2023). *Trade.* https://policy.trade.ec.europa.eu/eu-trade-relationships-country-and-region/countries-and-regions/china_en

Gehringer, A. (2023). *China's strategic foreign direct investment in Europe.* Flossbach von Storch Research Institute. https://www.flossbachvonstorch-researchinstitute.com/fileadmin/user_upload/RI/Studien/files/englisch/231002-chinas-strategic-foreign-direct-investment-in-europe.pdf

Gerstl, A. (2023, September 12). *The EU's de-risking strategy and its Global Gateway Initiative: Two strategic responses to China's Belt and Road Initiative and the China-CEEC cooperation.* Munk School of Global Affairs & Public Policy. https://munkschool.utoronto.ca/belt-road/research/eus-de-risking-strategy-and-its-global-gateway-initiative-two-strategic-responses-chinas

GT Global Times. (2023, September 08). *EU's FDI review mechanism poses increasing challenges and uncertainty for Chinese firms, investments: Commerce chamber.* https://www.globaltimes.cn/page/202309/1297853.shtml

Hale, T. et al. (2023, October 29). China suffers plunging foreign direct investment amid geopolitical tensions. *Financial Times.* https://www.ft.com/content/56294843-7eff-4b83-9fa2-c46fb4ac1278

Hong, S. (2021, February). *An overview of the China/EU Comprehensive Agreement on Investment.* Norton Rose Fulbright. https://www.nortonrosefulbright.com/en/knowledge/publications/1a85b7c4/an-overview-of-the-china-eu-comprehensive-agreement-on-investment

Huld, A. (2023a, April 04). *EU-China relations – Trade, investment, and recent developments.* China Briefing. https://www.china-briefing.com/news/eu-china-relations-trade-investment-and-recent-developments

Huld, A. (2023b, January 25). *Prospects for European companies in China in 2023.* China Briefing. https://www.china-briefing.com/news/european-investment-in-china-prospects-for-2023/

Kawamata, T. (2023). *Techno-nationalism/-globalism/-socialism over information and communication technology (ICT): The international political economy of US-China technological hegemony and EU's social shaping.*

KPMG. (2021, January). *Impacts of the EU-China comprehensive agreement on investment.* https://assets.kpmg.com/content/dam/kpmg/cn/pdf/en/2021/01/impacts-of-the-eu-china-comprehensive-agreement-on-investment.pdf

Kuo, M. A. (2023, June 26). *China's FDI in Europe.* The Diplomat. https://thediplomat.com/2023/06/chinas-fdi-in-europe/

Łasak, P., & van der Linden, R. W. H. (2019). *The financial implications of China's belt and road initiative. A route to more sustainable economic growth*, Palgrave Macmillan, Cham 2019.

Leahy, J., & Lin, A. (2023, December 14). China bets on security versus reform in 2024 outlook. *Financial Times*. https://www.ft.com/content/97ea31ae-2581-4139-b387-abfb1329bf67

Liang, A. (2023, November 14). Why businesses are pulling billions in profits from China. *BBC*. https://www.bbc.com/news/business-67353177

Mardell, J. (2023, November 03). Will the EU's global gateway launch a "Race to the Top"? *Internationale Politik, Quarterly*. https://ip-quarterly.com/en/will-eus-global-gateway-launch-race-top

McElwee, L. (2023, March 30). *The rise and demise of the EU-China investment agreement: Takeaways for the future of German debate on China*. Center For Strategic & International Studies (CSIS). https://www.csis.org/analysis/rise-and-demise-eu-china-investment-agreement-takeaways-future-german-debate-china

Merics & Rodium Group. (2023, May). *EV battery investments cushion drop to decade low*. Chinese FDI in Europe: 2022 update.

The Economist. (2023, October 17). *How China's belt and road initiative is changing: The many motivations behind Xi Jinping's key foreign policy*. https://www.economist.com/the-economist-explains/2023/10/17/how-chinas-belt-and-road-initiative-is-changing

World Bank. (2023, April 20). *The World Bank and China*. https://www.worldbank.org/en/country/china/overview

CHAPTER 5

The Sino-EU Sustainable Green Technological Competition and Cooperation

Abstract Despite the current geopolitical conflicts, there is potential for Sino-EU cooperation in the field of sustainable green technological development with a desire of both trading blocs to contribute to the Paris Climate Agreement (2015). Both the EU's Green Deal (2019) and China's 14th Five-Year Plan (2021–2025) are designed to provide policy frameworks for this with commitments to achieve a carbon-neutral future with a cleaner energy supply. The Sino-EU green cooperation can accelerate their commitment to zero emissions, give other countries an incentive for green technological development, and provide assistance where necessary to climate-vulnerable developing countries seeking to green their economies in accordance with the commitment of the 28th annual UN meeting on climate change (2023). Despite the Sino-EU green cooperation, there is increasing global competition for crucial resources and preservation of green energy supply chains to create clean technology needed to decarbonize the economy. The excessive concentration of China's supply chains plus its own clean technology needs as the largest emitter of greenhouse gases may pose risks that China will not be able to supply sufficient green technology to the rest of the world. Addressing these risks requires more global green cooperation, whether or not through a "green technology partnership" that, through a network of countries, takes responsibility for different parts of the supply chain that would increase the production of green technology above that of China, and at the same

R. W.H. van der Linden, P. Łasak, *Sino-EU Economic Relations*,
https://doi.org/10.1007/978-3-031-71814-4_5

time ensure that extraction, refining, and innovation are less concentrated in one country. In recent years, the EU has become increasingly dependent on the most advanced technologies from China, resulting in all kinds of vulnerabilities and threats. The digital economy plays a crucial role in accelerating economic development and achieving inclusive growth and sustainable development. The biggest challenge for the EU in this regard is to balance EU economic security with its decarbonization objectives. The growing role of modern technology also leads to greater cyber risks and creates more cybersecurity challenges that require greater international cooperation. However, so far, the Sino-EU cooperation on cybersecurity has been very limited due to differing policies and divergent Chinese state-led versus EU rights-driven digital regulations.

Keywords European Green Deal • 14th Five-Year Plan (2021–2025) • Carbon-neutral economy • Dual circulation strategy • "Clean compact and connected" cities • Digital technologies • Paris Climate Agreement • Sino-EU green cooperation • Green technology • High-technologies • EU Economic Security Strategy • European Economic Security Package • Made in China 2025 • Cyber economy • Market-driven regulatory model • State-driven regulatory model • Rights-driven regulatory model • Cybersecurity policy • Cybersecurity ecosystem

5.1 The Current Status of Sino-EU Sustainable Green Technological Progress and Collaboration Possibilities

China and the EU are united in their commitment to act against climate change and to implement the 2015 Paris Agreement under the United Nations Framework Convention on Climate Change. In 2018, the relevant policymakers from the EU and China focused their policies on climate change, and clean energy cooperation intensified in view of the necessary worldwide transformation towards a resource-efficient, sustainable, low-greenhouse gas emissions and climate-proof economy and society. The Sino-EU green cooperation is focused on the field of emissions trading systems, emissions modelling and long-term low-emissions development strategies, greenhouse gas emissions from vehicles and agriculture, climate-smart cities, scientific research, and technological development. The EU member states also have bilateral cooperative programmes with China on climate change, the environment, and clean energy. To contribute to the Paris Climate Agreement, the EU established the European Green Deal (EGD) in December 2019, while China has reviewed its climate commitments in the 13th (2016–2020) and 14th Five-Year Plans (2021–2025). The aims of the EGD are for Europe to become the first climate-neutral continent by 2050, boost the economy, improve people's health and quality of life, care for nature, and leave no one behind. Beyond its effect on the economy, one of the main impacts of the EGD will be to lessen the negative consequences of climate change and pollution for society. In addition, EU businesses could benefit from first mover advantages and gain in competitiveness on global green technology markets. The EGD also aims to ensure that economic growth, employment promotion, and decarbonization can go hand-in-hand. These ambitions make the EU a global frontrunner in green recovery efforts, fully subscribing to the goal of "building back better", the strategy to address short-term recovery and long-term economic and societal transition goals simultaneously. Reaching the EU target of climate neutrality by 2050 requires action by all sectors of the economy and intense coordination to exploit the available synergies across all policy areas (Fig. 5.1).

Each policy area of the EGD is accompanied by a precise and time-bound action plan. Table 5.1 features the EGD's main policy areas, guiding strategies, and key principles (EC, 2020).

In particular, China's 13th Five-Year Plan (2016–2020) paid close attention to sustainability issues, for example by increasing the use of non-fossil energy sources to 15 per cent in the period 2016–2020. This included planning to address the return of wind and solar energy to the grid and prioritizing renewable energy distribution policies. This makes this plan an important milestone in China's transition to a more balanced, better-quality, and greener growth path. Moreover, the central government explicitly highlighted the need to reform the GDP-oriented performance evaluation system for local government officials, while adding more indicators to assess progress towards green development. This has certainly paved the way for more attention to environmental protection in all provinces and to accelerating the transition to a greener environment and a more sustainable growth path (OECD, 2017). China's 14th Five-Year Plan and post-pandemic recovery present an even more challenging opportunity to accelerate the transformation to a carbon-neutral economy. This Plan focuses on innovation-driven growth, low-carbon development, and integration of urban–rural areas with deeper social inclusion. It

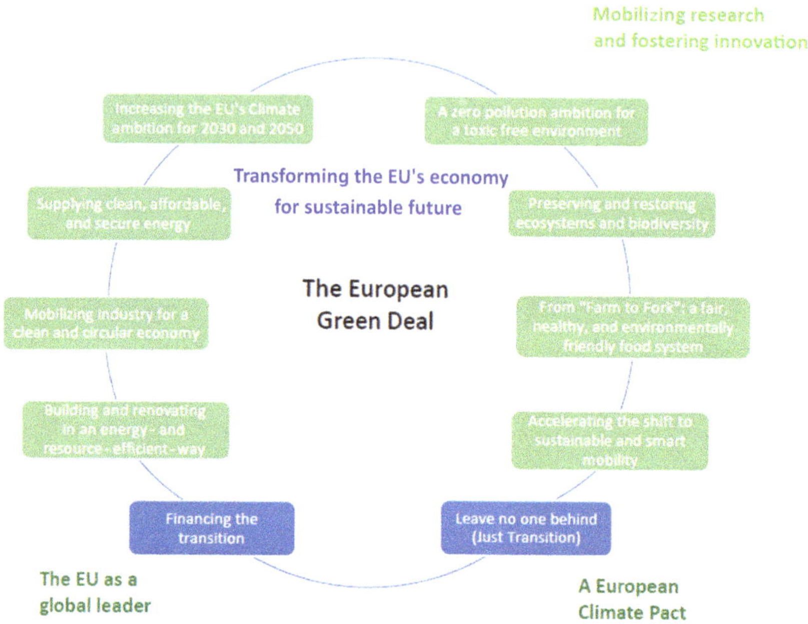

Fig. 5.1 The main elements of the European Green Deal. Source: own elaboration based on European Commission (https://eur-lex.europa.eu/legal-content/EN/TXT/HTML/?uri=CELEX:52019DC0640&from=EN)

highlights high-quality green development and emphasizes innovation as the core of modern development, relying on the *dual circulation* strategy as the growth paradigm coupled with reforms to increase living standards. Building on the achievements of the 13th Five-Year Plan, it aims to reduce the carbon intensity of the economy and peak carbon dioxide emissions before 2030. In the 14th Five-Year Plan it is crucial for achieving the goal of carbon neutrality by 2060, and if China can peak its carbon dioxide emissions by the end of this Plan's period, it would be in a better position to reach its carbon neutrality target. This can be achieved by accelerating many of the actions and investments that China will make to accomplish the transition towards a credible sustainable growth strategy. This will involve the structural transformation of industry towards higher skills and technology with less material input; new technologies, putting to work the extraordinary advances of recent times; re-designing energy and transport

Table 5.1 Main themes and key principles of the European Green Deal

Main themes of the EGD	*Key principles*
Clean energy EU Energy System Integration Strategy Hydrogen Strategy for a Climate Neutral Europe	– Prioritize energy efficiency and develop a power sector based largely on renewable sources – Pursue a secure and affordable EU energy supply – Work towards a fully integrated, interconnected and digitalized EU energy market – Promote green hydrogen to decarbonize sectors that are difficult to electrify
Sustainable industry Industrial Strategy Circular Economy Action Plan	– Economic processes need to be more circular, e.g. via a circular electronics initiative to promote longer product lifetime – New regulatory framework for battery recycling – Review of the directive of packing and packing waste – Sustainable products need to become the norm in the EU – EU aims to become the lead markets for climate neutral and circular products
Building & renovating Renovation wave	– Buildings account for 40 percent of energy consumed – hence present an enormous energy saving potential – The EU aims to at least double the annual renovation rate of existing building stock
Eliminating pollution EU Zero pollution strategy	– The EU Zero pollution strategy should be ready in 2021. – The EU will monitor, report, prevent and remedy pollution from air, water, soil and consumer products – The Commission will review EU measures to address pollution from large industrial installations
Biodiversity *EU Biodiversity Strategy for 2030* EU forest strategy (forthcoming)	– Establish protected areas for at least 30 percent of land and 30 percent of sea in Europe, with legally binding nature-restoration targets in 2021 providing stricter protection of EU forests – Restore degraded ecosystems at land and sea – Unlock EUR 20 billion per year for biodiversity
From Farm to Fork From Farm to Fork Strategy	– Make sure Europeans have access to healthy, affordable and sustainable food, and ensure a fair economic return in the supply chain – Tackle climate change, protect the environment, preserve biodiversity and increase organic farming – Initiative on substituting single-use packaging, tableware and cutlery

(*continued*)

Table 5.1 (continued)

Main themes of the EGD	*Key principles*
Sustainable mobility	– Transport is the second biggest source of GHG emissions. To achieve climate neutrality, a 90 percent reduction in transport emissions is needed by 2050 – The Connecting Europe Facility, Invest EU and other funds will finance the installation of one million charging points, clean fleet renewals by cities and companies, sustainable transport infrastructure and enable the shift to clean urban mobility – Investments in new technology, e.g. the EU battery alliance and the launch of the EU hydrogen alliance

Source: European Commission (https://eur-lex.europa.eu/legal-content/EN/TXT/HTML/?uri=CELEX:52019DC0640&from=EN)

systems; much stronger investment in natural capital and infrastructure than in the past; investment in human capital, through both education and health; and strengthening community and social institutions. This transition can establish China's competitive leadership in the global economy and set an example to the world on sustainable recovery and transformational growth following the Covid-19 crisis. The most important policy priorities for ensuring sustainable and green technology development in the 14th Five-Year Plan after Covid-19 consist of energy transition, new urbanization as a major driver of low-carbon economic growth, and investment priorities for ensuring post-pandemic recovery and long-term prosperity (Table 5.2). The following action points can be distinguished. First, the early peaking of emissions including carbon neutrality or net-zero emissions by 2060 and China's carbon dioxide emissions, which would peak before 2030 rather than by 2030. Second, clean energy transition with which China has committed to greening its major multi-country infrastructure and development project, the BRI, which ultimately also means that China will have to stop investing in coal-fired power stations at home and elsewhere in the relative short term. Third, geographical rebalancing and the new urbanization. In line with the *dual circulation* strategy as a major shift away from the export-led growth model since the start of the economic reforms in 1978, China now emphasizes deepening the supply-side structural reforms and innovative capabilities of the economy and increasing the reliance on the domestic economy (including domestic supply chains, indigenous innovation, and domestic demand) while

Table 5.2 Summary of key action points for China's 14th Five-Year Plan (2021–2025)

	Energy transition	*New urbanisation*	*Investment priorities*
Strategies/ Goals	Move away from coal Ensure Energy supply security Increase the penetration of renewable energy into grid utility	Towards sustainable urban development Reduce energy use and carbon emissions in cities A 'rebalancing' strategy that shifts activities from coastal areas to CCC cities in the interior	Invest in the four types of capital (physical, human, natural and social capital) for long-term prosperity; Invest in infrastructure and technologies that promote the energy transition and new urbanization.
Barriers/ Challenges	– Local governments of coal-dependent provinces; – Relocation of laid-off coal workers; – Dependence on oil and natural gas imports – Grid management – Electricity market	– Urban design issues highlighted by COVID-19; – Energy consumption and efficiency issues; – Migratory trends towards the existing coal megacities	– Prior emphasis on physical capital; – China's power and industry sectors as the prime targets for unlocking future emissions; – Reduce emissions while promoting strong and sustainable growth

(*continued*)

Table 5.2 (continued)

	Energy transition	*New urbanisation*	*Investment priorities*
Key action points	– Reform on local government taxation and accountability – Improve compensation policies and occupational retraining to affected coal workers – Ensure security of energy supply through investing in non-fossil fuel technologies – Upgrade grid infrastructure and technical standards; increase grid flexibility via various routes rather than adding more coal capacity – Push ahead with market-based economic dispatch	– Better urban planning and management; greater adoption of renewables, recycling and efficiency in public infrastructure; build climate-smart housing and efficient public transport networks; strengthen the quality and resilience of natural assets in cities, etc. – Implement best practices in energy and resource conservation in new buildings; retrofit existing buildings to improve energy efficiency; careful planning of land use; incorporate digital technologies into buildings; etc. – Ensure health and education services are evenly distributed; fiscal transformation in CCCs and existing megacities	– Integrate the recovery from the pandemic with the transformation of the economy in the medium to long term; focus on many sustainable projects that can be implemented quickly and create strong economic multipliers – Invest in energy-saving, clean energy and carbon removal technologies; invest in digital technologies to promote energy efficiency improvements across all major sectors – Stop building more coal-fired plants; redirect investment infrastructure and technologies to serve as the new driver of growth and secured jobs

Source: Hepburn, C., Ye Qi, Stern, N., Ward, B., Chumping Xie, and Zenghelis, D. (October 2021), *Towards carbon neutrality and China's 14th Five-Year Plan: Clean energy transition, sustainable urban development, and investment priorities*, Science Direct Environmental Science and Ecotechnology Volume 8, p.7

maintaining close engagement with the global economy. This rebalancing strategy can be enhanced through a shift from the export-oriented megacity "hubs" to smaller, well-contained "clean, compact and connected" cities (CCC) in the interior. By moving activities into the interior, China will generate employment and ensure a cleaner and healthier environment. Fourth, technological infrastructure investments focus on three aspects, namely information-based infrastructure, converged infrastructure for new digital technologies, and innovative R&D infrastructure. Some new technologies, such as hydrogen electrolysis, offer potentially huge export opportunities for China. The implementation of digital technologies across economic and social sectors can improve energy efficiency and promote a sustainable transition through systems innovations. Fifth, even before Covid-19, local governments in China were confronted with a debt spiral. Strong fiscal measures and reforms are needed to ensure that the stimulus and investment packages in response to the pandemic can embody and incentivize sustainability in finances, and do not lock in existing and environmentally damaging production patterns. Sixth, enhancing governance to deliver strong, sustainable, and inclusive growth. Administrative reform, both regionally and across government, will be required to realize the new form of sustainable growth and development. As part of the necessary reforms, clarity is needed on local spending assignments, as well as on financing mechanisms and the management of associated risks and liabilities (Hepburn et al., 2021).

As the EU and China have similar policy objectives regarding carbon reduction and commitment to green recovery initiatives in the wake of the Covid-19 pandemic, there is significant scope for both trading blocs to cooperate and exchange experiences in this area. In broad terms, the EU is recognized as a leader and "stabilizer" in low carbon development, and China is committed to following their lead, but with their own tailor-made policies. Collaboration can accelerate their green recoveries and commitments to zero emissions. Just as important, both the EU and China are well positioned to work together to convince other countries around the world to make similar commitments, and they can provide assistance where needed to developing countries who seek to green their economies. In this way, EU and Chinese leadership can help reform international institutions to not only steer the world towards emissions reductions but also to greening economic recovery responses. Both the EU's EGD and China's 14th Five-Year Plan are designed to provide policy frameworks for each economic bloc's commitments to achieve a carbon-neutral future and fulfill the promises of the 2015 Paris Climate Agreement. Further Sino-EU cooperation is necessary and possible in the following areas: managing a level playing field by investing heavily in fast-growing green industrial sectors including discussions on carbon border adjustment mechanisms; strengthening and reforming multilateral institutions to align on areas like debt restructuring/management, resilience, health/vaccine cooperation, and the evolution of global climate governance; maintaining open global markets to ensure critical supplies and components are available and diversified to prevent countries from being exposed or vulnerable to external disruption of critical resource and goods supplies as was the case during Covid-19; and developing aligned clean international economy standards in areas such as sustainable finance, clean technologies, and data/digital technology. In addition, the EU and China could aim to maximize synergies and cooperation on investment priorities in third countries in key sectors like energy, transportation, agriculture, and forestry (EC, 2020).

A new impetus for further Sino-EU green cooperation was given at COP28 (28th annual UN climate change meeting) in Dubai (November 30 until December 12, 2023), agreeing on financing, adaptation, mitigation, a Loss and Damage Fund, which would provide financial assistance to climate-vulnerable countries, and the implementation of the Paris Agreement. The crucial issue at COP28 was fossil fuels, with most parties disagreeing on how and when to phase out their use. As part of the final results of COP28, the parties were urged to transition "away from fossil fuels in energy systems, in a just, orderly and equitable manner, accelerating action in this critical decade, so as to achieve net zero by 2050 in keeping with the science" (UN, 2023). Despite the disagreements over ending the use of fossil fuels, however, the vast majority of countries have reached a consensus on phasing them out, charting a new path to better global green development governance. This is an area in which China and the EU have common interests and high cooperation potential looking at the promotion of green, high-quality, circular, and low-carbon development in EU's EGD and China's 14th FYP. The agreement of further Sino-EU green cooperation was further strengthened on November 24, 2023, when the China-France Carbon Neutrality Center was officially launched to facilitate the two countries' green transition. Moreover, on December 7, 2023, the 24th China-EU Summit reaffirmed the two sides' commitments to strengthen dialogue and cooperation in areas such as trade, the green economy, and the digital economy. They also agreed to work together to maintain the stability and security of industry and supply chains, and deepen cooperation on climate change, artificial intelligence, and other major global issues. One of the key messages from the summit was that China and the EU will continue their cooperation in some key fields to achieve net-zero emissions. China is now the global leader in new energy vehicles, and it has built the world's largest carbon market and clean power generation system, with high hydropower, wind power, solar power, and biomass power generation capacity. As such, China and the EU can build an open and collaborative green technology cooperation chain to reduce the cost of renewable energy while helping other countries, including developing countries involved in the Belt and Road Initiative, to make more stable and proper energy transitions. In addition, there is room for cooperation between the two sides in green technologies, which would reduce the use of plastic and better protect natural resources such as the oceans and forests, and help more countries achieve net-zero emissions. Given the trend of innovations through the fusion of artificial intelligence and other smart technologies, China and the EU have huge partnership potential in emerging industries such as cloud computing, visual image segmentation technology, electric vehicles, energy saving, emissions reduction technologies, construction, transportation, and chemical industries. China and the EU have accumulated lots of experience through years of cooperation in smart city construction and city-to-city relations, and should share their experience of building green cities and rural areas with other economies so they could learn from them and take practical measures to improve people's lives and living conditions. With regard to the Loss and Damage Fund, it can be stated that the historic decision on the fund is welcomed, but that this is only the first step and its success will depend on how quickly this fund gets off the ground. Furthermore, COP28 recognized nuclear energy for the first time as "green energy", but the possibility of nuclear energy being used by militaries, let alone terrorists, remains a huge threat to peace, especially in the current turbulent international situation (Ruixia, 2023).

5.2 The Preference for Deeper Sino-EU Sustainable Economic Development

The Significance of China's Sustainable Economic Development

In the field of sustainable economic development, Sino–EU relations are rather complex, especially since China's positions on these issues are often formulated in response to the US, with the EU playing a secondary role in the deliberations. In addition, these Sino–EU climate change relations are shaped by multiple interconnected and often sensitive issues, including the climate crisis and its ripple effects, global climate talks, international government aid and financing mechanisms, trade issues focusing on key components for the clean energy transition, and access to advanced decarbonization technologies. Nevertheless, cooperation in this sector remains pivotal, not just for the EU and China, but also for the global community. China, with 17.7 per cent of the world's population, and its 18 per cent contribution to the global GDP (according to the statistics for 2023), is the world's biggest emitter of greenhouse gases (27 per cent of the world's emissions in 2021) and the second largest in cumulative historical emissions behind the US. While the Chinese authorities have set ambitious goals for reducing China's carbon footprint (pledging to reach peak emissions by 2030 and carbon neutrality by 2060), its efforts on climate change are seen as "highly insufficient" and that could lead to a 3°C increase in global temperatures, far exceeding the global target of 1.5°C–2.0°C set in the Paris Agreement to limit global warming. On the one hand, China has been responsible for more than half of global coal consumption in the past decade (54 per cent of the world's consumption in 2021), consolidating its position as the world's leading user of coal. On the other hand, China has also established itself as a leader in the past fifteen years in the production and deployment of low-carbon technologies. Ultimately, this leads to more economic growth, increased global dependence on Chinese goods, and reduced production costs for these technologies. China, for example, now has the largest electric car industry in the world and three in every four batteries are made in China, giving the country significant control over their value chain. China is also the world's largest manufacturer of solar panels, accounting for 80 per cent of photovoltaic (PV) panel production, whose exports account for almost 7 per cent of China's total trade surplus. In addition, China has been the world leader in wind energy generation for more than a decade (Voita, 2023).

Current Risks of Faster Global Decarbonization in a Geopolitical Context

Despite rising geopolitical tensions, the EU, the US, and China agree on one goal, namely the need for all countries to replace fossil fuels with renewable energy, in order to cut the greenhouse gas emissions that are causing global warming. However, it is difficult to cooperate in the field of green technology trade in the context of current geopolitical tensions and geo-economic competition. The struggle for crucial resources to create the clean technology needed to decarbonize the economy creates new tensions and becomes a new source of rivalry. To pursue decarbonization as a global public good, greater alignment of the major economic powers is needed around a collective effort to accelerate the transition to renewable energy and electric vehicles. China wants to maintain its dominant position in global supply chains, while the US and EU are focused primarily on increasing their own supplies of clean tech, rather than improving the overall security of supply for all countries. For faster global decarbonization, two risks can be distinguished. The first arises from the excessive concentration of green energy supply chains in one country. China dominates the world supply chains for green energy products, including solar panels and electric vehicle batteries and, to a lesser extent, wind turbines. A problem arises here if China uses its dominant position in certain crucial raw materials to put pressure on other countries. Part of the EU and US response to reduce reliance on China is reshoring production, but this is economically inefficient given their limited access to critical raw materials and high production costs. Moreover, Chinese firms are far ahead of the rest of the world in green tech manufacturing and innovation, in extraction and processing. The EU can reduce this risk by building supplementary supply chains, rather than just reshoring crucial raw materials and production. The second risk arises from China's own clean-tech needs. China's decarbonization targets are a vital global interest because it is the largest emitter of greenhouse gases. Given China's massive investment in production capacity for renewables, the risk that China might be unable to supply sufficient green tech to the rest of the world appears currently to be low, but this risk could grow, and supply disruptions that would slow down global decarbonization remain a problem. To address both risks, a "green tech partnership" should be put in place. This would be a network of countries that take responsibility for different parts of the supply chain, according to their comparative advantage or, in other words, through coordinated specialization. It aims at creating a supplementary supply chain that would increase the production of green tech over and above that of China, while ensuring that extraction, refining, and innovation are less concentrated in a single country. The main challenge in designing such a partnership is how to align incentives for the governments and private sectors of participating countries, and how to keep it inclusive. In other words, the aim is not to substitute the China-centric green supply chain but to complement it by calling into partnership resource-rich countries and those with innovation capabilities or low-cost extraction, refining, or manufacturing infrastructure.

The Extent of the EU's Dependence on China for Clean Technology

While energy transitions in the US and EU tend to focus on access to critical raw materials, clean technology supply chains are complex and input needs for clean technology are multifaceted in terms of extraction, refining or processing, innovation, and manufacturing. Although the global extraction of global minerals is dispersed, China dominates mining and processing of key renewable energy mineral resources, many of which are central to the production of clean-tech goods such as natural graphite and rare earth elements (72 and 66 per cent of the world's extraction in 2019 and 2020 respectively). In addition to the domestic extraction of important minerals, China also has mineral network supply agreements that fuel the domestic refining industry, built through a series of cross-border acquisitions and trade agreements with countries in Africa, Oceania, and Latin America and with regional neighbours. China dominates the processing of rare earth elements, with a market share of more than 85 per cent, and of silicon and cobalt, all of which are integral to the production of high-energy density batteries and wind turbines and solar panels. The Chinese government's strategic goal to achieve dominance of the clean-tech industry is reflected in the fact that the Chinese share in metal processing is greater than its share in mining. For a long time, the US and the EU were content with moving the processing of crucial raw materials to China because for them it was too damaging to the environment and often depleted groundwater resources and it would now be difficult for them to restart processing on a large scale because of domestic political opposition.

Despite the ailing economy in recent years, China is still an advanced manufacturer of renewable energy goods, and through economies of scale (cost efficiency), China has a competitive edge in the production of many technically advanced goods including the three major types of clean tech, namely solar panels, wind turbines, and EV batteries. Firstly, in the field of solar panels, for more than a decade Chinese authorities have succeeded in developing a leading solar PV industry with a current global market share of approximately 85 per cent. By fine-tuning their advanced, highly automated manufacturing processes, Chinese solar PV firms are able to manufacture with superior precision, which has enabled them to achieve record efficiencies for commercial silicon cells in the last five years. More than 96 per cent of EU imports of solar panels came from China in 2022, with a high degree of dependence across the whole supply chain. It is striking that the EU is a sizeable net exporter of unrefined silicon to China, where it is processed and fed into the domestically captured value chain. Overall, the value chain is dominated by China, with European exports of unrefined silicon accounting for barely 5 per cent of the total. Secondly, as far as global production of lithium-ion batteries is concerned, it mainly takes place in China, Japan, and Korea, with China having a market share of approximately 60 per cent in 2022 (Herrero et al., 2023).

However, after major investments in EV battery factories in the EU and the US, among others, production will become increasingly regionalized. Nevertheless, it is likely that the extraction and refining of minerals, which is difficult to diversify, will remain focused on China in the short term. Imports of EV batteries into the EU currently mainly come from China. The EU is just one small participant in this supply chain, both in terms of finished and semi-finished products. Thirdly, EU-China trade in finished wind turbines is low relative to that in intermediate goods, because of the high cost of transporting wind turbine blades and towers between Europe and China. This favours localized production and has resulted in a regional fragmentation of the market. Although EU-China trade in completed wind turbines is low, there is a sizeable volume of trade in intermediate turbine components. While the EU's reliance on China is generally only moderate for most components, 91 per cent of EU imports of permanent magnets came from China in 2022, a dependence that extends to many other technologies, including electric motors (Wyk, 2023). In summary, it can be concluded that so far, Chinese companies have mainly taken the lead in production processes and cost efficiency. However, by investing more in domestic research into sustainable energy technologies, where so far the West still mainly holds the lead, Chinese companies aim to reinforce their grip on the export of innovation-driven higher-value goods.

Currently, it is difficult for the EU to reduce dependence on Chinese supply chains where it is virtually impossible to achieve decarbonization without importing a very large proportion of materials and finished products from China. There are two different types of risks associated with the concentration of Chinese supply chains, namely risks independent of the Chinese government and risks arising from decisions made in Beijing. Examples of the first form of non-political coincidental risks include potential exogenous shocks such as climate-related disasters, pandemics, or conflicts in mining regions that impeded exports from China. The second group of risks consists of two broad categories focused more on economic policy or based on political decisions. Among the former, China's decarbonization efforts figure most prominently. The country's domestic needs are considerable and will require a ramping up of production capacity and consistent pace of expansion of renewable energy infrastructure. At the moment, Chinese production is growing in response to increasing global demand. However, at some point, it might become difficult to meet the EU's demand for decarbonization goods if China cannot invest enough to keep on growing the supply of renewables, or decides to put its own needs first or serve other trading partners with which it may have signed preferential agreements. The second type of decision that the Chinese authorities make is retaliation. A recent example of this is the introduction by the Netherlands of export controls on semiconductor components (lithography machines), which in 2023 provoked retaliatory measures from China in the form of a halt to exports of gallium and germanium, which are essential inputs for high-quality semiconductors. Also, China's ambiguous position over the war in Ukraine, particularly the possibility of the EU imposing sanctions on Chinese companies exporting dual-use technology to Russia, could trigger retaliation.

The current situation shows that the EU needs climate policy which considers on the one hand the risks posed by climate change, but on the other hand should consider such aspects as the implications of the energy transition for jobs, economic growth, and industrial transition. According to this broader approach, the EU should strive to "de-risk" or reduce its dependence on its relationship with China (Mazzocco, 2023). The EU responded to the emerging challenges in 2023 by introducing new legislation. One part of the policy is to diversify sources of supply, as set out in the proposed EU Critical Raw Materials Act (CRMA) (EC, 2023a), while the second is reshoring manufacturing to the EU, as set out in the proposed Net Zero Industry Act (EC, 2023b). While the EU, for decarbonization purposes, needed to respond to the risks of excessive reliance on China, these two proposed laws are unfortunately unlikely to achieve this goal. The CRMA would set targets for domestic mining, refining, and recycling that are unlikely to be achieved because reshoring would be expensive and, in some cases, unfeasible because of European environmental protection rules. Furthermore, the bottlenecks in the supply chain for different types of green tech are so large that the EU's dependence on China cannot be solved exclusively through more access to refined critical raw materials. Even with such access, which so far remains elusive, reshoring the manufacturing of solar panels would not be cost effective, thus driving up prices of clean tech and making the energy transition even more costly (Herrero et al., 2023).

5.3 Critical Sino-EU Economic Sectors' Protection, Digitalization, and Ways to Cope with Cyber Threats

Sino-EU economic cooperation, deeper economic integration in both regions and between them, the acceleration of technological development, and certain economic flows (international trade and investments) and activities (the financial services offered with application of advanced technologies) lead to the need for some economic sectors' protection. There are two reasons for protecting the industry in both the European and Chinese markets. The first is the natural competition between China and the EU countries. The second is the consequence of the last Covid-19 pandemic which has spurred in Europe a debate about EU trade-, investment-, and supply chain-related dependencies. It targets the vulnerabilities of the EU's technological and industrial base and raises awareness of potential risks related to China's geopolitical aspirations.

The current research dedicated to Sino–EU economic relations and threats focused on six main areas:

- import-related vulnerabilities;
- supply chain-related vulnerabilities;
- market access-related vulnerabilities;
- competitiveness-related vulnerabilities;
- security-related vulnerabilities;
- vulnerabilities related to China's geopolitical aspirations.

From the European perspective all these enumerated areas relate to China's investment strategies and trigger several categories of risks such as political, economic, social, tech, legal, and environmental risks (Krpata, 2022). A closer look at the EU's dependence on Chinese-led-vulnerabilities provides the key areas with the greatest threats including:

- products connected to decarbonization goals: electric vehicles and solar panels;
- products connected to high-technologies: artificial intelligence (AI), advanced semiconductors, quantum computing, biotech industries, and other technologically advanced branches of industry;
- cyber risk connected to the technological and digital transformation of economies.

All of these areas require greater attention and special treatment as they define the geopolitical and geo-economic position of the EU on the world stage. The current situation wherein the EU finds itself dependent on China for certain products and activities is leading to appropriate protective actions. For this reason the EU is compelled to react in more protective ways and to securitize Chinese economic presence in Europe. For the EU perspective, especially important are critical minerals, closer scrutiny of foreign investment, and strategic tech exports to China. This also embraces implementation of anti-subsidy investigation into products like electric vehicles (Chen & Wu, 2024). Such actions sometimes put the EU in a difficult position. The biggest challenge for the EU is to balance the economic security in Europe with the decarbonization goals. The latter one comes from the EU policy oriented on the transition to climate neutrality with the Net-Zero Industry Act (EU, 2024). Industries like car manufacturing belong to the core European branches of industry but at the same time the Chinese producers of electric cars outcompete European carmakers. The situation with solar panels is even worse because 95 per cent of photovoltaic modules in the EU are imported from China. The panels produced in the EU countries are forty times more expensive than those made in China (Colnaghi, 2024). The whole situation is not easy and the EU must implement a sufficient policy which enables protection of its economic interests and at the same time continue the policy oriented on sustainability and protection of the environment (see Fig. 3.2).

The first step of the proper policy in the area is greater coordination at the EU level and implementation of its common industrial policy at a supra-national level. In this context, it is important that the EU countries act as one bloc and much less on an individual level as described in more detail in Sect. 7.4, and that the individual EU member states close the gaps in their fragmented national regulatory frameworks related to Chinese investments. R&D activities and research achievements should be protected from Chinese competitors, which include not only companies but also Chinese students who act as transmitters of advanced technology (Lau, 2024). It is a big challenge for the EU as economic security in European countries is part of national security and is a prerogative of member states. This means that it will be difficult to pass legislation beyond the inbound investment screening mechanism, which is part of the EU's trade policy. Regardless of these limitations, further work is needed to achieve the most far-reaching convergence in this area. This is necessary to protect the common market of EU countries.

Currently, apart from the protection of the most sensitive areas, connected with the decarbonization processes, the EU is interested in the application of a general policy oriented on resistance to the fierce Chinese economic competition in the technologically most advanced areas and thus protecting broader economic interests and providing long-term economic security. The best examples of such policy are the EU Economic Security Strategy of 2023 and the plan developed by the European Commission, called the European Economic Security Package of 2024. The EU Economic Security Strategy is based on a three-pillar approach: (1) promotion of the EU's economic base and competitiveness, (2) protection against risks, and (3) partnership with the broadest possible range of countries to address shared concerns and interests (EU, 2024[1]). The European Economic Security Package of 2024 is aimed at strengthening the EU's economic security over strategically sensitive areas. The regulations embrace crucial areas such as (Benston et al., 2024):

- tightening inbound investment screening rules;
- advancing export control conformity throughout the EU;
- contemplating the establishment of an outbound investment screening mechanism;
- scaling up dual-use and advanced technology research;
- protecting research and advanced technology from leaking to strategic competitors.

[1] Commission Recommendation of 3.10.2023 on critical technology areas for the EU's economic security for further risk assessment with member states.

The significance of protecting the EU market in these dimensions is confirmed by the examples of the German robotics company Kuka which was taken over in 2016 by the Chinese electrical appliance manufacturer Midea and the Finnish mobile games maker Supercell taken over by Tencent (Reuters, 2019). These are just two of many examples confirming that the EU has long been an attractive place for Chinese firms looking to invest and acquire assets, particularly in the key tech companies. For Chinese businesses it is beneficial and quicker to buy than to build a business in Europe. For this reason the regulatory protection of the EU market is a crucial priority for decision-makers.

The actions oriented on the regulatory issues, however, are overly focused on managing risks instead of increasing market share of the European companies. Such an approach when it is overly protective might be harmful for the efficiency, innovation, and increasing costs for consumers. For this reason it is important to trigger actions leading to the support of EU participation in the Chinese market. The reciprocity problem with China extends to restrictions at market entry (i.e. foreign companies are not allowed to invest in certain sectors) as well as formal and informal discrimination post market entry (i.e. companies can invest but face disadvantages operating in China compared to Chinese-owned companies). There are many such obstacles to a greater presence of EU companies in China. Among them are the negative Chinese treatment of foreign investors (non-tariff barriers), limited market access for European companies (prohibition of foreign investment), China's government subsidization of domestic companies, and infringement of intellectual property rights (Rahman & Habib, 2024). Despite the current situation, European business groups are emphasizing the potential of the Chinese market, particularly in sectors such as new energy and healthcare, and anticipating more cooperation and government support in further tapping into these opportunities. The support and enhancement of domestic EU investments in the Chinese market must, however, be strictly coordinated with the prevention of advanced research leakage (Hanemann & Huotari, 2018).

Not only the traditional processes occurring in the economy create threats for EU businesses, but also very important are the threats connected with the development of new technologies and the growing technological race and competition. Over the past couple of decades, China has made enormous progress in the technology sector. It has transitioned from a technologically underdeveloped country to a global technological leader. Apart from greater technological advancement the Chinese economy is largely subject to the digitalization processes. The process of digitalization of the economy nowadays is becoming a crucial driver of economic growth and development. The digital economy is playing a vital role in accelerating economic development, increasing labor productivity in the existing industries, cultivating new markets and new growth drivers in industries, and achieving inclusive growth and sustainable development. In the Chinese case the digitalization process currently plays a crucial role and enables the country to catch up with the US and EU economies (Huateng et al., 2021).

The last step of the transition of the Chinese economy started in 2015 when the CCP initiated a national strategic plan, Made in China 2025 (MIC). It was oriented on transforming this country from a manufacturing giant into a world manufacturing power with the key focus on technological development. The development is strictly interconnected with the processes of digitalization of the economy including technologies like AI, 5G, and Big Data. Apart from the MIC, also the China's 14th Five-Year Plan (2021–2025) focused on the development of new digital industries (see Sect. 5.2). Another initiative was the "China Standards 2035" or "Vision 2035 development" strategy, aiming to create a blueprint for the Chinese government and leading tech companies to set global standards for emerging technologies, such as 5G, Internet of Things, AI, quantum information, and semiconductors (Wu, 2020; van der Linden & Łasak, 2023). Digitalization is, however, also the EU's priority. In 2020, the European Commission launched the Digital Europe Programme, which is part of the Multiannual Financial Framework intended to shape the digital transformation of Europe's society and economy (Ghiretti, 2022). One of its goals is to enable a wide use of digital technologies across the economy and society, and to provide greater cybersecurity (European Commission, 2021).

Before focusing on the phenomenon of cybersecurity, it is important to understand the driving forces behind the transformation of the traditional economy into an economy based on digital technologies. Usually the processes are specific to the economy-type model. It means that the development of the cyber economy in different countries follows different paths and is adjusted to the general philosophy and model of economic development. For a full understanding of the current paths of digitalization and application of tech in economic processes, it is important to compare three solutions, namely the US, Chinese, and EU models. In the US the *market-driven regulatory model* is in force, which centres on protecting free speech, a free Internet, and incentives to innovate. The market-driven regulatory model places trust in tech companies' ability to self-regulate and embraces a limited role for the government (Bradford, 2023). In comparison, the Chinese and European models accept different basics of functioning. The Chinese model is called the *state-driven regulatory model*, while the European one is called the *rights-driven regulatory model*. The Chinese model seeks to harness technology in strengthening government control as opposed to protecting individual freedom. In the European *rights-driven model* tech companies need rules and those rules are established by governments. Moreover, in the EU, those rules are drafted to specifically reflected European values, oriented on protection of human dignity, data privacy, democratic discourse, or other core rights of European digital citizens. It means that in Europe the human-centric and rights-driven approach was adapted to digital regulation. It focuses on enhancing the individual and collective rights of European citizens in digital society and demonstrates the EU's unwillingness to align itself with either the US or China. In the European model governments play the central role in steering the digital economy and in using regulatory intervention to uphold the fundamental rights of individuals, preserve democratic structures of society, and ensure a fair distribution of benefits in the digital economy (Bradford, 2023; Kuo, 2023). It can be stated that the European rights-driven model has some important similarities to and differences with both the US and the Chinese model. It is situated somewhere in between these two more extreme solutions.

These three different models of steering the processes of digitalization exert an influence on the emerging, tech-based industries and their role in global competition. As Anu Bradford (2023) highlights, the US *market-driven regulatory model* is externalized through the worldwide presence of its tech companies, which have fuelled technological progress and shaped foreign societies economically, politically, and culturally. China's success in building tech companies has demonstrated that significant technological breakthroughs can also emerge under a *state-driven regulatory model*, and its command and control system propelled the country's tech industry into the leading global force it is today. In comparison, the EU model, which is connected with stringent regulations, has some significant weaknesses. The European digital regulations have had a significant impact on the daily operation of tech companies, including constraining the way they collect, process, or share data, design their products, or interact with Internet users or other businesses in their marketplace. In consequence, unlike American and Chinese entities, large European tech companies have not emerged out of Europe. It means that while the US and China are fighting over technological supremacy on the global level, transforming the global economic and geopolitical landscape, the European companies and economic sectors are lagging behind. On the other hand, the greater presence of foreign tech companies in the European market leads to greater threats for this market and its society. It creates a need for even greater regulation and protection of the domestic market (both from the US and the Chinese tech giants), and consequently, it creates a vicious circle of increasing regulations, which on the one hand ensure safety, but on the other hand hinder the development of tech industries.

Modern technologies, especially those which indicate the Industry 4.0 is leading to greater cyber risk and create challenges for cybersecurity. As highlighted in the literature, cybersecurity has become a complex and vexing challenge of the twenty-first century (Renaud et al., 2020). From the perspective of Western countries, cybersecurity embraces five layers of hierarchically organized areas (Fig. 5.2).

The pyramid highlights the different types of cybersecurity issues, coming from the basic security protection of individual consumers, through whole markets and global stability, and finally leading to such categories as democracy and human rights protection. The complexity and multiplicity of challenges in the area of cybersecurity make it necessary to look at this problem from many levels and address it through various regulations and through different institutions.

In the last couple of years cybersecurity has become a major interest both in the EU and in China. It has also become significant to global stability and the proper functioning of the global economy. It means that cybersecurity should not be considered separately for China and the EU, but should be considered as an international phenomenon. From such an angle it should be considered as a part of the EU–China relationship. It stems from the increasing relevance of global cyberspace to the societal, commercial, and military sectors in both the EU and China. Regardless, also the EU and the US share common threat perceptions and interests, they converge around a number of cybersecurity principles and norms, and they coordinate their actions in practice. This is a form of functional cooperation aimed at safeguarding common interests and avoiding the costs and vulnerabilities that arise from the EU-US interdependencies in the cyber realm (Anagnostakis, 2021). Despite the need to coordinate cybersecurity-oriented policies and define needs in this area, the practical

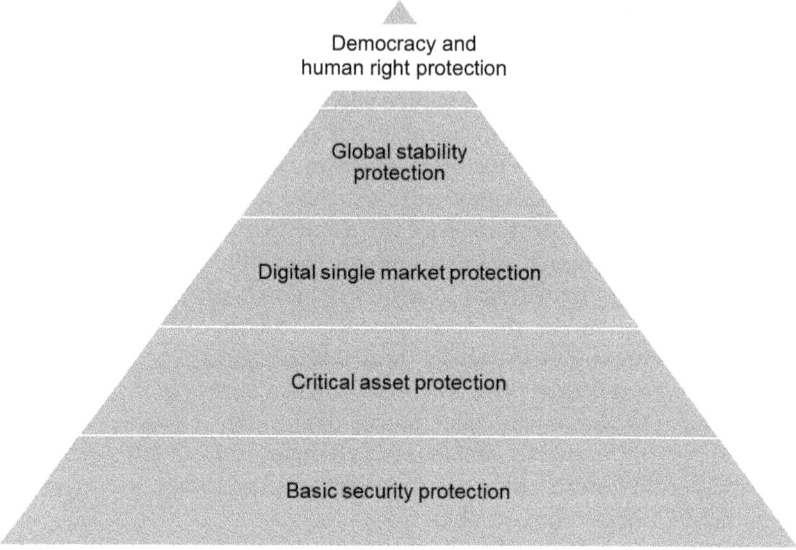

Fig. 5.2 The crucial layers of cybersecurity protection. Source: own elaboration based on European Network and Information Security Agency (ENISA), 2017

implementation of this policy encounters many obstacles and is often even impossible. This is confirmed by the different approaches of China and the EU to the issue of cybersecurity. Moreover, the current technological solutions support country-specific geopolitical and military goals, which leads to divergent goals and even to some conflicts between different nations.

Similar to other countries, the Chinese leadership treats cybersecurity as one of the most important security issues to be addressed in the twenty-first century. China's approach to cybersecurity is driven by the central objective of establishing cyber sovereignty within China and ensuring that the respect of national sovereignty becomes one of the guiding principles governing global cyberspace. In the Chinese approach security and control are prioritized rather than rights, openness, and freedom on the Internet. In consequence, the norms and logic related to cybersecurity in China and the EU are divergent. It means that the cooperation in this area between the EU and China remains largely at the level of rhetoric rather than practice. Despite some agreements (like the EU-China 2020 Strategic

Agenda for Cooperation) aimed to enhance cooperation, mutual trust, and understanding, and the joint economic interest in addressing cybercrime, in practice the approach to cyberspace and cybersecurity seems too opposed for any real action. It is related to such aspects as cross-border information sharing, norms and codes of conduct governing behaviour in cyberspace, or the freedom and openness of access to the Internet (Bersick et al., 2016). Moreover, in the Chinese agenda cybersecurity is divided into four main dimensions, which are not only oriented on the economic protection and technical aspects, but also related to ideological and social issues, as well as military aspects. They embrace (Bersick et al., 2016):

- capability build-up (focused on the technical aspects of cybersecurity);
- stability and domestic security, with a special focus on content and public opinion aspects;
- the military dimension;
- the international governance of global cyberspace.

These areas show that the Chinese approach implies China's "own control" over the enumerated processes. In such an approach not only the common benefits but also the conflictual nature and competitive partnership prevent far-reaching cooperation with other countries on cybersecurity issues.

The Chinese policy as well as the approach adopted in the EU excludes far-reaching cooperation with China in the field of cybersecurity. The EU's approach is based on three crucial pillars: (1) an institutional perspective, (2) as values-based actor, (3) as realpolitik dimension (Hasmath & Berzina-Cerenkova, 2022). All of these three pillars play a significant role in defining the specific nature of the EU cybersecurity policy. It is worth highlighting that currently cybersecurity is not only connected with technical risks coming from the application of advanced technology. Currently more often the cyber threats come from intended actions. State and non-state actors are prone to develop and use cyber tools, weapons, and strategies to deter and disrupt cyberspace (Basu et al., 2021; Sciacovelli, 2023). Cyberspace is also used for cyber espionage and industrial espionage to steal intellectual property. In such a context the cybersecurity policy must be carefully planned, coordinated, and implemented in many areas and many layers.

Such determinants as described above led to the current cybersecurity policy in the EU. The cyber threat perception and the approach to cybersecurity in the EU were originally fragmented, but have evolved over time and eventually they evolved into more coordinated policy with a concurrent legislative framework oriented on provision greater security (Bederna & Rajnai, 2022). Regarding the official beginning of the cybersecurity policy in the EU, it can be traced back to 2004 when the European Network and Information Security Agency (ENISA) was created. Since that time new institutions have been implemented and the EU cybersecurity policy was developed and processed. On June 23, 2021, a Joint Cyber Unit (ecosystem) was created which aims to coordinate a joint response to large-scale cyberattacks hitting EU member states. The cybersecurity ecosystem embraces three layers in four dimensions (Table 5.3).

The ecosystem operates separately from the other EU agencies and intervenes only in the case of widespread security incidents. Its main aim is to coordinate resources, communications, and joint response plans between existing EU bodies and state governments. Usually it is activated in such a situation when the incident has an impact in more than one state. The main idea behind the new structures is to establish and maintain secure communication channels and improve the capabilities of cyber threats detection.

The EU cybersecurity ecosystem confirms that the policy oriented on securing the European market from cyber threats plays an important role. However, it cannot be ruled out that there will be some form of joint cooperation between the EU and China in the future. It comes from the fact that is impossible to internalize every cyber threat, and as a consequence of the international tech and digital market, some issues must be solved on the international level. The growing role of Chinese tech companies in the global economy, and the political arguments for Sino-EU cooperation (discussion of various cybersecurity issues, joint investigation mechanisms, and joint actions oriented on mitigation of cyber threats, tension reduction, and damage minimization), led to the conclusion that finally cooperation of some kind in the cybersecurity area is needed. The only requirement is to provide safety for domestic consumers and eliminate an asymmetry when providing Chinese cyber technology companies access to EU markets, at the same time keeping Europe's own companies in check. It is imperative to provide a level playing field for entities from different countries.

Table 5.3 The cybersecurity ecosystem in the European Union

Layer/dimension	*Resilience*	*Law enforcement*	*Cyber defence*	*Cyber diplomacy*
EU citizens protection	EU Agency for Cybersecurity (ENISA) National Computer Security Incident Response Teams Cybersecurity National Authorities	Law Enforcement Agencies Europol (European Cybercrime Centre)	Ministers of Defence European Defence Agency European External Action Service	Ministers of Foreign Affairs Diplomacy Toolbox
EU Institutions protection	European Commission Computer Emergency Response Team for the EU Institutions, Bodies and Agencies Security Operation Centers			European External Action Service
Coordination	Cyber Crisis Liaison Organization Network Cooperation Group on Security of Network and Information Systems Horizontal Working Party on Cyber Issues Computer Security Incident Response Teams Cybersecurity National Authorities	EU Law Enforcement Emergency Response Protocol	Permanent Structures Cooperation (PESCO) European Defence Fund	

Source: own elaboration based on https://therecord.media/eu-announces-joint-cyber-unit-to-respond-to-large-scale-security-incidents

References

Anagnostakis, D. (2021). The European Union-United States cybersecurity relationship: A transatlantic functional cooperation. *Journal of Cyber Policy, 6*(2), 243–261.

Basu, A., Poetranto, I., & Lau, J. (2021). *The UN struggles to make progress on securing cyberspace*. Carnegie Endowment for International Peace. https://carnegieendowment.org/research/2021/05/the-un-struggles-to-make-progress-on-securing-cyberspace?lang=en

Bederna, Z., & Rajnai, Z. (2022). Analysis of the cybersecurity ecosystem in the European Union. *International Cybersecurity Law Review, 3*(1), 35–49.

Benston, E., Steinberg, F., & Alvarez-Aragones, P. (2024). *The European Union's Economic Security Strategy update.* Center for Strategic & International Studies.

Bersick, S., Christou, G., & Yi, S. (2016). *Cybersecurity and EU–China relations, security relations between China and the European Union: From convergence to cooperation* (pp. 167–186).

Bradford, A. (2023). *Digital empires: The global battle to regulate technology.* Oxford University Press.

Chen, L., & Wu, S. (2024, March). EU firms in China skewed 'disproportionately' towards risk management – Business group. *Reuters.* https://www.reuters.com/markets/eu-firms-china-skewed-disproportionately-towards-risk-management-business-group-2024-03-20/

Colnaghi, W. B. (2024, March 21). *The precarious political economy of European industrial policy.* East Asia Forum.

EC European Commission. (2020, October 19). *EU-China cooperation on green recovery and green stimulus: An overview of green recovery measures in the EU & their implications For EU-China relations.* https://climate.ec.europa.eu/system/files/2021-06/eu_chn_paper_green_recovery_20201019_en.pdf

EC European Commission. (2023a). *European Critical Raw Materials Act,* COM(2023) 160. https://single-market-economy.ec.europa.eu/publications/european-critical-raw-materials-act_en

EC European Commission. (2023b). *Net Zero Industry Act,* COM(2023) 161. https://singlemarket-economy.ec.europa.eu/publications/net-zero-industry-act_en

ENISA. (2017). *ENISA overview of cybersecurity and related terminology.* https://www.enisa.europa.eu/publications/enisa-position-papers-and-opinions/enisa-overview-of-cybersecurity-and-related-terminology

EU. (2024). *The Net-Zero Industry Act: Accelerating the transition to climate neutrality.* http://single-market-economy.ec.europa.eu/industry/sustainability/net-zero-industry-act_en

European Commission. (2021, March 23). *The digital Europe programme.* https://europa.eu/!JW33qU

Ghiretti, F. (2022). *Technological competition: Can the EU compete with China?* Istituto Affari Internazionali (IAI). https://www.jstor.org/stable/resrep30941

Hanemann, T., & Huotari, M. (2018). EU-China FDI: Working towards reciprocity in investment relations. *MERICS Papers on China, 3,* 9–25.

Hasmath, R., & Berzina-Cerenkova, U. (2022). Cyber technology and the European Union's gestaltian approach to China. *Stosunki Międzynarodowe–International Relations, 2*(10).

Hepburn, C., Qi, Y., Stern, N., Ward, B., Xie, C., & Zenghelis, D. (2021, October). Towards carbon neutrality and China's 14th Five-Year Plan: Clean energy transition, sustainable urban development, and investment priorities. *Science Direct Environmental Science and Ecotechnology, 8*, 100130. https://www.sciencedirect.com/science/article/pii/S2666498421000545

Herrero, A. G., Grabbe, H., & Kaellenius, A. (2023, October). *De-risking and Decarbonising: A green tech partnership to reduce reliance on China*. Breugel Policy Brief Issue nr. 19/23 (figure 9). https://www.bruegel.org/sites/default/files/private/2023-10/PB%2019%202023.pdf

Huateng, M., Zhaoli, M., Deli, Y., & Hualei, W. (2021). *The Chinese digital economy*. Springer.

Krpata, M. (2022). EU: China, a major driver in the push for greater resilience and autonomy. In J. Seaman, F. Ghiretti, L. Erlbacher, X. Martinand, & M. Otero-Iglesias (Eds.), *Dependence in Europe's relations with China: Weighing perceptions and reality. European Think-tank Network on China (ETNC) annual report*. French Institute of International Relations (Ifri).

Kuo, M. A. (2023, October 12). *'Digital Empires': The China-EU-US competition over tech regulations*. The Diplomat.

Lau. (2024). *EU's economic security plans take aim at China, China Watcher*. Politico EU. http://www.politico.eu/newsletter/china-watcher/eus-economic-security-plans-take-aim-at-china/

Mazzocco. (2023). *Balancing Act: Managing European dependencies on China for climate technologies*. Center for Strategic and International Studies (CSIS). http://www.csis.org/analysis/balancing-act-managing-european-dependencies-china-climate-technologies

OECD-DRC. (2017, June). *Industrial upgrading for green growth in China: Thematic focus on environment: Key findings and recommendations*. https://www.oecd.org/greengrowth/Industrial_Upgrading_China_June_2017.pdf

Rahman, M. S., & Habib, M. T. (2024). EU-China economic relations in the early 21st century. *Journal of Political Science*, 116–138.

Renaud, K., Orgeron, C., Warkentin, M., & French, P. E. (2020). Cyber security responsibilization: An evaluation of the intervention approaches adopted by the Five Eyes countries and China. *Public Administration Review, 80*(4), 577–589.

Reuters. (2019, January 28). *Germany's Weber: Chinese purchase of Kuka shows we must protect European firms*. https://www.reuters.com/article/idUSKCN1PM1DG/

Ruixia, J. (2023, December 27). New impetus for Sino-EU green cooperation. *China Daily*. https://www.chinadaily.com.cn/a/202312/27/WS658b5e5ea31040ac301a9a7a.html

Sciacovelli, A. L. (2023). *Cybersecurity challenges between the EU and China and the way forward: Thoughts and recommendations*. China and Eurasian Powers in a Multipolar World Order *2.0*, 202–210.

UN. (2023). *COP28 agreement signals "Beginning of the End" of the fossil fuel era*. UN Climate Press Release. https://unfccc.int/news/cop28-agreement-signals-beginning-of-the-end-of-the-fossil-fuel-era

Van der Linden, R. W. H., & Łasak, P. (2023). The digitalization of cross-border payment systems and the introduction of the CBDC. In *Financial interdependence, digitalization and technological rivalries: Perspectives on future cooperation and integration in Sino-American financial systems* (pp. 75–92). Springer Nature Switzerland.

Voita, T. (2023, November). Decarbonisation and climate negotiations. In *EU and China between de-risking and Cooperation: Scenarios by 2035*. Notre Europe Jacques Delors Institute. https://institutdelors.eu/en/publications/eu-and-china-between-de-risking-and-cooperation-scenarios-by-2035/andnegotiations

Wu, X. (2020). Technology, power, and uncontrolled great power strategic competition between China and the United States. *China International Strategy Review, 2*(1), 99–119.

Wyk, B. van. (2023, July 25). *China's wind power companies are giants, but they aren't going to take over the world—Yet*. The China Project. https://thechinaproject.com/2023/07/25/chinas-wind-power-companies-are

CHAPTER 6

Sino-EU Financial Cooperation and Perspectives for Reshaping the Global Financial Markets

Abstract Over the past decade, China has opened up its financial markets to the outside world and implemented many market-oriented reforms in the financial sector. Among the main accompanying processes are the promotion of Sino-EU financial cooperation through the BRI and CAI, deregulation of bilateral financial relations, and the acceptance of the RMB as the IMF reserve currency, which has stimulated RMB internationalization. Another accompanying trend in the more recent Sino-EU financial cooperation is green finance, where despite different approaches, both regions are stepping up their political, technical, economic, and scientific cooperation on climate change and clean energy. In addition, both trading blocs are taking the lead in aligning their sustainability taxonomies and tools, which could lead to the foundation for much-needed global standards in which the digitalization of both financial markets plays a crucial role. Regarding Sino-EU cooperation in the banking sector, it is important to distinguish between the local and global markets. While EU banks were initially strongly focused on traditional services to local markets, following the deregulation and liberalization of financial markets in the 1980s and 1990s, they have become global dynamic players with the largest cross-border lending of a full range of financial services. In contrast, Chinese state-owned banks immediately focused on lending to domestic export-oriented firms, which quickly gave them an international orientation and possibility to build up an extensive network of branches

R. W.H. van der Linden, P. Łasak, *Sino-EU Economic Relations*,
https://doi.org/10.1007/978-3-031-71814-4_6

and subsidiaries throughout the EU. This can be seen as a larger strategy to facilitate FDIs in the EU by circumventing some regulatory and operational restrictions in EU member states. Unlike the EU, despite a strong government deleveraging campaign, there is still a significant shadow banking sector in China that poses a variety of risks that could also have a potential negative impact on EU FDIs in China. Partly due to the increasing financial interconnectedness, there have recently been more initiatives for Sino-EU financial cooperation in areas of financial security and regulation, systemic risks, monetary policy, and sustainable development. The People's Bank of China has been taking the lead for some time with the introduction of the central bank digital currency or e-RMB for a more efficient payment system, RMB internationalization, retail payment system backup, and increasing financial inclusion in China. However, the slow and difficult implementation and acceptance of the e-RMB across China could be a warning signal for both the PBC and European Central Bank that there is still a long way to go to reduce USD dependence in the international payment and settlement system through the introduction of a digital yuan and digital euro respectively.

Keywords Central and East European • European Fund for Strategic Investments • Silk Road Fund • RMB internationalization • EU-China Comprehensive Agreement on Investment • Green finance • Multilateral cooperation • Green economy • Climate cooperation • Sino-EU financial cooperation • European Bank for Reconstruction and Development • Asian Infrastructure Investment Bank • Chinese FDI • State-owned banks • Global Financial Crisis • Shadow banking system • People's Bank of China • Special Drawing Rights basket • International economic and monetary system • Cross-Border Interbank Payment System • Digital RMB (e-RMB) • Cross-border transactions • Central bank digital currencydigital euro • QR codes • US dollar-denominated financial system • Bank for International Settlements • BigTechs • Word order • Global South • Cross-border settlement system • Distributed ledger technology • ECB Governing Council • European payment system

6.1 Sino–EU Financial Relations in the Twenty-First Century

Current Sino–EU financial relations in the twenty first century were originally fostered by the Chinese BRI. The BRI boosted continuous progress in China-EU bilateral cooperation not only in the real economy. It also resulted in establishing a multi-level investment and financing cooperation mechanism for the group "14 +1", a diplomatic platform coordinated by China, to support institutional coordination of relations between China and currently fourteen countries from the Central and East European (CEE) region. In parallel, the financial relations between China and its trading partners became significant (especially in relation to joint investment in the infrastructure fostering trade), and since the beginning of the BRI, Sino–EU relations have been continuously getting stronger. Apart from the group of CEEs, also other countries from the EU were interested in cooperation with China. In 2015 China and the EU started building a strategic connection between China's BRI and the EU's "Juncker Plan". In the next step China agreed to invest between EUR 5 and 10 billion in the European Fund for Strategic Investments through the Silk Road Fund as a participant in Europe's investment construction. In 2018, the Silk Road Fund and the European Investment Fund signed the "Memorandum of Understanding on Implementing the First Co-investment Fund and Further Strengthening Cooperation". It aimed to support the mid-sized companies with high growth potential in medical and high-end industries, consumer goods, and business services in Europe and China. In parallel, the group "14 +1" also has been improving the cooperation and communication mechanism between China and CEEC (see Sect. 4.3). Apart from these initiatives related to trade relations, both the EU countries and China were expanding the scope of cooperation at national level.

The next phase was related to Sino-EU investment and promotion of RMB internationalization. As a result, the European Central Bank, and some central banks (e.g. German, French, and Austrian) included the RMB as a reserve currency since 2017. These initiatives, together with some other activities, have helped to expand the international currency role of the RMB. In parallel with RMB internationalization new funding channels for investment and financing were created, as well as for diversifying the financial risk in the bilateral cooperation (Tang, 2020).

The next big step was the EU-China Comprehensive Agreement on Investment (CAI) (see Sect. 4.2) signed on December 30, 2020. One of the key areas which were included in the agreement were financial services. According to the settings, China had already started the process of gradually liberalizing its financial services sector and will grant and commit to keep that opening to EU investors. As key elements of the CAI, joint venture requirements and foreign equity caps have been removed for banking, trading in securities and insurance, as well as asset management. It is a significant step in Sino–EU financial relations as it promotes the opening up of China's financial sector, providing European companies with more opportunities in banking, insurance, and asset management capabilities, which can then provide better financial services to Chinese households with rising income levels.

In parallel with the financial initiatives, the Sino-EU cooperation which has occurred for the last couple of years embraces the process of deregulation for bilateral financial relations (opposite to the processes of stronger domestic regulations aimed to provide safety of financial markets). Here can be included such initiatives as QFII/RQFII quotas,[1] Stock Connect (2014),[2] Mutual Fund recognition (2015),[3] and Bond Connect (2016),[4] as well as the removal of all joint venture requirements in 2020. All such initiatives are for setting up wholly owned assets and wealth management firms, currency brokerages, and pension management companies in the country. The next big dimension of Sino-EU financial cooperation, apart from enhancing cooperation in traditional finance, is the green finance. Green finance is a broader phenomenon, connected with such terms as "low carbon", "climate finance", and "sustainable finance". All of them are related in some way to financing energy-efficient and climate-friendly

[1] The regulation implemented by the People's Bank of China and State Administration of Foreign Exchange called *Regulations on Funds of Securities and Futures Investment by Foreign Institutional Investors* (2020) to standardize and simplify administrative requirements on the remittance and repatriation of funds as well as currency exchanges by foreign institutional investors, aiming to better facilitate foreign investors' participation in China's financial market.

[2] A cross-boundary investment channel that connects the Shanghai Stock Exchange and the Hong Kong Stock Exchange.

[3] An initiative driven by the Hong Kong Securities and Futures Commission to promote the city as an international asset management centre. The Memoranda of Understanding were signed between Hong Kong and European countries like Switzerland, France, the UK, Luxembourg, and the Netherlands. Later they were followed by China, Australia, Malaysia, Taiwan, and Thailand.

[4] Bond Connect, launched in July 2016, is a cross-border investment channel that provides market access for bond investors between Mainland China and Hong Kong.

assets, and to the associated financial products to combat climate change. It is significant that both China and the EU are at the global forefront of the green financial policies (Larsen, 2022).

The idea of green finance is currently very popular all over the world, but China and the EU play a special role in this area. It stems from the fact that the EU and China are currently intensifying their political, technical, economic, and scientific cooperation on climate change and clean energy. They recognized the necessity of the worldwide transformation to a resource-efficient, sustainable, low-greenhouse gas emission, and climate-resilient economy and society. Currently, the EU and China must cooperate in particular on taxonomies, emissions trading, and their global engagements. The term "green finance" needs to be properly defined, as there is no commonly accepted definition and currently the EU and China have different approaches to defining this issue. However, China and the EU are working on harmonizing their green finance approaches as well as on the harmonization of the approaches on a global scale. Both China and the EU are active in different formats of multilateral cooperation. These are important activities. If China and the EU take the lead and align their sustainability taxonomies and tools, this could set the basis for the much-needed global standards. The joint Sino-EU work and thinking on energy transition and meeting climate challenges seems to be the area where both markets can have a common ground. It is very positive when compared to the developmental, commercial, and strategic differences between both markets (Anthony et al., 2021).

A project aimed at developing green finance taxonomy, related to Sino–EU relations, called "Common Ground Taxonomy", was launched on November 4, 2021. It is oriented on recognition of the green financial assets in China and Europe, contributing to the foundation of a new global standard on green finance products. This report is aimed especially to identify the similarities and differences in the approaches and outcomes of the existing taxonomies through an in-depth comparative exercise (Chan et al., 2023). The main differences between the EU and Chinese green finance approaches are presented in Table 6.1. As shown in the table, the policies and processes related to green finance in the EU and China have both similar and different characteristics. The main difference is that the approach in the EU case is bottom-up, while in the Chinese dimension it is a top-down approach. There are many other differences between China and the EU; however, they are not only connected with the local dimension, but also are significant on the international level. It is

Table 6.1 Summary of green finance approaches and characteristics in the EU and China

	Policy aspect	*EU*	*China*
Underlying governance system		Liberal democracy	Party-state capitalism
Policy approach	Expertise input	Inclusive: Broad range of selected experts	Inclusive: Broad range of invited experts
	Industry coordination	Thematic committees: e.g. High-Level Expert Group	Thematic committees: e.g. China Green Finance Committee
	Policy coordination	Overarching framework: Action Plan	Overarching framework: Guidelines
	Policy content development	Stakeholder consultation: Participation of varied interests	Technocratic: Participation of varied expertise
	Public access	Transparent: Policy drafts are continuously published	Closed-door: Limited release of drafts for consultation
	Regulator independence	Limited mandate: e.g. ECB independence	Non-limited mandate: e.g. PBoC non-independence
Market development	Development pace	Long-time horizons: e.g. green bonds' gradually developing since 2007	A mix of gradual and rapid: e.g. green bonds' explosive development since 2016
	Development model	Organic and industry-led: e.g. a majority of non-state issuers of green bonds	Command-and-control and state-led: Mainly state-owned issuers of green bonds
Conceptualisation of approach		Bottom-up market-facilitation	Top-down market-steering

Source: Larsen, M. L. (2023). Bottom-up market-facilitation and top-down market-steering: comparing and conceptualizing green finance approaches in the EU and China. *Asia Europe Journal*, *21*(1), 61–80

highlighted in the literature that China and the EU play different roles in green finance development in a global context. According to the assessment in the literature, the EU policy is treated as a standard-setter. It offers an organic and consultation-based approach. In contrast, China is not limited by many regulations and standards, which allows the country to be a pioneer in certain policies which other countries can adopt later (Larsen, 2023).

The differences between the Chinese and EU approaches to green finance result in collaboration through compatibility rather than harmonization. Both markets play different roles but also teach each other. As highlighted, the harmonization of green finance standards and taxonomies can be treated as the first step for further cooperation in the area. It is also significant that green economy does not require cooperation in one specific sector but rather a general strategy across industries. Finance is only one of these crucial areas of cooperation. Regardless of the scope of the challenges, China and the EU finally should join to achieve new goals in green development.

Sino-EU cooperation related to green finance is part of a bigger project. All the biggest economies, Europe, the US, and China, agreed on the need for all countries to replace fossil fuels with renewable energy. The main aim is to reduce greenhouse gas emissions and as a result decrease global warming (García-Herrero et al., 2023). The debate about climate protection and sustainability issues started in the 1980s and accelerated from 2000. For many years, despite the intensive academic discussion, it was difficult to reach an agreement between the biggest economic superpowers. The situation, however, has changed in recent years. The most symbolic step was the climate agreement between President Joe Biden and President Xi Jinping at the end of 2023 (described later in the chapter).

Sino–EU climate relations are not separated from the broader geopolitical relations and the sharpened competition in economic development. It can be expected that while supporting green finance, both markets will be also competing for the leadership positions in the low-carbon sectors, raw materials for green technologies, and the standards that govern them. It is important for both markets to care for their economic prosperity in the future, but also avoid undesirable dependencies. Such a need opens a broad area of economic relations between both markets. It is the reason why these countries will need to develop internationally aligned standards on clean energy, digital technology, and green finance. Adopting common taxonomy related to these areas is a crucial requirement for progress in future cooperation. Both China and the EU should also search for opportunities to combine a broader group of participants, especially such important partners as the US. Apart from the former steps related to the development of green finance policies in the EU and China, the crucial step would be if the US joins the initiatives. The US should play a key role in mainstreaming green finance, as the world's most influential financial market. Only the participation of most developed countries and biggest economies will enables green finance to expand and converge (Larsen, 2021). For this reason, some political cooperation aimed at fostering this goal is needed. An example of such initiatives is the latest summit of the Chinese and the US presidents in San Francisco in November 2023, and later the UN climate conference known as COP28. In consequence of the bilateral summit, the US and China agreed to resume a working group on climate cooperation and pledged a major ramp-up of renewable energy (Gan & Nilsen, 2023). During the UN COP28 climate summit in Dubai the world's two biggest polluters made a positive "gesture" to cooperate on climate change. The US and China agreed to accelerate the rollout of renewable energy to displace their heavy reliance on fossil fuels (Williams, 2023). The EU is their natural partner, however, with a relatively better situation in terms of dedication to climate issues. When assessing the situation in 2020, both China and the US were the largest emitters of net greenhouse gases. As shown in Fig. 6.1, the world leaders China, the US, and the EU are responsible for 30, 10, and 6 per cent of global emissions respectively (Froggatt & Quiggin, 2021).

It is expected that the world's biggest economies will start down a road leading to continuous cooperation in green finance. This is the only way to combat the common economic problems, connected with the side effects of the dynamic economic development of the biggest economies.

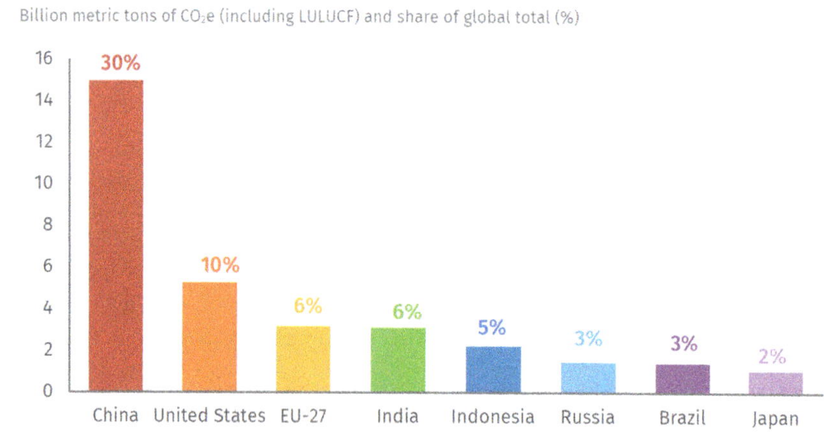

Fig. 6.1 Comparison of the world's largest emitters of net greenhouse gases in 2020. Source: Rhodium Group

Since financialization is one of the most important current economic trends, the financial markets play a crucial role here. As already highlighted, all three markets should set the direction and pace of change: the US with its most important financial market, the EU as the developed banking market, and China as the factory of the world, where the financial liberalization and opening currently plays a crucial role.

6.2 The Mutual Banking Sectors' Development and Interconnectedness

The first decades of the twenty-first century were the time when some drawbacks of the global monetary system became obvious. Firstly, the expansionary fiscal and monetary policy in the US triggered some global economic imbalances. Secondly, the global financial crisis (GFC) of 2008 undermined the confidence in international financial markets. Apart from other countries, both China and the EU reacted to these financial challenges by playing a more active role in global financial affairs and by tightening their ties in financial and monetary cooperation. They are aware that they are significant trade partners, and their further financial cooperation may bring substantial benefits to both markets. They also know that despite many advantages of strengthening Sino-EU financial cooperation, there are also many obstacles restricting this cooperation. Among them are the large gap between financial systems of both countries, various challenges confronting Chinese enterprises' investments in the EU, and the lower scale of EU-China financial cooperation than trade cooperation. In a longer, more advanced Sino-EU financial cooperation there is a risk of changes in the US dollar-denominated financial assets and deficiency in the Sino-EU mutual trust. Despite these obstacles, it is important that Sino-EU financial cooperation is supported by the officials and that the Chinese financial market is being opened. Financial cooperation between both markets, regardless of the threats involved, can bring many benefits to their economies in the long run. From this perspective the financial sector cooperation between the EU and China has gathered momentum in recent years (García-Herrero et al., 2017).

The EU and China are interconnected not only by trade and production ties, but also by financial relations. Increased mutual establishment of institutions fosters deep integration of these financial markets. It can be assumed that the current financial cooperation between China and the EU started on January 15 and 16, 2016. On January 15, 2016, China officially became a member of the European Bank for Reconstruction and Development (EBRD). On January 16 Chinese president Xi Jinping announced that the Asian Infrastructure Investment Bank (AIIB) had been formally established and open for business. Currently, one-third of its members are European countries. Both events contribute to current but also future Sino-EU financial cooperation (Ke, 2017). Apart from these two institutional changes, the Chinese regulatory institutions (among them the State Council, PBC, and the China Banking and Insurance Regulatory Commission) introduced measures to open the financial sector to the outside world. Among the most important initiatives are cancellations of requirements for foreign banks to keep a total assets minimum and relaxed restrictions on the proportion of Chinese shareholders in Sino-foreign joint venture banks. The scope of business access to foreign-funded banking has been expanded. Foreign banks are now allowed to issue, redeem, and underwrite government bonds on an agency basis, and to operate agency collection and payment business. Finally, the regulatory requirements for foreign banks have been improved and relaxed, and the administrative approval process has been optimized. In parallel to the banking sector, also the restrictions on the capital market and the insurance industry were relaxed in recent years. The restrictions on foreign shareholding in securities companies, fund management companies, and futures companies were lifted in 2020. In consequence, foreign financial institutions are now allowed to invest in setting up and taking shares in pension management companies. The business scope of joint venture securities companies is no longer separately limited, and the credit ratings industry has been further opened up. In the insurance industry, the restrictions on the proportion of foreign capital in joint-venture life insurance companies were lifted, and the market access conditions on foreign-invested insurance companies were further relaxed. Finally, the regulations on Chinese and foreign insurance companies have been further unified (Yang, 2022).

Banking activity in China and the EU should be considered from two dimensions. The first one is oriented on the local markets, the second one on the global market. When comparing the EU and Chinese banking markets, it can be concluded that they are completely different from each other. The European commercial banking sector has a long tradition, and banks constitute the backbone for the EU economies, whereas Chinese commercial banking was created from scratch in the 1980s. In consequence, the European banks were oriented for a very long time on provision of banking services to the local economies. After the process of financial liberalization in the 1980s and 1990s they became global players, which led to the current scenario that European banks are the largest cross-border lenders (García-Herrero et al., 2017). In contrast, banks in China were from the very first moment oriented on provision of the support for domestic export-oriented companies. Such orientation led to the situation that the Chinese banks entered international activity without any bigger problems. Moreover, in recent years the pace of opening China's financial industry has accelerated. In consequence, the Chinese banks not only were oriented on provision of support for Chinese national businesses, but also on entrance to other markets in foreign countries. They took advantage of the processes of financial liberalization and began to enter foreign markets from the beginning of the twenty-first century. A special investment opportunity was created by the GFC of 2008–2009, and later by the crisis in the Eurozone during 2009–2014. Some European banks from countries like Germany, UK, and France were experiencing financial problems (Khalaf, 2012). Taking advantage of the opportunity, Chinese banks have been building an extensive network of branches and subsidiaries across the EU. They are part of a bigger strategy, and their role is to facilitate Chinese FDI in the EU. The Chinese state-owned banks are coming to the EU to finance large Chinese and European corporate clients. It allows Chinese banks to circumvent some regulatory and operational constraints in the EU member states, and finally they serve the Chinese FDI inflow to the EU (Balmas & Dörry, 2023). At the same time China opened its financial markets to foreign investors. It also is keeping in check domestic capital outflows. Despite these described processes, it is significant that when compared to its role in goods and commodities markets, China's integration in international financial markets is still considerably lower (Fig. 6.2).

The EU and Chinese banking sectors are at different stages of development, but they share some common challenges. The majority of the EU member states, but also China, were originally characterized by a bank-based financial system. Since the GFC the financial systems of both regions have become more market-oriented, which is reflected in the rapid expansion of both capital markets. The size of their capital markets is similar and both the EU and China are planning to develop stronger bond markets. However, it is predicted that they will experience different development trajectories in the future. Each of them has its own institutional structure

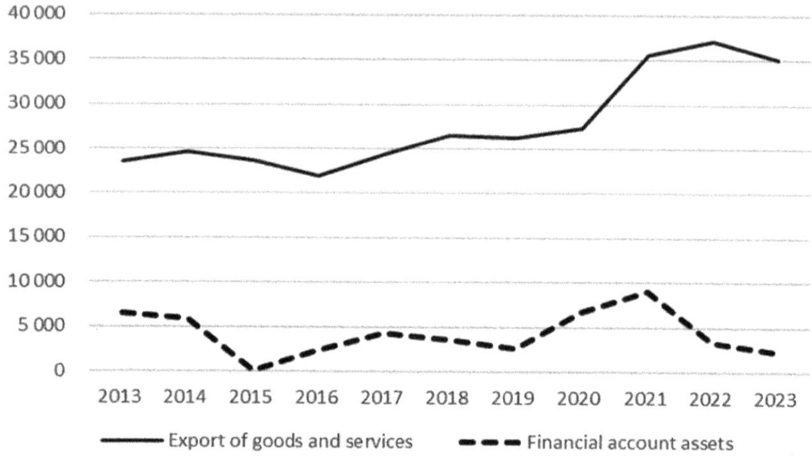

Fig. 6.2 The value of trade and financial flows in the Chinese economy in the period 2013–2023 (in 100 million USD). Source: own elaboration based on the time-series data of Balance of Payments of China, Chinese State Administration of Foreign Exchange

and own policy mechanisms. While the EU financial markets and institutions are mature, China's financial system is still going through numerous reforms. Growing China's economic interactions with the rest of the world causes the need for greater global integration of the Chinese market. The increased presence of Chinese enterprises in the EU requires more financial services support from financial institutions both in the EU and in China.

It is significant that both China and the EU are large, continent-sized economies, based on banking financing. The differences between the EU and Chinese banking sectors have become more important during the last few years. Whereas European financial markets historically were always based on the banking sector, in China the banking sector only after the economic transformation remains the dominant provider of finance. This causes some limits for financial services in China. In a situation where banks are unable to provide full financing at the expected level, a parallel, unregulated sector of shadow banks has developed. The estimates vary significantly, but it is estimated that the current shadow banking industry in China accounts for about 40 to 60 per cent of the country's GDP (Lahiri, 2024). The shadow banking system causes many risks and poses a systemic threat for the Chinese economy. Examples of institutions threatened by the shadow banking system in China embrace the biggest asset and wealth management company, P2P platforms, and others. Among entities which experienced problems in recent years might be included: Ezubao and Qbao.com (P2P lending platforms that experienced problems in 2016 and 2017), Zhongzhi (asset and wealth management company, became insolvent in November 2023), and the property developer Evergrande (defaulted in 2021, triggering a chain reaction). Such cases of defaults threaten the whole Chinese financial system and create a risk of contagion. They pose a threat to the traditional, incumbent Chinese banks, as there is strong interconnectedness between the Chinese traditional banking and shadow banking system (Łasak et al., 2019). The threat for the EU comes especially from the fact that the wavering of the Chinese shadow banking industry could potentially impact European FDI in China, in addition to other harmful impacts.

The Chinese and European authorities exchange their views about the respective financial safety and stability situations and the possible financial regulatory cooperation. An example of such initiatives is the *China-EU Working Group on Financial Cooperation* held in Beijing on March 18 and 19, 2024 (EU, 2024). The engagement of the EU institutions in the process of reforming and modernizing China's financial services industry will help to enhance the efficiency of the market and mitigation of systemic risk, enhance financial stability, and promote sustainable development. The rapidly growing Chinese economy and financial markets offer great opportunities for business development, both for Chinese and EU financial institutions. It creates a space for cooperation across a wide range of financial services. It can embrace capital market development (the issuing of bonds and listing of companies). For this reason, during recent years, cooperation and coordination both among financial institutions and among financial market regulators and financial policy authorities have become crucial dimensions. Moreover, it is also significant to cover global financial governance, monetary policy coordination, and financial regulation. All of these activities should lead to a reciprocal financial opening. The short-term aim for the EU and China is to promote cooperation in the financial market, financial infrastructure, financial regulation, and policy coordination, as well as global financial governance. In the long term, it is expected that the EU-China exchange-rate coordinating mechanism will be established.

6.3 The EU's and China's Search for Digitalization of Their Currencies and Consequences for Their Monetary Policy

The ECB and PBC pursue similar common goals (they are responsible for monetary policy) but differ significantly in many areas, especially in achieving price stability and promoting economic growth. The ECB focuses mostly on maintaining price stability in the Eurozone, defined as keeping inflation rates below, but close to, 2 per cent over the medium term. PBC is also focusing on maintaining the stability of the value of the RMB, but also on promoting economic growth and ensuring full employment. PBC is also focusing on managing the Chinese balance of payments. It is significant that while the ECB is an independent entity (the independence is enshrined in EU treaties), the PBC operates with a significant influence from the Chinese government and its policies are aligned with broader government strategies and economic plans. When comparing their policy frameworks, ECB primarily uses indirect tools (setting key interest rates, open market operations, and forward guidance), while the PBC combines direct and indirect tools (sometimes applying direct credit controls and guidance for banks). The differences also pertain to exchange rate policies. The ECB does not directly manage the euro's exchange rate, but the currency operates under the managed free-floating regime, and the ECB intervenes in the foreign exchange market only under exceptional circumstances. The PBC actively manages the RMB exchange rate through interventions in the foreign exchange market. China operates a managed float regime, allowing the RMB to fluctuate within a narrow band around a reference rate set by the central bank (Hess, 2020; Jones & Bowman, 2019; Rostagno et al., 2019).

The way of conducting monetary policy has significant consequences for both markets. Greater financial cooperation connected with monetary policy integration could increase financial asset diversification, enhance resilience, and enable risk diversification for participating entities. The partnership between the ECB and PBC might also lead to more coordinated exchange rate policies and stabilization of the EUR and RMB exchange rates. The increased use of the RMB in EU financial markets might accelerate its internationalization. Also, closer cooperation between the two central banks could lead to more aligned monetary policies and, in consequence, enable more coordinated policy responses. The limitation is that more coordinated action might constrain the independence of the

PBC and in particular the ECB, which is considered the most independent central bank in the world. If financial cooperation leads to significant capital flows, it might stress the exchange rates, necessitating interventions or adjustments in monetary policy to maintain stability (Marconi et al., 2016). While the cooperation on monetary policy between the ECB and PBC may be difficult, the two banks can cooperate more closely on climate issues. Both central banks focus on such issues and are planning to integrate climate considerations into their macroprudential regulations (Minas, 2022). Some attention should also be paid to the ECB's and PBC's plans to implement digital currencies. Cooperation in the area could spur the development and adoption of digital currencies, which are being planned by both of these central banks. Collaboration in the field might lead to innovative payment systems and greater implementation of financial technologies.

Currently, the global financial system is dominated by the US dollar (48 per cent of global settlements; 59.42 per cent based on share in total transaction value by SWIFT on May 2024). The euro has become the second most important international currency (31 per cent of global settlements; 12.9 per cent), while the RMB remains a smaller player (1.6 per cent of global settlements). However, China's growing role in the global economy results in an increasing desire to increase the share of the Chinese currency in international trade and financial settlements. For this reason China created a plan and exerts a pressure to include its currency in the SDR basket. Europeans also supported the IMF's decision in 2015 to allow the RMB into the basket of currencies that make up Special Drawing Rights (SDRs), following China's efforts to internationalize the RMB (García-Herrero et al., 2017). In consequence of this decision on October 1, 2016, the RMB was officially included in the SDR currency basket. It was assessed as an amplifier of the further development and internationalization of the Chinese economy. This step enabled the RMB to develop its status as a reserve currency. This is the first step towards the internationalization of the Chinese currency. However, much more needs to be done for the yuan or RMB to become an international currency. This especially depends on whether and how the Chinese authorities will continue to open up their markets and modernize their market infrastructure. It means further liberalization and allowing greater access to the RMB both onshore and offshore (Zöllner, 2016).

After the decision to introduce the RMB to the SDR currency basket and when China became a more significant member of IMF, the country continued the strategy to strengthen its role in the international economic and monetary system. RMB internationalization has become one of the crucial goals of the Chinese government over the last several years. It embraces a combination of activities and conditions to increase the acceptance and use of the RMB in global financial markets and trade, solidifying its status as a key international currency. Among the activities might be included: (1) establishing bilateral swap agreements between China and numerous countries to facilitate the use of the RMB in trade and investment, (2) development of offshore RMB markets, (3) encouraging the use of the RMB for trade settlement, (4) creating channels for foreign investment in RMB-denominated assets, (5) gradual liberalization of China's financial markets, (6) implementing regulatory reforms to improve transparency, governance, and risk management in China's financial system, thereby increasing confidence in the RMB among international investors, (7) establishing and promoting RMB international payment systems like the Cross-Border Interbank Payment System, and (8) gradual relaxation of capital controls to allow for more free movement of the RMB across borders. The process, however, is slow and meets many obstacles. The Chinese monetary authorities are searching for a balance between greater presence of their currency in the international markets and government control over the currency. Apart from this crucial currency determinant, there are many more, like appreciation, which can exert negative impact on the export-oriented policy, responsibility for the management of the international monetary structures, and political obstacles created by foreign countries afraid that the RMB will receive status of international currency. Putting together the obstacles with the current technological advancement and the growth of the volume of digital payments, it becomes more obvious that the creation of the digital RMB (e-RMB, electronic Chinese yuan, e-CNY) and its internationalization is a strategy which can replace the traditional Chinese currency and encourage the process of its internationalization. When compared to traditional RMB internationalization, digital-RMB (e-RMB) internationalization refers to efforts by China to promote the global use and acceptance of its digital currency. This strategy involves leveraging digital technology to enhance the international status and accessibility of China's currency. Key aspects of this strategy include: (1) facilitating cross-border transactions using digital RMB, allowing for faster, cheaper, and more efficient international payments compared to traditional methods, (2) conducting pilot programs and trials of digital RMB usage in cross-border transactions with selected partner countries and regions, (3) promoting the use of digital RMB in offshore markets, (4) encouraging international businesses, financial institutions, and individuals to adopt digital RMB for cross-border transactions, investments, and payments, (5) ensuring interoperability between China's digital RMB system and existing international payment systems to facilitate seamless cross-border transactions and enhance global acceptance of digital RMB, (6) developing clear regulatory frameworks and standards for the use of digital RMB in international transactions, and (7) leveraging digital RMB to promote financial inclusion, especially in regions with limited access to traditional banking services.

Such e-RMB will be issued by the PBC and be controlled by the institution (Table 6.2). It means that the payment clearing and settlement will be done through a centralized approach rather than by the distributed

Table 6.2 The difference between the CBDC in China and in the Eurozone

Characteristic feature	*China*	*Eurozone*
Current phase of advancement	Has initiated a pilot phase (since April 2020) of the CBDC implementation (primarily in large coastal cities, but is progressing towards an official launch across all of mainland China)	ECB is in a research phase (since November 2023); it moved beyond assessing citizens' interest in a digital euro to finalizing its design, and it is on a regulatory draft
Main objectives of creating CBDC	The creation of e-RMB reveals an ambitious plan to create domestic payments efficiencies, compete with Western private players, support the internationalization of the RMB, and prevent effects of the Western sanction's regime. There are some other goals like (1) improve the efficiency of the central bank's payment system, (2) provide a backup for the current retail payment system, and (3) enhance financial inclusion across China The target market for the digital yuan is domestic, but the PBC is exploring foreign use as well	Mitigating the risks of financial instability, increasing the power of the euro as an international currency, and establishing strong regulatory frameworks for the digital monetary system

(*continued*)

Table 6.2 (continued)

Characteristic feature	*China*	*Eurozone*
How the CBDC will work	The currency is treated as a substitution for cash. There are no plans for CBDC to replace cash, but it should co-exist with it. The current payment system will not be disturbed, and commercial banks will not be eliminated from participation in the payment system. China has chosen two-tier operation architecture where PBC is the issuer, financial market participants create the first tier, and financial users (customers) create the second tier	The digital currency was designed to simplify digital payments. It would help strengthen the monetary sovereignty of the euro area and promote competition in the European payments sector. The digital euro will be a free, secure, and private means of electronic payment, similar to cash, usable in all euro area countries. It will work by storing amounts in an electronic wallet created by users at their bank or a public intermediary. This is not the end of the paper euro. It will always be possible to use physical currency or private payment cards
Advantages of the CBDC	There are many motivations which include promoting safe, inclusive, and adaptive retail payment infrastructures, the declining usage and costs associated with cash, and enhancing the efficiency of central bank payment systems, and maintaining monetary sovereignty. Among the main advantages might be enumerated: 1. Reduction of transaction costs 2. Programmable features of CBDC could help enhance the effectiveness of monetary policy tools in China 3. The CBDC helps prevent financial crimes like financial scams, money laundering, and other illegal activities 4. Foster the process of internationalization of the Chinese currency	1. The digital euro could be used as a monetary policy tool if issued with interest rates 2. Digital euro could support some of the Eurosystem's objectives, such as maintaining the availability of optimal monetary items, improving cross-border payments, and allowing exchanges with other currency areas 3. CBDC could also substantially reduce criminal risks, such as money laundering or frauds that are very common with the use of cryptocurrencies

(*continued*)

Table 6.2 (continued)

Characteristic feature	*China*	*Eurozone*
Risks related to CBDC	The Chinese government will have access to daily transactions of e-RMB users, which limits the anonymity of these transactions The implementation of the e-RMB in the whole country will be a slow process because it must be connected with the educational process and cultural shift	1. Bank disintermediation risk which would occur in the event that the holders of commercial bank accounts find it more convenient to replace their deposits with the digital euro 2. The ECB would be exposed to the possible risks of changes in the size and composition of the Eurosystem's balance sheet, as well as exposure to financial liabilities as an operator of a retail payment system 3. The digital euro infrastructure could be vulnerable to cyber-attacks that carry financial and commercial repercussions

Source: own elaboration based on literature

approach (Van der Linden & Łasak, 2023). In such a newly created system, the e-RMB will become a legal tender in China. E-RMB is the digital version of fiat currency issued by the PBC and operated by authorized operators (Progress of Research & Development of E-CNY in China, 2021). It is a value-based, quasi-account-based, and account-based hybrid payment instrument, with legal tender status and loosely coupled account linkage.

When considering the use of e-RMB in the internal market, it has the features typical of other CBDCs. China's digital currency is a legal tender, issued and backed by the central bank. It will be an attractive replacement for notes and coins and have all the functionality of paper currency, a medium of exchange, a unit of account, and a store of value. It is significant that the implementation of e-RMB in China is not something completely new in the payments space. During the last two decades China experienced dynamic growth of such means as Alibaba's Alipay and

Tencent's WeChat Pay. Later the Chinese payment ecosystem was dominated by QR codes and digital wallets (Subrahmanyam, 2023). All of these means of payment transformed the Chinese society from cash level to the electronic means of payment. It is also significant that China bypassed the development of such traditional forms of payment as credit cards and other banking solutions that are typical in other countries.

When considering the international role of the e-RMB, many arguments support the project. Firstly, it will help China to gain a stronger foothold in the global financial system. It will reduce China's dependence on the US dollar-denominated financial system. It also will allow China to leverage its position as the leader in CBDCs. This is a significant argument, as many societies around the world are becoming cashless. There are also some obstacles connected with the implementation of the e-RMB at the international level. One of them is legal issues. The role of traditional currencies which are in circulation is strictly defined by law. The idea of CBDC is a new one and triggers a need for development of suitable legal frameworks. Such frameworks are already being developed by the Bank for International Settlements and by some central banks. However, it might take some time to put them into force.

When considering the motives for introducing digital e-RMB, it should be clearly emphasized that in the first place these were motives resulting from national needs. The main goals of introducing CBDC in China embrace the need for increased traceability and oversight of digital transactions and the recentralization of monetary authority from third-party vendor monopolies. There are, however, many more arguments in favour of digitizing the Chinese currency. The Chinese approach treats money as means of payment, but also as an instrument used for economic policy and even social policy. Among the main motives for implementing the e-RMB, especially important are the following three points: (1) improve the efficiency of the central bank's payment system; (2) provide a backup for the current retail payment system; and (3) enhance financial inclusion across China (Table 6.2). Regarding the internal use of e-RMB, it is assessed that this electronic currency can be used to improve the efficiency of central bank payment systems as more secure and connected with an inclusive retail payment infrastructure. It also can be used as the best tool that meets the public's demand for cash in the digital economy era. Secondly, the CBDC provides a backup or redundancy to the retail system. For the last several years an important part of the payment infrastructure in China was been developed by BigTechs such as Alibaba, Baidu, and Tencent.

Now what is important are the risks connected with the functioning of such giants as the enumerated BigTechs. In such a situation the CBDC offers a more secure and efficient payment system (free of economic risk associated with the activity of BigTechs) and sets the e-RMB a status of legal tender (BIS, 2022). It will also be used to stimulate domestic consumption during worse times from the perspective of economic development. Digital currency can be used as a useful monetary policy in the hands of the PBC, especially when there is a need to increase or decrease money supply, because of the economic situation. It can also be treated as a tool that increases a bank's short-term liquidity. In the case of the purpose oriented on enhancing financial inclusion, paradoxically, this applies not only to the excluded local citizens, but also to foreign visitors staying in China, who often have no access to the mobile-dominated electronic payment system (Orcutt, 2023).

These enumerated motives are important determinants for the development of the CBDC project. According to the project, the electronic Chinese yuan (e-RMB or e-CNY) replaces the traditional paper currency. The CBDC in China has been piloted in several cities in China since 2020. It is electronic cash of the PBC available both to the public and to foreign visitors of China. It is available through account-based interfaces (Aneja & Dygas, 2023). In 2014 China's central bank began research on the digital currency. One year later the State Council approved the development of the digital currency, in partnership with commercial banks and other organizations. In October 2019 the PBC announced that a digital RMB would be released after the preparation period. The next phase, spanning from 2020 to 2023, marks the period during which the e-RMB has been tested and consequently introduced in a greater number of regions. In this period the PBC is taking consecutive steps towards testing and assimilating the e-RMB within its domestic financial system. One of the features is that the e-RMB has an expiry date. It means that either it is spent or it will vanish in a certain time frame. Such a solution compels users to spend it, thereby boosting internal consumption (Aneja & Dygas, 2023).

The use of the e-RMB in the international monetary system has significant consequences for the world order. According to some assessments, it will leverage the Chinese economic influence abroad. It is a similar situation as in the past in the US, when the USD became the dominant international currency in foreign exchange reserves and cross-border transactions. It is expected that the e-RMB will be firstly used abroad via the BRI. The Chinese currency could take advantage of the agreements mandating digital yuan payment for all these debtors, borrowers, and contractors (Elston, 2023). Enabling access to electronic payment, China can easily convince the countries from the Global South to use e-RMB. Greater concerns related to the Chinese initiative appear in the developed countries, and especially in the US. The monetary authorities in this country are afraid that the development of the e-RMB may create a threat to the dominance of the US dollar. The acceptance of e-RMB on a broader scale and creation of cross-border settlement system could lead to de-dollarization. Currently the dollar is not only a reserve currency, but also is treated as a highly liquid bridge between different currencies, as an instrument of borrowing as well as global trade. However, it seems that despite the possibility to introduce e-RMB at the international level, there are some constraints to accepting the Chinese currency on a greater scale. Among such constraints are liquidity and capital obstacles (Kumar, 2023).

The interest in CBDCs has been progressively increasing as economies undergo digitalization, with financial systems also being embraced by this trend. Apart from the Chinese initiative leading to the digitalization of the RMB, also central banks in other countries were interested in this initiative. At the end of 2023 eleven countries already had CBDC in operation. A few other countries have also decided to launch their currencies in the digital form and are in the advanced pilot stage of the process (Demertzis & Martins, 2023). Significantly, the ECB is also working with other national central banks of the euro area to develop a European solution for implementation of digital euro currency. This project is treated as a new phase of the process of development of a European single currency. Moreover, it is assessed that when changed into digital currency, it would be more separated from the payment processors from outside the EU. It is also highlighted that the idea is that the digital euro retains the properties of traditional cash, such as anonymity, offline payments, and high inclusion (Schwarz, 2023). The wholesale CBDC in the EU has existed for a few decades and was used by financial institutions for settlements in central bank money, while the retail version of CBDC is a new concept. The current initiative is aimed to introduce CBDC which will be used by retail customers (citizens and businesses). It is significant that the new, digital euro will also have an important impact on the current wholesale payment system. Moreover, also the use of distributed ledger technology (DLT) for the CBDC is a new solution. It enables the implementation of the digital euro, which will be treated as a complement and an equivalent to physical cash. It means that it will be a digital substitute for cash.

There are more reasons to issue the digital euro, but also the new solution requires greater consideration than in the Chinese case. The euro currency is a consequence of a long process of economic and monetary integration and is based on particular regulatory solutions, related to the process. For this reason the replacement of the traditional euro with its digital version is not as easy as in China with the replacement of the RMB with e-RMB. Among the motives for implementation of the digital euro might be enumerated: complementing cash and deposits, creating synergies with payment industry, supporting digitalization in the European economy, ensuring access to central bank money, avoiding risks of unregulated payment solutions, and pre-empting uptake for foreign currencies. There is also an idea that the digital euro can foster economic growth, especially in times of recession or crisis. For this reason the majority of physical money (cash) should be replaced by digital money. Such a situation means that instead of keeping money in their hands, people keep digital money in deposit accounts. In such a situation the ECB can introduce a policy of negative real interest rates upon deposits. It is a policy leading to the growth of consumption and can be efficient in economic growth stimulation. Moreover, the new system may lead to the substitution of commercial bank deposits with central bank money and could increase the financing capacity of central banks and reduce that of commercial banks. It also could become more expensive for commercial banks to lend to the private sector, because the banks would have to pay higher interest rates on their deposits or rely more on capital markets, in direct competition with other financial intermediaries. As already highlighted, the crucial aspect is the legal status of the digital euro. For this reason the next phase of its implementation requires development of a legal framework for the implementation of the digital euro.

Despite the very early stage of development of this project, some radical steps have already been implemented. In October 2023 the Governing Council of the ECB decided to move to the preparation phase of this project (as shown in Table 6.2). This phase will lay foundations for a potential digital euro. According to the plan, the digital euro, as a digital form of cash, could be used for all digital payments throughout the euro area. The preparation phase will have two years and then the ECB Governing Council will decide whether to move to the next stage of preparations. The decision-makers still have not yet made any final decision on the underlying technology framework (both centralized and decentralized solutions have been considered). The main differences between centralized and decentralized digital currencies lie in the control of information, privacy, and transparency. The decentralization leads to a situation where the power is being moved from one single organization to a network to avoid giving control to any single authority, such as the central bank. Such a solution might be implemented by Distributed Ledger Technology (DLT). Everyone who is participating in the network can see all transactions made and received by any user since all revenue streams are placed on a public chain, called blockchain. In the context of the EU legislation it is crucial to change the regulations as according to the current legal status it is impossible to introduce digital euro by the ECB that is directly accessible to consumers through national central banks. For this reason a new legislation would have to be drafted for the ECB to introduce a CBDC system with direct consumer access (Mooij, 2023). It also must be mentioned that the digital euro is associated with some challenges. The most important might embrace: disintermediation of commercial banks, expansion of central banks' balance sheets, financial instability and volatility of capital flows, and reputational risks (Passacantando, 2021). It means that the digital euro might be an opportunity to greatly improve the efficiency of the European payment system, but also is connected with some significant challenges. The proper implementation of this solution requires good planning, hard work and coordination during the implementation phase, and development of the new, sufficient regulations.

It must be highlighted that despite the strong intentions, the mass-adoption of e-RMB has failed hitherto (Sekiguchi & Lejun, 2023). It will still be a long time until the e-RMB is widely accepted throughout China. The internationalization of e-RMB is an even longer process. This should be a warning signal for the EU and ECB that the process of digital currency implementation is not an easy one. It means that the full implementation of such currency will take longer than expected. It also means that both markets, China and the EU, must still wait with the aim to reduce their dependency at the international level on the US dollar and the dependency on the payment rails of the US-domiciled Visa and Master Card duopoly.

References

Aneja, R., & Dygas, R. (Eds.). (2023). *Digital currencies and the new global financial system*. Abingdon, Oxfordshire: Routledge.

Anthony, I., Yuan, J., & Xia, S. (2021). *Promoting China-European Union cooperation on green and sustainable finance*. SIPRI policy brief, no. 29591.

Balmas, P., & Dörry, S. (2023). Chinese bank networks in Europe: FDI-oriented by legal and strategic design. *Eurasian Geography and Economics*, 1–27. https://doi.org/10.1080/15387216.2023.2182805

BIS. (2022). E-CNY main objectives, guiding principles an inclusion considerations. In BIS Papers chapters in: Bank of International Settlements (Ed.), *CNDC in emerging economies* (Vol. 123, pp. 45–48).

Chan, K. J. D., Wilson, M. L., & Shing, T. (2023). *Common ground taxonomy: Premium and spillovers in corporate green bonds*. https://doi.org/10.2139/ssrn.4496153

Demertzis, M., & Martins, C. (2023). Progress with the digital euro. *Intereconomics, 58*(4), 195–200.

Elston, T.-B. (2023). *China is doubling down on its digital currency*. Foreign Policy Research Institute. https://www.fpri.org/article/2023/06/china-is-doubling-down-on-its-digital-currency/

EU. (2024). https://www.eeas.europa.eu/delegations/china/eu-china-working-group-financial-cooperation-held-its-first-meeting_en?s=166

Froggatt, A., & Quiggin, D. (2021). *China, EU and US cooperation on climate and energy. An ever-changing relationship*. Research paper: Energy, Environment, and Resources Programme, Chatham House.

Gan, N., & Nilsen, E. (2023). US and China pledge to ramp up renewables in place of planet-warming fossil fuels ahead of Biden-Xi summit. *CNN*.

García-Herrero, A., Grabbe, H., & Kaellenius, A. (2023). De-risking and decarbonising: A green tech partnership to reduce reliance on China. *Bruegel Policy Brief Issue, 19*(23).

García-Herrero, A., Kwok, K. C., Xiangdong, L., Summers, T., & Yansheng, Z. (2017). *EU–China economic relations to 2025: Building a common future*. A Joint report by Bruegel, Chatham House, China Center for International Economic Exchanges and The Chinese University of Hong Kong, The Royal Institute of International Affairs.

Hess, P. (2020). China's monetary policy: Institutional setting, tools and challenges. *Monetary Policy Implementation in East Asia*, 13–30.

Jones, B., & Bowman, J. (2019). *The PBC's objectives and operational framework*| RDP 2019–11: China's evolving monetary policy framework in international context.

Ke, Z. (2017). China-EU financial cooperation and the Asian infrastructure investment bank. In M. Telo, D. Chun, & Z. Xiaotong (Eds.), *Deepening the EU-China partnership*. Routledge.

Khalaf, R. (2012, September 17). Top Chinese banks target Europe. *Financial Times*.

Kumar, A. (2023). Domestic and global implications of China's digital currency. *Intereconomics, 58*(4), 185–188.

Lahiri, I. (2024). *What are shadow banks and why are they failing in China?* https://www.euronews.com/business/2024/02/27/what-are-shadow-banks-and-why-are-they-failing-in-china

Larsen, M. L. (2021). Intersecting interests and coincidental compatibility: How China, the EU, and the United States can coordinate their push for globalizing green Finance. *Georgetown Journal of International Affairs*. https://gjia.georgetown.edu/2021/07/15/intersecting-interests-and-coincidental-compatibility-how-china-the-eu-and-the-united-states-can-coordinate-their-push-for-globalizing-green-finance/

Larsen, M. L. (2022). Driving global convergence in green financial policies: China as policy pioneer and the EU as standard setter. *Global Policy, 13*(3), 358–370.

Larsen, M. L. (2023). Bottom-up market-facilitation and top-down market-steering: Comparing and conceptualizing green finance approaches in the EU and China. *Asia Europe Journal, 21*(1), 61–80.

Łasak, P., Szyszko, A., & Pagacz, P. (2019). The interconnectedness between traditional banks, shadow banking and non-performing loans in the Chinese economy. *Bank i Kredyt, National Bank of Poland, 50*, 347–374.

Marconi, D., Bencivelli, L., Marra, A., Schiavone, A., & Tartaglia-Polcini, R. (2016). *Offshore RMB markets in Europe: Prospects for greater financial integration between Europe and China*. Bank of Italy Occasional Paper, (334).

Minas, S. (2022). Financing climate justice in the European Union and China: Common mechanisms, different perspectives. *Asia Europe Journal, 20*(4), 377–401.

Mooij, A. M. (2023). A digital euro for everyone: Can the European System of Central Banks introduce general purpose CBDC as part of its economic mandate? *Journal of Banking Regulation, 24*(1), 89–104.

Orcutt, M. (2023). What's next for China's digital currency? *MIT Technology Review*. https://www.technologyreview.com/2023/08/03/1077181/whats-next-for-chinas-digital-currency/

Passacantando, F. (2021). *The digital euro: Challenges and opportunities*. The (near) future of Central Bank digital currencies, *113*.

Progress of Research & Development of E-CNY in China. (2021, July). *Working group on E-CNY research and development of the People's Bank of China*.

Rostagno, M., Altavilla, C., Carboni, G., Lemke, W., Motto, R., Guilhem, A. S., & Yiangou, J. (2019). *A tale of two decades: The ECB's monetary policy at 20.*

Schwarz, M. (2023). The digital euro in the digital age: Can we really digitise cash? *Journal of Payments Strategy & Systems, 17*(4).

Sekiguchi, K., & Lejun, W. (2023). *China's digital yuan struggle underscores challenges for central banks.* Nikkei Asia.

Subrahmanyam, V. (2023). China's digital currency: The hopes and fears of the e-CNY, *22*(3) chinacenter.net/2023/china-currents/22-1/chinas-digital-currency-the-hopes-and-fears-of-the-e-cny/

Tang, L. (2020). China-EU investment and financing cooperation under the belt and road initiative. *China Economic Transition= Dangdai Zhongguo Jingji Zhuanxing Yanjiu, 3*(4), 115–120.

Yang, P. (2022). *China Promotes Reform by Opening up: The Prospects of Financial Opening up and Economic and Trade Cooperation*, China Watch, Vol. 2, No. 3.

Van der Linden, R. W. H., & Łasak, P. (2023). The digitalization of cross-border payment systems and the introduction of the CBDC. In *Financial interdependence, digitalization and technological rivalries: Perspectives on future cooperation and integration in Sino-American financial systems* (pp. 75–92). Springer Nature Switzerland.

Williams, A. (2023, November 15). US and China agree to boost green energy in climate action 'gesture'. *Financial Times.*

Zöllner, P. (2016). *The renminbi in the SDR basket and its future role in the international financial system.*

CHAPTER 7

The Current Sino-EU Cooperation Options in the Context of the Current Geopolitical Environment

Abstract This chapter describes potential policy area opportunities and threats for Sino-EU cooperation and competition with an emphasis on the global value chains (GVCs). It is presented against the backdrop of contemporary geopolitical conflicts that are increasing the EU's dependence on crucial raw materials mainly from China. The chapter is deeply embedded in the geopolitical-economic context and also takes into account the new situation resulting from the upcoming US elections. Over several decades, globalization, initially driven mainly by multinational corporations, has facilitated the formation of GVCs, strengthening market liberalization and economic interdependence. However, recent disruptions such as the Covid-19 pandemic, the Sino-US trade and tech war, and other geopolitical conflicts have exposed vulnerabilities in these GVCs, which has led to greater awareness of the interdependence between countries. The increasing fragmentation of the global trade landscape due to the deglobalization or regionalization trend in recent years has dramatically changed the trade patterns of the world's major economies, resulting in greater supply shortages worldwide. For the EU, this new international trend meant a strategic adjustment towards ensuring the resilience of supply chains, especially with regard to Critical Raw Materials (CRMs). In the EU's pursuit of a more low-carbon economy without protectionism, several policy measures are available to promote security of supply of CRMs such as gradual market-driven supply diversification, innovative

R. W.H. van der Linden, P. Łasak, *Sino-EU Economic Relations*, https://doi.org/10.1007/978-3-031-71814-4_7

substitution, incentivized and mandatory recycling, and stockpiling. As part of the EU's "de-risking" strategy, a range of economic instruments have also been developed in recent years to both reduce dependence on China and defend against its divide-and-rule strategy in various EU member states. In response to China's more dominant role in global trade, the EU has recently introduced several primarily defensive measures aimed at limiting foreign companies' access to crucial aspects of the European economy and neutralizing their competitive advantages derived from market distortions partly caused by Chinese trade policies. The EU's defensive call to reduce risks must also be accompanied by a more offensive EU-wide industrial policy that focuses on both Europe's industrial core and a long value chain strategy including EU's neighbours and selected partners in the Global South, which are closely linked to EU initiatives such as the Global Gateway and the Green Deal to achieve a smooth transition to climate neutrality. While it is extremely difficult to design a comprehensive and consistent long-term common EU China strategy with limited consensus between and even within EU member states together with numerous business decision-makers and stakeholders, it's obvious that the EU needs an overall strategic framework for dealing with China in the coming decades.

Keywords Global value chains • Global supply chains • Multinational corporations • Electric vehicles (EVs) • Digital technologies • Climate-neutral economy • Critical Raw Materials (CRMs) • Green Deal Industrial Plan • Net-Zero Industry Act • CRM Act • Inflation Reduction Act • Rules-based international order • China-centric world order • 5G capabilities • International Organization for Standardization • International Electrotechnical Commission • Standard-essential patents • Standards-setting bodies • Divide-and-rule strategy • Strategic autonomy • Foreign investment screening • International procurement instrument • Foreign subsidies regulation • Anti-coercion instrument • Outbound investment controls • Artificial Intelligence Act • "Country neutral" policy • Global decarbonization partnership • Free trade agreements • Strategic Technologies for Europe platform • "Cooperation partner" • "Economic competitor" • "Systemic rival" • Dual-use Items • Export Control Regulation • EU-US Trade and Technology Council's working groups • Trilateral Security Partnership Between Australia • UK and the US • Upstream value chain

7.1 The Post-Pandemic Global Value Chains and Economic Importance of Critical Raw Materials for the EU

Since the rise of globalization in the 1980s and 1990s, the organization of trade in global value chains (GVCs) or global supply chains has gradually facilitated market liberalization and efficient allocation of goods and services between sectors and countries while increasing their interdependence. A GVC involves cross-border manufacturing and distribution of goods and services which integrates various processes, from acquiring raw materials to delivering completed products to customers, which could encompass a product idea, design, marketing, and after-sales services. These linkages constitute complex, diversified, fragmented, dynamic, and developing organizational systems. The rise of GVCs, mainly driven by multinational corporations but also increasingly incorporated by small and medium-sized enterprises , has been stimulated by removing trade barriers, expanding technological breakthroughs, liberalizing investments, and developing Asia as a global industrial centre, especially after China's accession to the WTO in 2001 (EP, 2023).

Recent shocks in international trade such as Covid-19, the Sino-US trade war, the Russia-Ukraine war, and the Israel-Hamas war with attacks on Western ships in the Red Sea have led to disruptions of the GVCs and an increased awareness of the mutual dependence between countries. This development also highlights the sensitivity of trade flows to trade barriers, which can be to the detriment of the entire economy. These disruptions to GVCs have also highlighted the vulnerability caused by the EU's dependence on complex import and export chains. Covid-19 in particular has led to more efforts in digital technologies to restore the resilience and recovery of the economy, such as access to the labour supply for certain industries, especially through the service sector. The outbreak of Covid-19 has revealed the interdependence of countries in terms of the supply of inputs and final goods. The demand for some manufactured goods and services, such as airlines, tourism, restaurants, sports, and other face-to-face communication-dependent services, dropped significantly, leading to a decrease in demand for all parts of the production chain linked to these goods and services. The US-China trade war has also caused disruptions that are spreading through the value chain and has led to increased protectionism through increased bilateral tariffs and non-tariff measures for the countries concerned and their most important trading partners including those of the EU. The ongoing Sino-US trade conflict was combined from 2020 with Covid-19 pandemic reinforcing each other's effects on increased uncertainty in trade policy. Additional non-tariff burdens induced by the trade tensions and the Covid-19 pandemic mainly affected firms that were less able to diversify their production inputs or use additional inventories. Moreover, these external shocks and geopolitical conflicts have sparked new debates over the past decade about a reorientation of the benefits and risks associated with GVCs. With the advent of more protectionist measures, especially between the major trading blocs, there has clearly been a shift in recent years from globalization to deglobalization or regionalization, whereby a shift to more localized production would provide better protection against disruptions, which often result in supply shortages and uncertainty for consumers and companies.

China, the US, and the EU are the largest contributors to the global economy and GVCs, which play by far the largest role in the global supply of goods services. For example, in the intermediate market, the three regions exported 10.2 per cent, 10.3 per cent and 29.9 per cent of the world's total intermediate goods and services, respectively. The intermediate import share of these three regions is 14.7 per cent, 9.9 per cent, and 28.2 per cent respectively. China supplied 24 per cent of Europe's imports of finished goods and services from outside the continent but only 13 per cent of its imports of intermediate goods in terms of bilateral trade flows, represented as links between exporters and importers. The EU imported more intermediate products from the US (17 per cent), and 20 per cent of the US's imports were from the EU. In contrast, for final consumption, the US and the EU were more reliant on supplies from China. China provided 25 per cent of the rest of the world's imports of final products, while China and the US each supplied 14 per cent of the rest of the world's intermediate product imports according to the Asian Development Bank in December 2021.

Despite the trade tensions, significant changes ("trade diversion") have occurred in the geography of the trade over the period 2017–2022. In response to the tariff increases by the US, China shifted its export focus to East Asia and Pacific and Europe and Central Asia, and the US increased its exports to Mexico and Canada, Europe, especially the UK, and Central Asia. Since the Sino-US trade war and the Covid-19 pandemic, the trade patterns of the world's major economies have changed. This has helped to increase EU trade with both China and the US, mainly due to Germany's increased trade with China, the US, and Poland, but at the same time it led to a reduction of its trade with France. During this period China has become the world's leading auto manufacturing and consuming country, accounting for approximately 31.8 per cent of global production and 32.9 per cent of global sales in 2022 thanks in part to electric vehicles (EVs). Chinese government has provided support to new-energy vehicle producers to promote domestic auto production. In the meantime, the tariffs imposed by the US on Chinese-made auto parts significantly impacted US imports from China, resulting in declines in their bilateral trade flows. Mexico was a beneficiary of the Sino-US trade tensions because the decline in imports by the US of auto parts from China was accompanied by a corresponding increase in imports from Mexico.

The Covid-19 pandemic and related disruptions to the movement of products and people have exacerbated challenges to globalization. The collapse of GVCs during the pandemic has led to concerns about the ongoing availability of key commodities, and policymakers have considered various responses to increase resilience, including regionalization and reshoring. Moreover, the pandemic came during a period in which GVC expansion was already slowing down ("slowbalization") because of several factors such as rising trade costs and trade policy uncertainty, rising trade tensions which led to tariff increases between major trading economies, eroding wage differences between developed and developing economies that decrease the returns to offshoring, and last but not least the technological progress in areas like automation and artificial intelligence.

In an increasingly interconnected and rapidly changing world, GVCs face numerous challenges that can disrupt operations and impact global economies. Digital infrastructure and technologies offer a promising means of enhancing the resilience of supply chains, promoting rapid adaptability, and thereby enabling businesses to thrive in volatile environments. Firstly, the development of the digital economy itself can enhance economic resilience by increasing the size of the economy. The rise of digital industries, such as the platform economy and the Internet economy, has increased the number of industrial forms in numerous countries, expanded employment options, and spread regional systemic risk, all of which can help countries to combat external shocks. Secondly, digitalization improves transparency and the allocation of resources. Digital technologies can help reduce information asymmetries, lowering search costs for producers and dramatically increasing the circulation of resources. Information sharing can strengthen the connection between suppliers and buyers, and facilitate collaboration among stakeholders, thereby reducing friction along the value chain. Digital platforms enable seamless communication, information sharing, and coordination among suppliers, manufacturers, distributors, and customers. Technologies like the Internet of Things, (cloud computing, and Big Data analytics enable businesses to streamline processes, monitor operations in real-time, and make data-driven decisions. Thirdly, digitalization can help manage the risks and improve the security of GVCs. Increased visibility enables early detection of potential disruptors and the appropriate adjustments to mitigate risks swiftly and effectively. By creating an interconnected ecosystem, businesses can quickly identify bottlenecks, resolve issues, and make informed decisions, thereby fostering resilience and adaptability (WTO, 2023).

The EU's trade policy remains an important tool to address supply chain vulnerabilities that can contribute to the resilience of supply chains through four channels: first, the EU's trade policy strategy and specific policy instruments should contribute to the stability, predictability, and transparency of rules for businesses; second, EU's industrial policy measures, bi- and plurilateral agreements, and its unilateral trade defence aim at diversifying sources of supply; third, the EU should work with trade partners and other organizations, including the G-20, WTO, OECD, to monitor critical supply chains, and ensure fair and equitable access; and fourth, the EU should make supply chains more sustainable assuming the supply chains will thebe more resilient to disruption. In connection with this last channel it can be stated that in a transition to a climate-neutral economy through a turn to renewable energy and e-mobility solutions, the global economy is moving towards replacing reliance on fossil fuels with reliance on raw materials. Assuming that global demand and competition for raw materials will continue to grow, the associated increased dependence on raw materials could also lead to a range of problems of its own, such as heavy metal pollution, habitat destruction, and resource depletion due to the higher mining intensity. In line with the US and China, the European Commission launched the European Raw Materials Initiative in 2008, a strategy that includes targeted measures to secure and improve access to raw materials in the EU, including a publishable list of Critical Raw Materials (CRMs) that is updated at least every three years. In the most recent updated list on September 3, 2020, the so-called rare earth metals, bauxite and lithium, which are key components for batteries in electronic devices and electric vehicles, were listed for the first time. Many of these are defined as CRMs because they play a key role in the economy and industrial production, a role that is destined to grow even more in the wake of the ecological transition and the move away from fossil fuels. Furthermore, their supply chain is subject to strategic risks, due mainly to the fact that they are mostly extracted in non-European countries, some of which are authoritarian and/or countries with low quality of market institutions, often in problematic social conditions (e.g. exploitation of workers, underage labour) and using methods with a high environmental impact.

In addition to the CRM Act, on February 1, 2023, the EU introduced the Green Deal Industrial Plan, which aimed to increase the competitiveness of the EU-neutral industry and achieve a smooth transition to climate neutrality. One of its pillars, the simplification of the regulatory framework to stimulate strategic projects, should be achieved through two regulations proposed by the Commission: the Net-Zero Industry Act (NZIA) and the CRM Act. The main objective of the NZIA is to boost the production and competitiveness of clean technologies within the EU to achieve climate neutrality by 2050. The NZIA aims to reduce dependency on important energy and critical materials while promoting sustainable economic growth and job creation. The CRM Act is built around four main goals: defining priorities and objectives for EU actions; improving its monitoring, risk management, and governance in the field of CRM; strengthening the EU CRM value chain in a global context; and ensuring a sustainable level playing field across the single market. Combined, these legislative acts will shape the EU's CRM strategy and direction for years to come. The proposal clearly seeks to enhance the EU's production capacity of net-zero energy solutions to reduce the risk of raw material supply shortages and dependencies. The regulation will simplify and speed up the process of obtaining permits for production sites and develop uniform European standards. It will also include the possibility of cooperation with like-minded partner countries, to strengthen and diversify supply chains.

CRMs are indispensable for modernization including digitalization of an economy. Minerals such as lithium, cobalt, and copper are essential for renewable energy technologies and for the further deployment of electric vehicles. Ultimately, the value added (VA) of CRMs for the EU is mainly determined by, first, its economic importance in terms of end-use applications and the VA of corresponding EU manufacturing sectors and, second, the delivery or supply risk reflected in the risk of a disruption in the EU supply of the material based on the concentration of supply from raw materials-producing countries, considering their governance performance and trade aspects. Within the EU the following technologies make use of

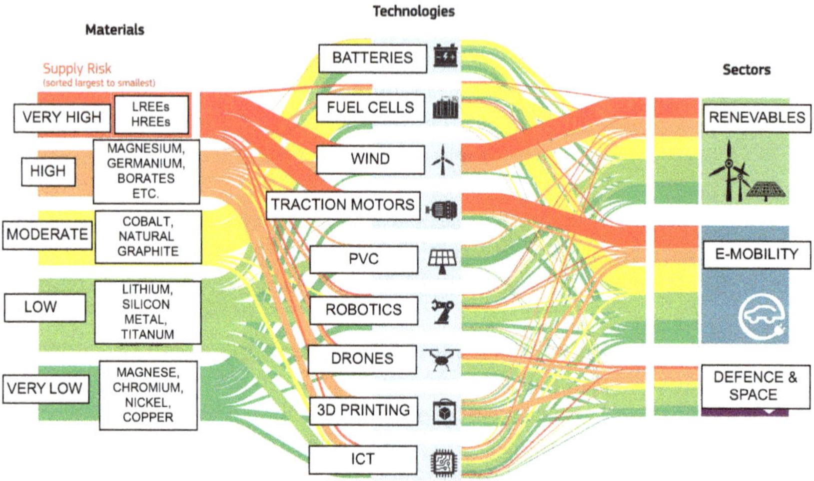

Fig. 7.1 Semi-quantitative representation of flows of raw materials and their current supply risks to the nine selected technologies and three sectors (based on twenty-five selected raw materials) in 2023. Source: EP (March 2023)

CRMs: batteries, fuel cells, wind energy, traction motors, photovoltaics (PV), robotics, drones, 3D printing, and ICT. All those technologies are strategic in so far as they are central to sectors such as renewables, e-mobility, defence, and space. Those technologies use intensively an array of raw materials that face varying degrees of supply risk (Fig. 7.1). Therefore, they are subject to potential disruptions due to possible lack or shortage of input supplies. Moreover, many of those technologies compete for the same raw materials.

According to the European Commission, supply risk considers the degree of diversification of supply sources at the country level, the quality of governance in supplier countries, applicable trade restrictions, the degree to which the EU relies on imports of a given material, the impact of its extraction and processing on the environment, and recycling or substitution potential.

Figure 7.2 shows the largest supplier countries of CRMs to the EU. China in particular has by far the largest percentage (98 per cent) of rare earths, demand for which is expected to increase tenfold by 2050, due

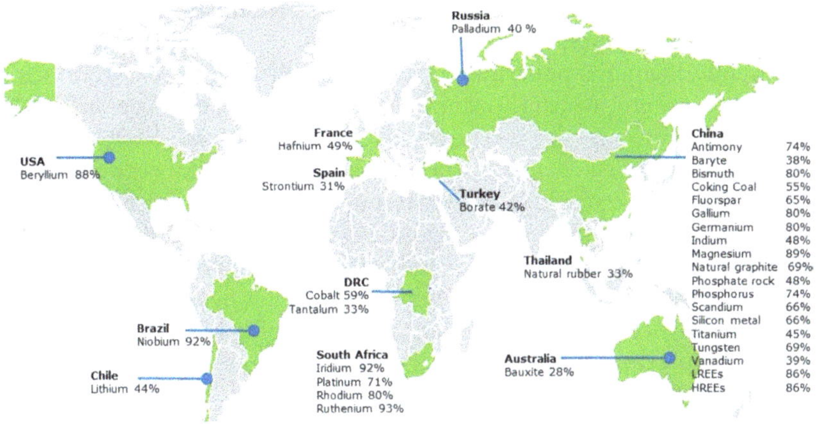

Fig. 7.2 Largest supplier countries of CRMs to the EU. Source: EP (2023)

to the production of electric vehicles, digital technologies, and wind generators alone. It's more worrying that some CRMs are concentrated in countries and regions characterized by low governance standards (e.g. Congo, Russia). The dependence on those countries for CRMs entails many risks, such as volatile supply security, risks of armed conflicts, and a rise in environmental and social problems (e.g. human and labour rights violations). Moreover, given the aforementioned shift towards alternative power sources, energy, and the increasing reliance on semiconductors, the demand for CRMs will likely increase substantially.

The EU will need to address and mitigate these supply risks by diversifying supply sources through responsible and sustainable sourcing from non-EU countries, combined with removing international trade distortions and strengthening rules-based open trade. This will be a crucial part of the EU strategy as the EU will remain dependent on imports for many of the raw materials on the CRM list even in the medium and long term. To fulfil this diversification goal, the EU needs to ensure undistorted access to a wider range of global markets for raw materials, utilize trade policy tools (such as Free Trade Agreements with key source countries), enhance enforcement by swiftly addressing third countries not meeting international obligations, and collaborate with international organizations to prevent distortions in trade and ensure that investments in raw materials support its commercial interests (EP, 2023).

Recently, many EU policymakers have been pursuing a low-carbon self-sufficient economy, which should not lead to a new dependence on China for CRMs. However, the extent to which a sudden loss of CRMs from China is critical in an economic sense is debatable. The real economic risk for the EU may be wasting taxpayer resources in unnecessary attempts to follow the US in its decoupling from China. In practice, CRMs are only an input to specific, although often important, GVCs where a sudden cessation of their supply would not immediately result in an economy-wide decline in activity but might only impact individual industries. The overall negative impact of crucial trade restrictions on raw materials is therefore much smaller than that on fossil fuels, for example. In the EU's drive towards decarbonization, several policy measures are available to promote security of supply of CRMs. Firstly, this concerns diversification subsidies. China's current dominant position in many of these markets is not due to the fact that the raw materials themselves are only available in China, but rather to the fact that Chinese extraction and processing of its raw materials are used for the specific capabilities they provide to the low-carbon products they are part of, whether lithium, nickel, or cobalt in batteries, or rare earth metals in the permanent magnets in wind turbines or EV engines. This means that the demand for a certain CRM is subject to innovative substitution as scientists discover new and cheaper materials with the same potential to replace them. The incentive for private actors to pursue innovation substitution is directly linked to the price of a given CRM, and puts a de facto limit on likely future price increases, and also makes it commercially risky to invest large amounts in new extractive capacity for "critical green raw materials" that can replace innovation in the future. For example, the price of cobalt, which is highly sought after for use in automotive batteries, has fallen by more than 60 per cent since early 2022 as new cobalt-free, iron phosphate-based battery technologies have emerged. Similarly, sodium batteries are increasingly competing directly with traditional lithium batteries, effectively imposing a price ceiling on the latter's main component as lithium prices have fallen by more than 75 per cent since the end of 2022. Future innovative breakthroughs are likely to lead to new advancements, as well as cheaper and more available materials to replace expensive CRMs. EU governments can actively promote replacement innovation by funding basic materials research at universities and private entities. A third option to maintain supplies would be for the EU to encourage and make recycling of CRMs mandatory. CRMs can be recycled for safe domestic supply, but recycling may not be a viable strategy for certain rare earth minerals where only small amounts are used in individual products, which can add excessive costs to the process. As a final option, security of supply concerns can also be addressed through incentivized or mandatory minimum stocks. Governments can choose to do this by simply purchasing and stockpiling the raw materials they deem sufficiently important, or they can incentivize companies to do so through tax breaks or prescribed inventory levels at the corporate level. In short, the EU has several cost-conscious policy measures at its disposal to address concerns about longer-term supply constraints, such as gradual market-driven supply diversification, innovative substitution, incentivized and mandatory recycling, and stockpiling. In order to become less dependent on future CRMs, it is therefore not necessary for the EU to implement the same protectionist, "forced exit" from Chinese sources policy as the US with massive expensive national security-driven subsidies via the Inflation Reduction Act (IRA) (Kirkegaard, 2023).

7.2 A Shift in the EU's Policy Approach Towards a More Dominant China

Recently, China has increasingly come to view the EU as part of a hostile "Western" bloc with the US at the helm instead of an independent pole towards a situation of equilibrium against US policy objectives. China's continued disregard for the liberal rules-based international order has led to an attempt to create an alternative Sino-centric world order that better suits its preferences and interests and reflects its values. Their increasingly aggressive economic actions and political and economic support for Russia's invasion of Ukraine pose immediate risks to European economic and security interests. Over the past three decades, the EU and its member states have prioritized trade and investment considerations over security and values-based concerns, believing that engagement would encourage China to open its markets and increase transparency. However, this EU wish about the development of a future China has not come true. Chinese industries have moved up in the GVC, while strategic barriers to market entry remain. China has intensified violations of the human rights of its citizens while supporting authoritarian leaders who threaten the EU's security.

At the same time, unbalanced Sino-EU trade flows, substantial Chinese infrastructure investment, and their increasing pursuit of greater national economic security leave European countries potentially vulnerable to China's economic coercion. The unbalanced trade flows undermine European competitiveness through market distortions caused by China's unfair trade practices including anti-competitive actions like firm subsidies and below-market price distortions, intellectual property theft through malicious cyber activities and forced technology transfers, and protectionism through market access restrictions and non-market interventions that bolster and concentrate production within China. Due to these practices, the EU's aggregate trade deficit with China tripled from USD 151 billion in 2012 to just under USD 417 billion in 2022. This expansion was primarily driven by China's increasing exports to the EU, including in high-value products like green technology, EVs, and telecommunications equipment. While the EU also sells some high-value goods to China, including machinery and vehicles, which comprise 52 per cent of China's imports from Europe, the benefits of this trade accrue unevenly and tend to concentrate within a small set of firms and countries. The impact of China's unfair trade practices is becoming apparent as European producers face rising export competition with Chinese producers in high-tech sectors, including wind turbines and EVs. China already dominates the global market for rechargeable batteries, and it has become the world's top auto exporter at the expense of European carmakers' global market share in terms of total units sold. China's growing success in Europe is due to China's unfair trade practices as well as European policy inducements. Chinese EV producers operate in a highly protected and subsidized market at home, encounter low EU tariffs when exporting their cars to the European market, and also reap the benefit of EU subsidies since many EU countries' EV subsidies apply to imports as well as locally produced cars. Moreover, the EU's 2035 ban on the sale of new combustion engines that do not run on CO^{2}-neutral fuels has sharply increased demand for EVs, particularly Chinese EVs, which are highly competitive with European cars due in part to these Chinese and European policies. China is expanding its coercive capacity over Europe through investments in critical European infrastructure, including logistics networks, ports, and 5G capabilities. Chinese logistics companies are expanding into European transportation networks to capitalize on Europe's booming e-commerce market and move outside of China's slowing domestic economy. Additionally, Chinese investments in European ports have increased as

China seeks to expand sea trade traffic to accommodate its growing economic power and influence under the Belt and Road Initiative. Two Chinese state-owned enterprises, COSCO and China Merchants Group, maintain sizeable shares in four of Europe's top five busiest ports. Several European ports have also entered into agreements with LOGINK, China's state-run logistics data management system, granting access to international shipping data that China could aggregate for commercial or security advantage. Finally, Chinese telecommunications play a prominent role in several European countries' 5G networks. Countries like Austria, Germany, Italy, Poland, Portugal, and Spain have continued to buy large amounts of Chinese-made 5G equipment despite efforts by the EU and European countries to limit Huawei and ZTE's presence in their networks. China's growing investments in European critical infrastructure give it access to and leverage over Europe's communications networks and supply lines, which leaves Europe vulnerable to attempted economic coercion through pressure on these networks. This indirectly impacts the US, which also depends on European logistics networks to source and deliver goods from Europe and other trading partners.

As part of its efforts to gain a dominant position in key emerging industries, China is increasing its leadership roles and committee participation in international standards-setting bodies at the expense of some EU countries. By acquiring leadership positions in standards-setting organizations, including the prominent International Organization for Standardization (ISO) and the International Electrotechnical Commission (IEC), China is better positioned to set the technical agenda and shape the standardization process towards its interests, in some cases to the detriment of European industries. In addition to expanding its leadership positions, China is also increasing its participation in standards development committees within the ISO and IEC to exploit first-mover advantage by establishing its preferred technical standards in key industries, including rare earths, transaction assurance in e-commerce, and smart grid user interface, among others. By joining these bodies, China seeks to make its exporting firms more competitive and induce European dependence by locking European firms into Chinese technical standards. China seeks to promote its own set of technical standards for critical and emerging technologies, such as in 5G, through the adoption and enforcement of Chinese standard-essential patents (SEP) in international and regional standards-setting bodies. SEPs protect firms that develop novel standards by requiring firms that adopt these standards to pay royalties to the SEP holder. By popularizing Chinese-developed standards in international organizations, China can force foreign companies to pay royalties to Chinese SEP holders and induce dependence on Chinese technology. This practice presents significant challenges to European firms working in emerging technology fields, like the Swedish telecommunications firm Ericsson, which faces strong and increasing competition in international standards organizations from the Chinese firm Huawei (USCESRC, 2023). Moreover, if Chinese standards are not interoperable with European products, then European firms will either need to adjust to Chinese standards or lose market share. If left unaddressed, both US and EU companies face the potential of becoming dependent on Chinese technology that is incompatible with US- and EU-produced goods. In addition, a lack of coordination between the US and EU on technical standards vis-à-vis China may lead to fragmentation in standards, thus reducing the pace of shared technological development and limiting the potential for economic growth.

For several years now, China has been trying to interfere in the politics of the EU and its member states, sometimes sowing division through its divide-and-rule strategy via media influence, disinformation campaigns, subversion of EU institutions, and coercion of individual member states and policymakers. It is common for China to use its extensive economic relationships to create competitive incentives among individual European countries to reduce their capacity and propensity to respond adversely to Chinese policies through their national policies. A good example of this is the relationship between China and Germany. Germany has the largest economy in the EU, and in 2022 it was the second-largest EU importer of Chinese goods and the largest EU exporter of goods to China. In the same year, German foreign direct investment in China reached a record high of USD 10.5 billion in new investments, while Germany received a third (USD 1.9 billion) of all Chinese foreign direct investment to the EU. Because Germany has long been sensitive to and also dependent on its economic ties with China, Germany has taken a rather moderate approach in its China policy compared to the EU and many other EU member states. Although the German government aims to "raise awareness of the risks associated with China", which is now called a "de-risking" strategy in the EU, many large German companies are trying to reduce their exposure to political risks by localizing production in China, which means expanding investment and future growth. Such a position removes responsibility from the German government to act while undermining the effectiveness of the EU's de-risking approach, given large German firms' willingness to sustain investment in China despite rising political risks and continuing barriers to market participation (USCESRC, 2023). In light of these challenges and shifts, EU and individual European states' strategic assessments of China are rapidly shifting from primarily seeing China as a potential policy partner and geographically distant economic competitor to increasingly seeing it as a multidimensional systemic rival with an active presence in Europe in opposition to democratic norms and values. Although this shift is bringing EU policy approaches into greater convergence with the US, particularly as it relates to China's growing economic threat via unfair trade practices and strategically motivated investments in sensitive infrastructure and technologies, important differences remain. The EU is a collection of 27 member states, and "European" policy towards China can at best be seen as a combination of EU policies alongside the positions of the member states and the positions of European countries that do not belong to the EU. In that sense there is a difference between the EU and "European" policy and the policy of the individual EU member states towards China. Diversity in views between and within EU countries makes consensus-building slow and may limit the scope, speed, and depth of fundamental change in the EU's collective policy approach to China. The complexity of this EU policy in dealing with China poses challenges for the US and could undermine the EU's China policy due to the limited space created for a viable policy cooperation. After all, China has often responded to the diversity in European approaches in the past by undermining EU action through selective measures to increase involvement with individual member states rather than the EU as a whole. At the same time, many of the EU's common policies fail to adequately address China's practices and also present challenges for the US. In a way, the EU is an important centre of geostrategic competition between the US and China. Like the US, the EU also aims to increase economic resilience and reduce dependency on China. Although the EU is developing a number of economic instruments to mitigate China's unfair trade practices and economic coercion, these instruments are often voluntary and have a more limited scope than the corresponding US mechanisms, which limits the effectiveness of transatlantic coordination activities. In addition, this transatlantic policy coordination is also complicated by significant differences of opinion between the EU and the US on the economic policy to be pursued, including differences over preferential subsidies, even though this was more problematic under Trump than under the Biden administration (USCESRC, 2023).

7.3 Possible EU Policy Options to "De-risk" China

The EU is increasingly pursuing strategic autonomy and economic security that must be accompanied by reduced critical dependence on "systemic rivals" such as China. The most important policy areas of Sino-EU cooperation and competition are presented in Table 7.1. European Commission President Ursula von der Leyen has called for risk reduction, including "testing our relationship to see where the biggest threats lie to our long-term resilience, prosperity and security". The EU should produce at least 40 per cent of its clean technology, taking into account economic security interests when exporting to China. In June 2023 the

Table 7.1 Potential policy area opportunities and threats for more Sino-EU cooperation and competition in this decade

Policy areas	*Sino-EU cooperation (opportunities)*	*Sino-EU competition (threats)*
Market potential	The Chinese market has become too large to be avoided. Europe is more economically exposed to China than the US and in the medium term, most business opportunities will be greater in China than in the US	Europe is dealing with lingering apprehensions over Chinese dominance of vital resources, market access barriers, and trade imbalances. Currently the EU is opting for strategic autonomy and economic security; it leads to a reduction of dependence on "systemic rivels" like China
Industry structure and investments	There are some branches of industry where closer cooperation with China is needed as the Chinese market offers a lot of investment opportunities (see Sect. 4.4) A very large share and value of Chinese investments are located in some European countries, such as Germany, France, and the UK	The need to mitigate risks, diversify partnerships, reconfigure commercial interactions, and relocate operations to reduce dependencies in critical sectors
Institutional basis for cooperation	The EU and China are interconnected by institutional cooperation (it embraces such institutions as AIIB, EBRD, and WTO)	The lack of a comprehensive uniform strategy of Sino-EU cooperation, presented by the entire EU

(*continued*)

Table 7.1 (continued)

Policy areas	*Sino-EU cooperation (opportunities)*	*Sino-EU competition (threats)*
Green finance and technology	An important area for Sino-EU financial cooperation is created by green finance. Both China and the EU are at the global forefront of green finance policies China and the EU are united in their commitment to act against climate change and clean energy cooperation. They are convinced of the necessary global transformation towards a resource-efficient, sustainable, low-greenhouse gas emissions, and climate-proof economy and society	China creates threats in some areas as products connected with decarbonization goals (electric vehicles and solar panels), products connected with high-technologies (AI, advanced semiconductors, quantum, biotech industries, and other technologically advanced branches of industry)
Priorities for international cooperation	BRI gives great opportunities to promote Sino–EU relations based on win-win cooperation. Cooperation between China and the EU embraces trade and investment, but also peace, security, and people-to-people exchange	The Chinese support for Russia in the war with Ukraine entails direct risks for the EU's economic and security interests The BRI has also shown some drawbacks, such as the "debt sovereignty trap" of some recipient countries (e.g. Sri Lanka and Zambia)

Source: own elaboration

European Council also recommended that the EU should "reduce critical dependencies and vulnerabilities, including in its supply chains, and where necessary and appropriate, reduce and diversify risks". A dilemma in this European drive for more autonomy is that China is so dominant in important strategic sectors and products that a partial or total "decoupling" does not necessarily mean that the risks are reduced, but is on the contrary a very risky undertaking.

European dependence on China has increased rather than decreased. For every five containers shipped from China to the EU, only one is exported to China. Compared to 2012, imports had tripled by the end of 2022, and the balance deteriorated further during the Covid-19 years and after Russia's invasion of Ukraine. In certain sectors there is hardly an alternative to China. Dependence on rare earth elements is 98 per cent and on antibiotics 79 per cent, and almost 90 per cent of global solar panel production is in Chinese hands. China's prominent position in GVCs is also the main reason why companies are so wary of "decoupling", as this would essentially mean leaving the world's second-largest economy behind. Inevitably, decoupling will reduce the already limited competition in China and give an even greater share to Chinese businesses. It would make the EU more dependent on state aid, potentially increasing friction between European countries, and would slow down not only the EU's but also the world's ongoing efforts to decarbonize its economy. Of course, this does not mean that the EU strategy of "de-risking" is a bad alternative as long as the West remains vulnerable to the weaponization of trade by China. A good example of this is the recent faster-than-expected Chinese ban on the export of gallium and germanium to the EU in response to the Dutch export ban on semiconductor technology to China (Schaus & Lannoo, 2023). In recent years, the EU has developed a range of economic instruments to reduce dependence on China. In general, the EU's measures seek to limit foreign firms' access to critical aspects of the European economy, neutralize the competitive advantage foreign firms derive from distortive trade practices and a lack of market reciprocity, and coordinate an EU response to economic coercion against any member country. This concerns the following EU measures or instruments:

- *Inflowing foreign investment screening mechanisms* to review the security implications of inflowing investment in critical sectors like infrastructure, nuclear technologies, semiconductors, and defense, among others.
- *International procurement instrument* to penalize bidders on EU contracts if European firms do not have reciprocal access to the bidder's market.
- *Foreign subsidies regulation* giving the EU the ability to penalize foreign firms operating in the European market that receive distortive financial contributions from their home governments.
- *Anti-coercion instrument* which allows for the application of trade restrictions on countries attempting economic coercion based on a

majority vote of EU member states, including increased duties, import or export licenses, and public procurement restrictions.
- *Outbound investment controls* for European companies operating in high-tech industries, including AI, quantum computing, and biotechnology.
- *Artificial Intelligence Act* to establish safeguards for the application of AI by categorizing uses based on perceived risk (USCESRC, 2023).

"De-risking" China essentially means limiting economic vulnerability to factors arising from Chinese control over crucial aspects of global economic exchanges through diversification. Although the EU's "de-risking" strategy towards China had become commonplace in 2023, it has very different meanings for different countries. While the US understanding focuses on national security, the EU takes a more economic approach, aiming to reduce excessive dependence on China for the sourcing of CRMs and manufactured goods. EU member states hold different views regarding the risks of dependence on China, ranging from Hungary's outright rejection of the need to de-risk to Lithuania's calls for fast action to reduce the chance China will retaliate. Germany's China strategy sits in between these two extremes (Merics, 2024). EU member states may implement the above economic measures or instruments as an effort to build resilience and reduce risks, rather than an attempt to limit economic ties with China. The above-mentioned EU risk management instruments are limited in scope, but broad in reach, which means they are not sufficiently successful to adequately address Chinese practices due to the policies' voluntary application or high levels of support required for the policy to operate. Uneven application and high thresholds for operation present China with the opportunity to manoeuvre around EU measures by operating just under thresholds for government response or working through countries with less restrictive regulations. In addition, the EU's defensive economic tools are often limited in scale and scope due to the EU's arduous consensus-building process. In negotiations on the anti-coercion act, EU members reduced the effectiveness of the instrument by purposefully "watering down the executive power of the European Commission" to enact the measure by requiring a qualified majority vote from the European Council. While this dilution of power increases the instrument's appeal among member states, it also creates an opening for intra-European division and the possibility for China to manipulate this division to its advantage. The EU is deliberately pushing for a "country-neutral" policy that can be applied to other countries, including the US, which could potentially undermine US-EU cooperation on their China policy. This neutrality benefits the EU in several ways, including by making their policies WTO compliant, avoiding pushback from targeted countries, and giving the EU versatility to apply policy to a broad set of actors. The country neutrality can be interpreted as both a diplomatic choice to avoid singling out China and a subtle warning to the US to reconsider policies with which the EU disagrees, such as the IRA. Moreover, country neutrality gives the EU the option of equally applying these policies to the US. Finally, the broad applicability of the EU's policies reduces trust and the potential space for US-EU cooperation on China (USCESRC, 2023).

The major challenge for the EU is how to "de-risk" China. The following three options can be considered. Firstly, the EU needs a much more integrated and coherent industrial policy to support the green and digital transitions. This involves coordinating national R&D programmes and increased funding at EU level, jointly forecasting industry trends and coordinating investments in strategic sectors. Taking advantage of this improved internal coordination, this also means defining the EU's role in a kind of global decarbonization partnership, which would include the creation of complementary supply chains for all decarbonization efforts. Global green demand will continue to increase and green production in China will simply not be able to keep up. Most importantly, this partnership would help avoid technological dependency and enable the further development of more effective technologies for the benefit of the EU and the world including China. Such a partnership should rely on coordination of incentives with international partners based on common standards. However, the EU's green initiatives are seen as biased or protectionist by some partner countries. Cooperation would thus require continued and joint EU efforts on global sustainability, which could translate into supporting strong accompanying measures (capacity building and financial arrangements) in partner developing countries.

Secondly, the EU needs a much more comprehensive approach to de-risk and diversify. This would require extensive consultation and coordination between EU institutions and industry to clearly set the stage for reducing risks and providing predictability and certainty for the EU's more resilient supply chains. The hierarchy of risk reduction priorities would be politically determined, together with the insights of companies on the ground, taking into account the variety and specificity of sector-based and individual risk reduction strategies, based on commercial and increasingly geopolitical reasons. It is important for companies to know which areas need to be de-risked and which are the unproblematic areas for cooperation with China. Diversification requires new markets and further trade opportunities that can only be achieved through a joint EU approach with entirely new free trade agreements (FTAs) (Schaus & Lannoo, 2023). The EU has built an extensive network of preferential trade agreements, but because the trade pattern in CRMs is different from the EU's overall trade pattern, it is important to understand the extent to which the EU's current FTAs cover the major suppliers of CRMs. Given the scarcity of resources within the EU, it is also important to look at outward EU foreign direct investment in resource-rich countries, through EU member states' bilateral investment treaties, which set out the conditions for private investments abroad (EP, 2023).

Thirdly, the EU must establish procedures for visits and statements on its "systemic rival" to ensure that China cannot divide and rule. In principle, the intention is for the EU to speak out with one voice, even if the individual member states do not always allow the EU to take a united position. The EU High Representative should take the initiative to reach consensus in the Foreign Affairs Council and act together with the European Commission (Schaus & Lannoo, 2023).

7.4 Sino-EU Economic Ties and the Complications of a Coordinated Joint EU-China Policy

The dilemma of the EU is that it has deep economic ties with both China and the US, making the continent a place of geostrategic competition between the two superpowers. The EU's approach to China influences the scope and impact of US policies aimed at limiting exposure to and dependence on China, maintaining a free and open Indo-Pacific region and protecting the liberal rules-based international order. From the point of view of the Chinese authorities, the EU is primarily seen as an important region to support its economic development and other political and geostrategic goals, but also as a region that is increasingly resistant to Chinese policies, coinciding with a greater convergence with the US. For China, maintaining and expanding the EU market is essential as the economy shifts to a higher value-added production. China has historically supplied the EU market with relatively low-quality manufactured and consumer goods, but the Chinese composition of exports to the EU has gradually changed from relatively low-value to higher-quality and technologically advanced products. In fact, in 2022, four of the EU's top five imported goods from China were high-tech, including telecommunications equipment, automatic data processing machines, electrical machinery, and electronic components. A possible further Sino-EU cooperation could be intensified in the "green transition" to strive for a cleaner environment. As China continues to dominate clean technology industries, the EU is likely to become dependent on exports of Chinese environmentally friendly products, especially in the areas of EV and other green technologies. Although Chinese investment flows to the EU as a whole have declined over the last five years, this is less the case for Germany, France, and Hungary, with China trying to gain access to more sensitive European technologies through targeted acquisitions, such as German robotics and Dutch equipment for the production of semiconductors. Ultimately, these events led to the establishment of a unified EU approach to the foreign investment screening mechanism in 2020 (USCESRC, 2023).

Besides the fact that the EU's risk reduction instruments have a limited scope, there is also limited consensus between and even within the EU member states on a joint or common or unified EU China policy, let alone a consistent long-term China strategy, that not only prepares the EU for the various potential future scenarios, but also helps Europe shape those scenarios and China's future choices, in order to preserve the liberal world order and peace. By geography, Baltic countries, informed by their experiences under the Soviet Union and proximity to Russia, tend to hold more hawkish views and desire closer coordination with the US, particularly in addressing security issues related to China. Southern European states tend to be more open to engagement with China, as China was able to exploit these countries' dissatisfaction with the EU's and Germany's handling of the Eurozone crisis in 2009 to expand its economic ties with the region.

After the Covid-19 crisis, the relationship of Southern European countries with China is more limited as the EU has given these countries more budgetary support during the pandemic. In between these extremes sit several of the EU's largest economies, including France, Germany, and the Netherlands. These countries' views and approaches are driven in large part by their business communities, which harbour complex and competing interests arising from firms' various levels of connectivity with the Chinese market. Finally, there are a number of EU and non-EU European countries with declining democratic institutions motivated by economic opportunism, such as Hungary and Serbia, which see China as a viable partner and useful "card" to negotiate with the EU and its member states. This diversity of perspectives and views on a joint China policy makes it difficult to achieve a coordinated, effective EU China policy.

In 2022, China was the top supplier for both the US and the EU markets, comprising 16.5 per cent of imports to the US and 20 per cent of imports to the EU. That same year, EU goods comprised only 10.5 per cent of China's imports, while US goods comprised just 6.5 per cent of China's imports. Similarly, while aggregated reciprocal FDI flows have hit a recent low, a small set of large European countries and their largest multinationals dominate the European investment landscape in China. German, Dutch, and French firms comprised at least 70 per cent of annual EU investment inflows into China from 2017 to 2021, with most funding flowing to one of five sectors: autos, food processing, pharma/biotech, chemicals, and consumer products manufacturing. Despite rising risks, European multinational companies remain invested in China to benefit from the promise of its growing consumer market and its research and development (R&D) ecosystem, especially as Europe's market growth stagnates. Despite its long-term challenges in encouraging and expanding domestic consumption, China's consumer market has grown significantly, with household expenditure nearly tripling from USD 2.6 trillion in 2011 to USD 6.8 trillion by 2021. By comparison, the EU's household expenditure rose from USD 8.7 trillion to USD 8.8 trillion over the same period (USCESRC, 2023).The current size and future growth potential of China's domestic market is large enough to draw in Europe's largest companies, even if the majority of Chinese consumers are not fully engaged. In addition to revenue, European firms invested in China report benefiting from China's rapidly developing R&D ecosystem. China's dynamic R&D environment is a substantial draw for European companies, and many that remain invested in China report plans to expand their R&D activities and further integrate them with global strategies to capitalize on China's competitive talent pool, speed of commercialization of new tech, and "potential of combining European hardware excellence with Chinese software expertise". Despite the EU strategy of "de-risking", large and powerful European companies remain embedded in the Chinese market. European multinationals may further frustrate the EU's attempt to economically de-risk through investment restrictions by siloing production in China, a type of firm-level political de-risking. Siloing occurs when a firm sections off productive activities and sales in a given market by developing a supply chain and distribution strategy that is unique to the market and that minimizes contact between operations in the siloed economy and other economies. European and US firms are increasingly siloing production in China as a way to reduce exposure to political risks, including the potential for import tariffs, outbound investment screening, new regulations, and other economic sanctions. This siloing increases European firms' entrenchment in the Chinese market, reducing the effectiveness of economic sanctions and trade restrictions while also reducing Europe's ability to effectively de-risk from China through a coordinated joint or common EU China strategy (USCESRC, 2023). Unfortunately, the EU has never jointly pursued such a strategy until now. Even when EU–China relations were characterized by their strategic partnership and there were fewer tensions, Europe lacked a comprehensive long-term China strategy. The EU simply hoped that trade and economic ties would help democratize China, but it lacked a plan to help bring about such an evolution. In March 2019, the European Commission published "EU–China – A strategic outlook" (EC, 2023). In this strategic outlook, China is described as a partner, "an economic competitor in the pursuit of technological leadership" and a systemic rival. The sectors that the Chinese government deems strategically important are often equally important to the EU and individual European countries. Technology can be "strategically important" in at least two different ways. Either the technology is sensitive for reasons of national security, such as military and dual-use goods, or the technology is important to preserve Europe's economic competitiveness (Clingendael, 2022). However, the failure to agree on significant funding for the Strategic Technologies for Europe (STEP) platform (June 2023), with only EUR 1.5 billion to support the development and production of strategic technologies (advanced clean-, digital-, and biotechnologies including their value chains), reflects the reluctance of member states to commit to a European industrial policy. The Commission's January 2024 economic security package does not address the need for major public or private funding for early-stage, capital-intensive critical technology projects and the EU continues to lack a strategy for serious innovation funding. In an era of economic security, the single market cannot simply be built on strict competition rules, but it should be seen as a space of capacity mutualization (Jacques Delors Institute, 2024). The European Commission is currently focused on building European "strategic autonomy" by developing an assertive industrial policy and reducing its strategic economic dependencies. This means that Europe risks sharing or even losing key technologies to a "competitor" and a "rival", thus creating one-sided dependencies with Beijing (Clingendael, 2022). Since 2019 the EU has introduced a series of policies, mainly economic, that are meant to protect it from threats or risks that could come from China (see Sect. 7.3). However, these are primarily defensive measures and are not driven by any long-term goal, being the product of current issues or risks that have been identified. Neither is de-risking a strategy; it is merely a tactic meant to protect the EU from crises or negative scenarios, whilst doing nothing to defend the liberal world order or preserve peace. The EU's "partner-competitor-systemic rival" narrative simply describes EU–China relations, but this can certainly not be referred to as a strategy either. While designing a comprehensive and consistent long-term China strategy among twenty-seven member states together with countless decision-makers and stakeholders is extremely difficult, the EU needs a general strategic framework for dealing with China over the coming decades (EP, 2024).

7.5 Possible Future Policy Areas for Sino-EU Cooperation or Competition

While the EU is committed to de-risking, with a combination of industrial policy and trade diversification providing targets and incentives for European companies, the risk of further fragmentation of the global trade landscape over the next decade will thus require a high degree of adaptability. Like the US, the EU will remain committed to a society based on a rules-based liberal international trade system. Sino-US relations in particular will therefore determine possible future relations between China and the EU, consisting of more cooperation or competition. For that matter it will make a big difference which US president will be elected in November 2024. The following possible future theoretical scenarios of varying degrees of Sino-EU coordination and its policy implications for the EU can be distinguished.

The following overview of the possible future cooperation or competition between China and the EU is based on the three pillars of the multifaceted EU classification of the complex relationship with China, as formulated in the EU-China Strategic Strategy Outlook 2019, namely China as a "cooperation partner" , "economic competitor", or "systemic rival".

First, "cooperation partnership". Over the next decade, it is likely that further Sino-EU cooperation on climate and sustainability will get a higher priority. In addition, it is expected that further cooperation in the field of reforms of the WTO and other multilateral institutions will receive more attention as well. Although serious high-level climate dialogues have been taking place between the EU and China for several years, these conversations often consist of an exchange of both sides' positions on countering climate change and sustainable development, rather than providing actually meaningful platform coordination in this area. The desire for more Sino-EU cooperation in the field of climate change also risks becoming overshadowed by increasing concerns about the EU's growing dependence on China for products, resources, and technologies that are vital to the green transition. China's dominance in the production of solar panels, batteries, and electric vehicles, as well as related rare earths and other essential materials such as solar-grade polysilicon, is not only a growing source of concern in the EU for fossil energy dependence on the Middle East and Russia, but also for green dependence on China.

Second, "economic competitor". This pragmatic "economic competitor" approach partly reflects the fact that many European national governments have struggled to reach agreement on their own domestic China policies. Differing China-critical or security-conscious perspectives and China-accommodating or commercially oriented views among national EU member state authorities have competed to find their way into national strategies and approaches with regard to formulating a common China policy. The EU is increasingly introducing EU policy instruments relevant to China to increase access to the European market and unilaterally enforce economic reciprocity with China by making continued access to the Chinese market in Europe conditional, where possible, on access to the European market in China. This so-called toolbox of aforementioned economic policy measures (instruments), so far primarily composed of the active FDI Screening Mechanism, International Procurement Instrument,

Dual-use Items Export Control Regulation, etc., lies mainly in the area where the EU's powers are the largest, namely in economic and trade policy. While the EU's new trade and reciprocity tools are a huge step towards standing up to detrimental and unfair Chinese economic practices, many more steps need to be taken to leverage these tools to increase the EU's international strategic influence and economic reciprocity compared to China. Furthermore, the proposed CRM Act, announced by Commission President Von der Leyen at the State of the European Union in 2022, and the proposed Chips law are indications of the increasing priority given to security of supply, in addition to reciprocity in EU policymaking aimed at the EU's external economic relations, especially with China. The aim is to diversify supply chains outside of China and collaborate with alternative partners around the world. The EU trade reciprocity toolbox will, depending on the political will to implement it effectively, increase Europe's capacity to protect itself against unfair Chinese economic practices and raise the EU's ability to act internationally, but this may also come with an economic cost due to Chinese countermeasures and potential price increases. However, as there has been an internal trend in China towards greater economic autonomy and decoupling of GVCs for a long time, combined with the intensification of market distortions, it is inevitable that this will increasingly require a reorientation of a more competitive EU China policy.

Third, "systemic rival". This negative scenario for Sino-EU cooperation raises the question as to what extent a uniform European foreign policy response will follow possible Chinese aggression against Taiwan. To what extent is the EU prepared, whether or not in coordination with the US, to implement a comprehensive sanctions regime against Beijing? It is desirable that there is a common EU position specifying the EU's "red lines" and the type of sanctions that would trigger China if it decided to cross them. However, it remains to be seen whether individual member states can be convinced to take a strong common position on Taiwan in the absence of a major crisis in the region for the foreseeable future. Moreover, as the use of these sanctions will continue to depend on unanimity, it would be difficult to devise a plan that could fully ensure EU's decisiveness if one of the feared scenarios comes true, further increasing the critical uncertainties around the Taiwan Strait. In any case, diversifying supply chains for crucial resources, rare earth metals, batteries, and solar panels would go a long way to improving future EU resilience in preparation for worst-case scenarios (Wieringen, 2022).

In future intensified cooperation between China and the EU, it is important to distinguish between mutual economic relations and the area of national security policy. The defensive mechanisms launched by the EU, like the FDI screening mechanism and the anti-coercion instrument, are considered important tools for managing the economic relations. In the field of security policy, countries must recognize and address the challenges of China and find unified positions on crucial geopolitical issues such as China's support for Russia and the pressure exerted on Taiwan. At EU level, capacity building must be central to managing relations with China. This means that analyses, strategies, and information are shared among the EU member states and an effort is made to achieve a common EU China policy. The US, the EU, and its individual member states face similar challenges from China, including bilateral trade deficits, a lack of market reciprocity, widespread intellectual property theft, uncooperative diplomacy, and the pervasive disinformation campaigns of the CCP's leaders. By coordinating a response to the growing economic and security threat from China, and pursuing joint US-EU development in key and emerging technologies such as AI, the EU and the US will be more effective vis-à-vis China. However, latent tensions in US–EU relations and differences between EU member states remain an obstacle to effective coordination of the confrontation with China. Beijing's increasingly aggressive actions towards the EU, as well as the EU's and European countries' changing views on China, provide an opportunity for the US to expand and strengthen the transatlantic partnership (USCESRC, 2023). There may already be a division among EU member states about how the "de-risk" China strategy should be interpreted. Even though all EU member states agree with the basic idea of reducing risks, they differ greatly in how they view its size and scope. While Western Europe is grappling with the implications that an economic withdrawal from China could bring, it is clear for northeastern member states including the Baltic states, but also other countries in Central and Eastern Europe, that economically painful decisions must be taken to outweigh the geopolitical risks of overreliance on China. Geopolitics, however, is at the forefront of the de-risking debate in northeastern EU member states due to the decades of Soviet occupation (the Baltics) and Soviet-imposed control (Poland). Ukraine's fight to preserve its sovereignty and align itself with European and Western values echoes the recent history of these northeastern European nations, who similarly reclaimed their statehood and are cognizant of their geopolitical vulnerability. China's stance following Russia's full-scale invasion of

Ukraine in 2022 has not resonated well with these member states. Far from opposing Russia, Xi Jinping showcases Vladimir Putin as a top guest at important events, including the Third Belt and Road Forum that concluded in Beijing in October 2023. For northeastern Europeans, these are signals that China's geopolitical vision is not one that makes the world safe for small EU members. Thus, when it comes to the European debate on de-risking, most economically smaller EU members with little to lose are willing to go further than their larger Western EU member states like Germany, France, and the Netherlands. On the one hand, it is important that the EU's geopolitical awakening following Russia's invasion of Ukraine offers hope that an EU-wide, top-down political consensus can bring about change. On the other hand, it is also important not to apply the "de-risking" China strategy one-on-one to EU businesses, fundamentally rearranging GVCs without any incentive or support that could harm European competitiveness. For example, EU carmakers are still going to China, which means "re-risking" rather than "de-risking" the relationship, because China offers a robust technology ecosystem, regulatory incentives for electric vehicles, and a sophisticated upstream value chain (VC). The EU's call to reduce risks must therefore be accompanied by a robust EU-wide industrial policy that focuses on both Europe's industrial core and a long VC that includes the EU's neighbours, and selected partners in the Global South firmly linked with the EU's industrial policy initiatives, such as the Global Gateway and the Green Deal. In order to achieve this, the EU needs not only strong leadership and consensus, but also a radical policy push towards an EU-wide industrial policy that follows in China's and the US's footsteps (Merics, 2024).

For a successful implementation of a strategic approach to China, it is not only important to seek greater coordination within the EU, but this should also be accompanied by greater agreement with like-minded partners, in addition to the transatlantic relationship between various EU member states and the US and possibly also relations with their selected "neutral" partners in the Global South (e.g. India, Brazil, South Africa). Despite the many challenges, the strong interconnections between the EU and China require equally strong diplomatic efforts and continuous engagement. China remains a necessary partner to tackle global challenges. The EU must keep engaging with Beijing at different levels, while also upholding fundamental principles, such as a commitment to free trade, fair competition, and the rule of law. On the bilateral level, the EU should find new venues of collaboration, such as scientific cooperation, coordination, on climate change and other global commons. Continuing to build a stronger and fairer economic relationship through bilateral agreements is key to removing trade and investment barriers. On the multilateral level, a functioning rules-based international system with the WTO at its core is essential to deal with the potential distortions posed by countries like China. Efforts to constructively engage China in the reform of the WTO as well as in other multilateral fora are important. In addition, the EU should encourage plurilateral efforts to deal with unfair trade practices, including the trilateral talks on industrial subsidies between the EU, the US, and Japan and ongoing cooperation under the G7 on export controls, coercion, and supply chain resilience. In addition, the EU must continue actively coordinating with its most important like-minded partners, the US and the UK, on common challenges posed by China through existing cooperation fora like the EU-US Trade and Technology Council's working groups on investment screening, misuse of technology threatening security and human rights, export controls, secure supply chains, and global trade challenges like economic coercion (AmCham EU, 2023).

7.6 The Sino–EU Relationship in Light of the Upcoming US Presidential Elections

The possible future theoretical scenarios for further cooperation or competition between China and the EU largely depend on the outcome of the US elections in November 2024, which is an exciting battle between the previous and current US presidents, Trump and Biden respectively.[1] For both representative parties, the Republicans and the Democrats, China represents the biggest challenge for US national security interests and world order. While there are differences between and within these parties in how they see the nature of the Chinese military threat and ways to deal with it, the ambition to prevail in the US-China strategic rivalry will drive

[1] When writing paragraph 7.6, it was assumed that the US presidential elections were a battle between the previous president Trump and the current president Biden. Trump was officially nominated as the Republican Party's presidential candidate on July 18, 2024, and Biden withdrew from the election race on July 21, but will complete his term as president. Although Biden has recommended vice-president Harris as his successor, the Democratic presidential nominee will be officially chosen at the Democratic Party convention on August 19–22, when this book is already in production and out of editing. In the text below, whenever Biden is mentioned, it should be assumed that his successor on behalf of the Democratic Party will continue similar policies to Biden.

the US's foreign policy regardless of which party wins the presidency in 2024. This consensus is strongly pronounced in the economic realm, where both parties are focused on succeeding in the technological competition with China. From China's perspective, it is not easy to make a trade-off between the pros and cons of a new Biden or Trump presidency. On the one hand, Trump's presidency from 2017 to 2021 saw a profound shift in the US's policy through several forms of decoupling. His administration deployed tariffs in an attempt to reduce US's trade deficit and protect jobs. It redefined the domestic debate in the US, with China portrayed as a political, technological, and military adversary. On the other hand, Biden's more systematic approach to governing has posed a different kind of threat to China than that of Trump's first term. During Biden's presidency, the US has kept the Trump tariffs in place, which rose on average for Chinese companies from 3 per cent in 2018 to 21 per cent at the end of 2019, when the two countries entered into a truce. However, on top of that the Biden administration also built a comprehensive system for restricting Western technology flows to China, and by investing in the US's security partnerships and alliances, from Australia and India to the Philippines and South Korea, it has rejuvenated an Asian security system to deter and contain China. According to Goldman Sachs estimates, the overall net trade effect of the US-China trade war as a percentage of GDP is negative for China and positive for the US, although there is still a significant trade surplus for China versus the US. It should also be noted that the Sino-US trade war eroded the real incomes of both Chinese and Americans by raising prices, disrupted financial markets in each country, and led to policy uncertainty that curbed business spending. Partly due to the strict Covid-19 measures and other unfavourable geopolitical disputes, the Chinese economy and financial markets are in a worse position in 2024 compared to 2018, and it is likely that a new Trump presidency focused on a more "balanced bilateral trade" situation will further intensify the trade war with both countries raising their (non)-tariff barriers, resulting in a negative effect on their real income growth with limited flows of Sino-US foreign direct investments. Judging from the possible trade barriers in the event of a second Trump presidency, it is likely that the Chinese authorities would prefer a Biden victory since it is far less likely than a Trump administration to trigger a destabilizing trade shock. However, the Biden administration increased import restrictions on Chinese electric vehicles (EV) with a 100 per cent border tax in May 2024 as a response to unfair policies and intended to protect US jobs. The US government also further hinders the flow of US advanced technology to China in areas such as semiconductors, artificial intelligence, and quantum computing. While from a purely economic perspective the Chinese policymakers may have a slight preference for an extension of the Biden rather than a new Trump administration in the short run, this does not necessarily apply to the different positions between Biden and Trump regarding the strategic geopolitical and military Sino–US relationship in the long run. For example, Xi Jinping is very sceptical about the Western-led world order and wants to turn China into an alternative power centre. Trump's tempestuous relationship with US allies in Europe and Asia could undermine cohesion with them on a joint or common China policy if he is re-elected. Also, Trump's disdainful remarks about NATO, including his recent suggestion that he would not provide US protection to allies, including Japan and South Korea, that do not spend enough on defence, are viewed favourably in China. Another reason why China might favour Trump over Biden is that a Trump administration might unwind the work Biden has done to nurture Asian partnerships. China's authorities are watching with suspicion how Biden created a new grouping, *Trilateral Security Partnership Between Australia, UK and the US* known as AUKUS, aimed at strengthening cooperation with Australia and the UK in responding to the security challenge posed by China's navy in the Indian Ocean and Pacific. AUKUS involves exactly the kind of long-term, rather than transactional, relationship that Trump dislikes. Similarly on Taiwan, Trump may be preferable for China. During his first term, Trump has shown far less commitment to "democratic" policies than Biden, who has repeatedly said US troops would defend Taiwan if China invaded. Above all else, Xi Jinping wants social stability. Biden's approach to China is likely to be more predictable but better organized and enforced, and perhaps a bigger threat in the long run. Trump's unpredictable potential for chaos and excesses could create opportunities for China to outmanoeuvre the US but also bring the instability China fears (*The Economist*, 2024).

It is very likely that future China-EU coordination will be strongly determined by the outcome of the 2024 US elections. Although the European alliance with the US has been the central feature of its foreign and security policy for a long time and the EU–US relationship under the Biden presidency may be closer than that under Trump, US foreign and security policy has changed significantly over the past decade, which means that the transatlantic relationship with the EU is no longer always the US's first priority.

Beyond the broad agreement between Republicans and Democrats on successfully addressing technological competition with China, important differences remain in how the parties view the role of allies in the US-China competition. A new Trump presidency would likely take a more unilateral approach towards China, penalizing European allies if they do not play along. It is likely that a second Trump presidency will deepen divisions between the US and EU. Any future Republican administration will be more transactional in its relationship with the EU and will make its trade policies vis-à-vis Europe dependent on the EU's strategic industrial policy on China. The current Republican frontrunners, especially the Trump supporters, are also more likely to push for a faster redeployment of military resources away from Ukraine to the Indo-Pacific. However, in the event of a second Biden administration, the US is more likely to continue to engage allies to contain China. In any case, for either a second Biden or new Trump presidency, the US will increasingly expect the EU to align its strategic industrial policy on China with that of the US, while demanding greater European contributions to military and security matters in Ukraine in order to free up US military resources for the Indo-Pacific.

Also with regard to policy themes of energy and climate change, international institutions and cooperation, and allies and alliances, it may be of great importance to the EU whether 2025 opens up for a second Biden or a second Trump administration. First, as of January 2021, the Biden administration has taken several steps in tackling the climate crisis including rejoining the Paris Agreement and adopting new ambitious goals for reducing US greenhouse gas emissions and achieving a net-zero economy by 2050. If re-elected, Biden will push for allies and partners to follow the US's lead on the IRA and subsidize the energy transition in their own countries or regions, transforming their economic model in favour of renewable generation and energy efficiency. Driven by its objective of domestic renewal to compete with China, climate friendly investments and technology competition will continue. In contrast, a new Trump administration will reintroduce a pro-fossil fuel policy. Among the tools at that president's disposal will be deregulation in favour of oil and gas, increased numbers of drilling permits, the dismantlement of the Environmental Protection Agency, and the provision of tax incentives for the oil and gas industries. Internationally, it is likely that this new Trump administration would ally with fossil fuel producers and promote fossil fuel exports with new partners in the Global South as well as the EU member states. Second, if re-elected, Biden would continue to work to shape the system of international organizations, diplomacy, and agreements, with the end goal being to reform but ultimately conserve it since Democrats view this as an opportunity for leverage. However, increased competition with China and the war in Ukraine continue to erode multilateral frameworks of cooperation, while the Global South has become increasingly transactional with the rapid transformation of the world order. In contrast, it is unlikely that a second Trump administration will allow itself to be influenced by agreements made by international organizations, but he will likely renew his deal-making ambitions focused more on negotiating new bilateral or regional agreements. Third, Biden believes in the value of allies and alliances in strengthening the US's position as a global leader. The US's strategic investments in its high-end and green technology industry (with its Chips Act and the IRA) have caused friction with the EU members who worry about the long-term consequences of the US gaining such a competitive advantage and skewing the rules of global trade in its favour. As the EU member states are losing economic and military ground to the US and the security situation in Europe worsens, the risk of becoming vasal states is growing. In contrast to Biden, Trump openly vilified traditional US alliances and cheered on the prospect of additional member states leaving the EU after Brexit. His scepticism views allies as free-riders on US security and established a consensus within the Republican Party base that NATO allies should pay up for their defence (Belin et al., 2023).

If a Biden administration is extended, it is more likely that the US and EU will cooperate more and thus pursue a more similar China policy than with a new Trump administration. If this comparison is applied to more economic classification described in Sect. 7.5 where China can be seen from the EU's perspective as a "cooperation partner", an "economic competitor", and a "systemic rival", then it is likely that under a Biden presidency China will be approached more as both a "cooperation partner" and an "economic competitor", while under a Trump presidency the emphasis is more likely to be on that of a "economic competitor" and a "systemic rival". However, a completely different reality emerges if the Biden-Trump presidency comparison is made more on the basis of geopolitical differences. In that respect, the US and the EU are much closer to each other in the Biden approach towards China than with a Trump presidency. It could therefore be more attractive from a geopolitical point of view for China in its relationship with the EU if Trump wins the US elections so that this gives Chinese policymakers more room to enter into a separate relationship with the EU and/or individual EU member states, independent from their relationship with the US.

References

AmCham EU. (2023, December 08). *EU-China: How to manage an increasingly challenging economic relationship.* https://www.amchameu.eu/blog/eu-china-how-manage-increasingly-challenging-economic-relationship

Belin, C., Ruge, M., & Shapiro, J. (2023, May). *Brace yourself: How the 2024 US presidential election could affect Europe.* European Council of Foreign Relations. https://ecfr.eu/wp-content/uploads/2023/05/Brace-yourself-How-the-2024-US-presidential-election-could-affect-Europe.pdf

Clingendael. (2022, August). *Sino-European joint ventures and the risk of technology transfers.* Clingendael Alert-Datenna. https://www.clingendael.org/sites/default/files/2022-08/CA_Datenna_0.pdf

EC European Commission. (2023, March 12). *EU-China – A strategic outlook.* https://commission.europa.eu/system/files/2019-03/communication-eu-china-a-strategic-outlook.pdf

EP European Parliament. (2023, March). *Global value chains potential synergies between external trade policy and internal economic initiatives to address the strategic dependencies of the EU.* https://www.europarl.europa.eu/RegData/etudes/STUD/2023/702582/EXPO_STU(2023)702582_EN.pdf

EP European Parliament. (2024, March). *EU-China relations: De-risking or de-coupling – The future of the EU-strategy towards China.* https://www.europarl.europa.eu/RegData/etudes/STUD/2024/754446/EXPO_STU(2024)754446_EN.pdf

Jacques Delors Institute. (2024, February). *Shield up: How China, Europe, Japan and the United States shape the world through economic security.* Policy paper number 298. https://institutdelors.eu/wp-content/uploads/2024/02/PP298_Comparing-_Economic_Security_Strategies_Fabry_Kohler-Suzuk_Lamy_Sibona_EN.pdf

Kirkegaard, J. F. (2023, December 01). *Europe's fear of dependence on China for critical minerals is overblown.* Peterson Institute for International Economics (PIIE). https://www.piie.com/blogs/realtime-economics/europes-fear-dependence-china-critical-minerals-overblown

Merics. (2024, January 04). *Expert debate on: What does it really mean for Europe to 'de-risk' its relationship with China?* https://merics.org/en/comment/expert-debate-what-does-it-really-mean-europe-de-risk-its-relationship-china

Schaus, M., & Lannoo, K. (2023, September 07). *The EU's aim to de-risk itself from China is risky… yet necessary.* CEPS. https://www.ceps.eu/the-eus-aim-to-de-risk-itself-from-china-is-risky-yet-necessary/

The Economist. (2024, February 20). *How scared is China of Donald Trump's return?* https://www.economist.com/china/2024/02/20/how-scared-is-china-of-donald-trumps-return

USCESRC US-China Economic and Security Review Commission. (2023, November). *Chapter 5: Changing relations with Europe, Taiwan, and Hong Kong, section 1: Europe-China relations: Convergence and divergence in transatlantic cooperation.* https://www.uscc.gov/sites/default/files/2023-11/Chapter_5_Section_1%2D%2DEurope-China_Relations.pdf

Wieringen, K. van. (2022, December). *EU-China 2030 European expert consultation on future relations with China.* European Parliament. https://www.europarl.europa.eu/RegData/etudes/STUD/2022/739240/EPRS_STU(2022)739240_EN.pdf

WTO. (2023, November). *Impacts of trade tensions and COVID-19 on global value chains.* https://www.wto.org/english/res_e/booksp_e/05_gvc23_ch2_dev_report_e.pdf

CHAPTER 8

Concluding Remarks and Some Recommendations: The Consequences of the EU's "de-risking" Strategy for the World Order

Abstract The US and the EU have benefited enormously in recent decades from the rise of China as a driving force in the global economy. It was rapidly transformed from a low-wage manufacturing to an advanced high-tech industrial country, spurred by initiatives such as "Made in China 2025", and its self-reliance-oriented "dual circulation" policy. China's more dominant role on the world stage initially spread its foreign policy and political values through "soft power" without the use of coercion, but in recent years increasingly through an assertive "hard power" approach which through its economic, technological, and military strength also has caused increasing global tensions. This change in the structure of China's more innovation- and high-tech services-oriented economy has intensified competition with the EU, especially in sectors crucial to the EU's green and digital transition. Now China has a comparable share of global GDP in this decade as the US and the EU and other emerging markets are following suit, there is a greater desire for a multipolar (Chinese-centric) world order. In such world countries refrain from interfering in the internal politics of other countries, the notion of "universal values" is viewed with scepticism and the hegemony of the Western-led order dominated by the US and its allies no longer applies and liberalism and democracy can no longer be taken for granted. The EU's "de-risking" approach in this context can also be seen as a response to the trend towards a more multipolar economic and security world order. It is a way to simultaneously find

R. W.H. van der Linden, P. Łasak, *Sino-EU Economic Relations*,
https://doi.org/10.1007/978-3-031-71814-4_8

a better balance between the transatlantic alliance with the US and cooperation with China, by seizing opportunities and managing risks through a "three-pronged approach" consisting of the pillars of protection, promotion, and partnering. In the coming years, it will therefore be a complex and delicate balancing act for EU policymakers to strike a skilful balance between being neither too defensive nor too offensive in addressing the dependencies, risks, and vulnerabilities in supply chains, without falling into too much protectionism and threatening the current world order.

Keywords "Soft power" versus "hard power" approach • China's industrial policy • "Made in China 2025" strategy • Middle-income trap • "Dual circulation" policy • "Self-reliance" in strategic sectors • Innovation-driven economy • "Civil-military fusion" • Risk mitigation approach • EU's three-pronged approach • Proactive common industrial policy • Multipolar world order • Strategic independence • Dual-use technologies • Global economic and security order • Multilateral organizations • EU-US-China triangle • Global Gateway strategy

The US and the EU have benefited enormously in recent decades from China's rise as a driving force in the global economy, both in terms of trade and investment. Initially, China's foreign policy and political values were mainly spread through "soft power" without the use of coercion, but in recent years China's more assertive "hard power" approach fuelled by its economic, technological, and military strength is also increasingly creating some geopolitical risks that have provoked global tensions. China has become one of the EU's most important trading partners, accounting for roughly 9 percent of EU exports and 20 percent of goods imports. The Sino-EU economies were once largely complementary, but have now transitioned to an era of more direct competition. Since 2010, China's industrial policy has transformed from supporting a model focused on low-wage manufacturing and heavy industry to one that focuses on high-tech industries and higher value-added manufacturing segments aimed at global leadership in the growing industries of the future. Since 2015, with the publication of its *"Made in China 2025"* strategy, China's policymakers have focused on improving its technological self-reliance and controlling ever-larger segments of value-added production chains for its strategic emerging industries such as telecommunications, energy and biotechnologies, advanced materials and robotics and more recently AI, advanced semiconductors and quantum computing technologies.

Similarly, new industries are important for the EU's energy and digital transitions towards a more sustainable future, but also one that continues to guarantee enough economic progress for its own citizens. The resulting more direct economic competition with China is a driving force behind the search for a common EU China policy, which is not an easy goal to achieve with 27 individual member states with varying Sino-relationships. The EU's concerns about its current relationship with China mainly relate to the trade and investment interdependencies and the market disruptions in a number of crucial sectors with a Chinese supply chain dominance ranging in solar photovoltaics, lithium-ion batteries, and electric vehicles that this has caused. In addition, the influence that such dependencies create for China and its willingness to use this influence as well as the broader ambitions of their leadership in the current geopolitical landscape have not been conducive to the recent Sino-EU relations. Compounding concerns over supply chain dependencies are the perceived vulnerabilities created by China's investments into critical infrastructure in Europe, from ports to critical mineral processing to undersea cables to all kinds of input that the EU needs in its efforts to achieve a carbon-free green transition at relatively low costs through its *"Green Deal"*. While China's industrial strategy is driven in part by a social and political imperative to escape the ***middle-income trap*** and ensure continued growth and prosperity for its people, it is also motivated by ambitions to change the world order from which it can more effectively exert its influence and pursue its geopolitical interests. From 2020 onwards, the *"dual circulation"* policy approach aims to achieve "self-reliance" in strategic sectors in order to reduce dependence on foreign technology, strengthen resilience, and reduce vulnerabilities. In line with this, China will increasingly focus on developing *domestic* value chains to fuel China's consumption and innovation-driven own economy, while stimulating higher value-added technology exports and capturing global market share. These recent developments, reinforced by a "civil-military fusion", are increasingly taking place in a political environment in which purely economic priorities are increasingly subordinated to those of national security. In addition, the geopolitical environment is increasingly characterized by territorial disputes and tensions between more democratically and more autocratically governed countries with differing visions of the future world order, making Sino-EU cooperation increasingly difficult (EP, 2024).

Since the Second World War, it can be argued that the US and its Western democratic allies have created the current world order and thus US hegemony, consisting of the United Nations and its numerous agencies, as well as institutions such as the World Bank, the IMF, and the WTO. While around 1995 the US global GDP share was still well above that of the other major advanced economic countries in the world, this is by no means the case in this decade, with China having a similar global GDP share to the US and EU-27 (see Fig. 2.1). The US-led unipolar multilateral and transatlantic world order has thus been steadily evaluated towards an inevitable new multipolar multilayered and culturally diversified world order translated into shifting global supply chains, which will make global governance much more complex and is by no means a guarantee for multilateralism (Geeraerts, 2011). In recent years, with varying degrees of success and without intervening, China has increasingly taken the initiative as a mediator in geopolitical conflicts such as those between Russia and Ukraine and between Hamas and Israel. This strategy, which can partly be seen as a response to the unconditional support for Israel in the past by the US and to a lesser extent by the EU, is attracting a growing number of countries to Beijing's dream of a new, multipolar Sino-centric world order in which the hegemony of the West no longer applies and liberalism and democracy are no longer self-evident. This Chinese "goodwill" strategy abroad claims not to interfere with other civilizations and other political systems (Table 8.1).

While quietly watching European and American societies become polarized over geopolitical conflicts, China is successfully pursuing its own ideal of a post-Western, multipolar world order. Beijing is aiming for a multipolar world order in which countries refrain from interfering in the internal politics of other countries in which the notion of "universal values" is viewed with scepticism, and where the US is just one of the players. In this new world order, democracy and liberalism are no longer a universal ideal, but only hold sway over certain parts of the world. The liberal world order will transform into a regional order. Autocratic forms of government will no longer be rejected out of hand, and the rules in this multipolar world order will mainly be set by China and its partners (Dams, 2024). For example, the Shanghai Cooperation Organization and BRICS are not based on liberal values and member states can have autocratic governments just as well as democratic ones. The reshaping of the new world order has translated into the expansion of BRICS+ from five to ten members since January 2024 including Egypt, Ethiopia, Iran, Saudi Arabia,

Table 8.1 Comparative analysis of a different world order from the EU and Chinese perspective

Criteria of the different world order	*EU perspective (democracy)*	*Chinese perspective (autocracy)*
The defining principles	"Rules-based approach" that is based on such principles as diplomacy, state sovereignty and territorial integrity, and non-interference in the international affairs of states.	The global governance system is understood as a new world order which justifies "unilateral sanctions" and "bloc confrontation".
The understanding of the multipolar world order	Greater EU autonomy could serve as a counterbalance to US dominance in global affairs, potentially leading to a more multipolar world order.	Multipolar Sino-centric world order in which the hegemony of the West no longer applies and liberalism and democracy are no longer self-evident. A multipolar world order in which countries refrain from interfering in the internal politics of other countries in which the notion of "universal values" is viewed with scepticism, and where the US is just one of the players. In this new world order, democracy and liberalism are no longer a universal ideal but only hold sway over certain parts of the world.
The way of behaviour	The approach is oriented towards limiting exposure to and dependence on China, maintaining a free and open Indo-Pacific region	The confrontational approach assumes repressive actions and tight control over some territories (Taiwan Strait, Hong Kong)
The axis of cooperation with other countries	The EU should deepen and expand its coordination with like-minded partners and its partnerships with the Global South not only to ensure the development of more resilient, diversified, and more independent supply chains but also to ensure that economic security policies will not lead to a new wave of protectionism and nationalism.	China's BRI strengthens the development of the world order or China's autocratic democracy-free model of development.

(*continued*)

Table 8.1 (continued)

Criteria of the different world order	*EU perspective (democracy)*	*Chinese perspective (autocracy)*
The understanding of the role of the opposite partner	The EU considers China in a more realistic, assertive, and multi-faceted approach when compared to the past.	China has increasingly come to view the EU as part of a hostile "Western" bloc with the US instead of an independent region.
The relation towards the opposite market	In the coming years, it will be a delicate balancing act for EU policymakers to find a skilful balance between being neither too defensive nor too offensive in addressing the dependencies, risks, and vulnerabilities in the supply chain without veering into protectionism.	The EU is primarily seen as an important region to support its economic development and other political and geostrategic goals, but also as a region that is increasingly resistant to Chinese policies. Maintaining and expanding the EU market is essential as the economy shifts to higher value-added production coinciding with a greater convergence with the US.
The approach to competition in business activity	The EU is the world's largest trader of industrial goods and services. The current approach involves diversifying supply chains, identifying alternative sources of goods and services, and implementing measures to reduce exposure to potential disruptions.	Originally relatively low-quality manufactured and consumer goods gradually changed from relatively low-value to higher-quality and technologically advanced products as part of the "Made in China 2025" strategy

Source: own elaboration

and the UAE. Together, these ten nations account for around 40 percent of both crude oil production and exports. They also account for one-quarter of global GDP, two-fifths of global trade in goods, and nearly half of the world's population. It is clear that BRICS+ can shift the world order in terms of energy (more opportunities to influence energy prices outside the Western-led financial system); trade networks (increasing intra-BRICS+ market access and circumventing Western sanctions related to Ukraine war); Infrastructure and development finance (e.g. New Development Bank (NDB), BRI, AIIB); Monetary policy (BRICS+ are keen to develop greater independence from the Western-led international monetary system, e.g. the NDB has issued about a fifth of its loans in RMB); technological cooperation (e.g. to improve their ability to create intellectual property and adopt alternative technical standards) (BCG, 2024).

Beijing is convinced that the US will succumb to the tension between the military, diplomatic, and moral responsibilities it has assumed in the world and the care for its own people. China is therefore not pursuing the same kind of hegemony that the US once enjoyed but has a different kind of agenda. Beijing wants to be a military superpower, especially in Southeast Asia, and to have economic influence in other parts of the world and to offer countries an alternative to the US. According to Xi, the liberal world order, which, especially in China, is very focused on a global economic and security order, is based on arrogant Western standards, such as democracy as the ideal political system. These values and standards were first imposed on many countries by the European colonial powers and subsequently, and often hard-handedly, by the Americans. Ultimately, after the Second World War, this mainly benefited the US and other rich capitalist and democratic countries, but in the current era, China, Russia, and other more autocratic countries like North Korea and Iran have the power to influence and shape that world order according to their own wishes. So it is not so much about throwing away the current world order, but about adapting it in a transition from a unipolar to a multipolar system (Dams, 2024).

In March 2023, the European Commission introduced a *"de-risking"* approach to protect the EU's strategic autonomy against risks in cooperation with China on supply chain resilience, national security, defense of political values, and sustainability issues and technological competitiveness. The EU's "de-risking" approach can also be seen in part as a response to the trend towards a more multipolar world order, with the US, China, and the EU27 having the largest global GDP shares in this decade. Unlike "decoupling" of economic ties in China-US relations, the China-EU "de-risking" strategy is a more nuanced and moderate concept of risk management intended as a way to achieve a better balance between the transatlantic alliance with the US on the one hand, and the cooperation with China on the other, by seizing opportunities and managing risks. The vast majority of economic interactions with China do not pose a security risk, and over-reacting to those that do exist could have profound consequences for European interests. For the Commission, a risk mitigation approach is an essential part of a broader economic security strategy aimed at strengthening European resilience and intended as a guideline in the complex journey towards a common EU-China policy. The economic security framework identifies four types of risks, namely (1) risks to the resilience of supply chains, including energy security; (2) risks to the physical security and cybersecurity of critical infrastructure; (3) risks related to technology security and technology leaks; and (4) the risk of weaponizing economic dependencies and economic coercion. A *three-pronged approach* addresses these risks through the pillars promotion, protection, and partnering. The first pillar promotes EU's competitiveness by strengthening the internal market, boosting innovation, strengthening technological and industrial capacities together with digital and green transitions. The second pillar protects economic security through a combination of new and existing tools and the third pillar addresses shared security concerns, diversification and improvement of trade agreements, strengthening of international rules and institutions and investing in sustainable development.

In recent years, the EU has increasingly faced dependencies and vulnerabilities in global supply chains, leading to an increased debate about the role of the state in the market and in particular the use of state aid to achieve strategic policy objectives. In contrast to China and recently the US under the Biden presidency, the European internal market is often built around a strong common competition policy with the necessary restrictions on state intervention. China's proactive state aid industrial policies have not only generated enormous amounts of waste and overcapacity, but have also helped strengthen the country's economic and technological position, putting the EU at a competitive disadvantage (EP, 2024). The European economic integration, on the other hand, has been incomplete over the past thirty years, meaning that the financial sector, energy companies, and telecommunications have always lasted under national control. As a result, the EU has remained fragmented in those areas, and little or no EU umbrella companies or sectors have been built up that cover the entire EU. Also, the high-speed train has been developed quickly and effectively, but has remained within national boundaries, except on the Paris-Brussels-Amsterdam route. Another shortcoming in EU integration is the large amount of state aid that some member states, such as France and Germany, give to their own industries instead of spending this on a more "pan-European" basis (Letta, 2024). For the EU, it is therefore essential in its pursuit of offensive risk reduction where individual member states pursue their own industrial policies to strike a balance between enhancing its competitiveness, maintaining European cohesion, controlling inequalities between and within EU member states and avoiding a broader turn to economic protectionism and nationalism. While the EU seeks to increase its resilience through a proactive common industrial policy (Fig. 3.2), it is also increasingly seeking to enhance its economic security and manage risks by developing a number of defensive instruments aimed at countering market distortions such as anti-subsidy and anti-dumping instruments intended to support global trade rules by promoting a level playing field and enforcing reciprocity. In addition, the EU is seeking to develop guidelines, toolkits, and policy coordination mechanisms aimed at insulating strategic and critical industries such as infrastructure from malign foreign influences, countering the weaponization of dependencies and preventing sensitive technological leakage or the unwanted transfer of technology from wind turbines and solar energy to high-speed rail and telecommunications. The third pillar of the EU's approach to de-risking and broader economic security is the deepening of relationships with "reliable partners" to address economic security concerns and more generally to bolster resilience through a diversification of supply chains which can be considered synonymous with EU's "de-risking" strategy. Ultimately, this idea of diversification of the EU's economic ties or "de-risking" is aimed at EU's pursuit of greater sovereignty or strategic autonomy from other countries in a variety of policy areas ranging from defense and foreign policy to economic affairs, and it also includes preserving and improving democratic values. Although there is a lack of consensus among member states on the exact nature of the EU's strategic autonomy, whether or not to transform as a major geopolitical power alongside the US and China, there is nevertheless a broad consensus that what matters is the EU's ability to manage its own dependencies and thus contribute to its long-term economic security. From China's perspective, the EU's pursuit of autonomy is interpreted as a challenge to Sino-EU relations aimed at the EU's geopolitical distance from the US in the areas of politics, security, values, and economics. The Chinese interpretation goes beyond such a view and also highlights the positive aspects of this autonomy. According to this approach greater EU autonomy could serve as a counterbalance to US dominance in global affairs, potentially leading to a more multipolar world order in which China's influence is more easily accepted. In its pursuit of greater strategic independence in line with some of China's global strategic interests, it therefore poses a complex challenge for European policymakers to balance its need for autonomy with the reality of existing transatlantic alliances and their geopolitical implications (EP, 2024).

Amid the escalating Sino-US strategic technology competition, there is a danger that the EU and its member states will become increasingly entangled, with US putting increasing pressure on its allies to join its China policy. An example of this is the contribution of advanced semiconductors from Western companies to China's military build-up, the flow of which the US has restricted as a security measure given Beijing's increasingly assertive political and military policies, especially towards Taiwan. Although the EU and its member states have taken similar measures to those of the US among the EU's dual-use export control regulations, this EU framework is more limited and less coherent with regard to economic security. While the EU's technology restrictions clearly distinguish between "purely" commercial and dual-use technologies, in contrast, China's military-civil integration and the central role that commercial technologies play in military development is becoming increasingly essential for its national economy and security in the battle for technological leadership. While many EU member states share US concerns about the security threat from China, coordination on this issue between both the EU and the US and between EU member states is too limited. Unlike the US, the common security policy towards China is too fragmented where the role of strategic commercial technologies and trade therein are not clearly related to European security. In this regard, it is not only essential that the EU rebalances its trade, investment, and security policies this decade, but a more robust European strategic technology doctrine will also need to be developed to enable better coordination between its member states. Given the complex challenges that the EU faces in the coming years, it is therefore essential that the EU develops its comprehensive geopolitical vision and consistent, coordinated, joint long-term strategy on the future of its relations with China with a possibly partly more matching, but partly also deviating world order. The ongoing Sino-US trade and tech war has put increasing pressure on the global economic and security order, increasingly calling into question the added role of multilateral organizations such as the WTO. In recent years, there has been an increasing mismatch between the way in which powerful states are using economic means to pursue geostrategic ends, and the institutions available to manage such competition safely. In this geopolitical environment, the EU must first formulate a common security policy and could form a mediating role as a countervailing power in the EU-US-China triangle, so that possible reforms of the WTO once again could gain added value in managing strategic competition between the trading blocs and settling their disputes (Gehrke & Ringhof, 2023).

While China has increasingly promoted its role in various perspectives on a new world order in recent years, the EU has been less successful in formulating and selling a competing vision, especially for the Global South, with the notable exception of the emerging *Global Gateway* strategy that is still in its infancy stage. The multipolar world order puts the informal and heterogeneous Global South in repeated opposition to the West on a broad range of issues and in demands for more influence, which will have wide consequences for global security, stability, economy, institutions, and norms. In the coming years, it will be a delicate balancing act for EU policymakers to find a skilful balance between being neither too defensive nor too offensive in addressing the dependencies, risks, and vulnerabilities in the supply chain without veering into protectionism and threatening the current world order. At the same time, the EU should deepen and expand its coordination with like-minded partners and its partnerships with the Global South not only to ensure the development of more resilient, diversified and more independent supply chains, but also to ensure that economic security policies will not lead to a new wave of protectionism and nationalism. The EU's Global Gateway development initiative with a balanced combination of feasible pragmatism and a sustainable approach can play an important role in this regard by not only supporting to diversify supply chains, but also responding effectively to local development needs and their stakeholder's interests. It is essential here that the EU will not promote the Global Gateway as a geopolitical response or competitor to China's BRI, but rather focus on implementing concrete projects that can draw lessons from the BRI's drawbacks of the past decade such as the creation of "sovereign debt traps" of its recipient countries (EP, 2024).

As part of the EU's three-pronged approach, it makes sense to increasingly invest in sustainable energy projects in partnerships with like-minded countries and those in the Global South. In recent years, it has become increasingly apparent that the EU has become overly dependent on China for the green technology needed to decarbonize its economy, risking Chinese dominance and military-civilian integration of production sources. An alternative solution to reduce this risk on a country-by-country basis may be to create a green technology partnership envisaged as a supplementary supply chain not intended to replace but to complement the existing China-centric supply chain, aimed at increasing both the scale and diversity of supply of renewable energy technologies. As there is a crucial dependence on China for all stages of the supply chain, from extraction, refining to production and even high-end innovation, a sustainable supplementary supply chain can provide a solution through a coordinated specialization based on comparative cost advantages in terms of production subsidies and carbon pricing of the participating partner countries. While it is now difficult to reach a multilateral Sino-US agreement and their allies in the current geopolitical environment, it is essential that the EU and its member states reach coordinated agreements with various partner countries to increase the production of green technology through "de-risking" decarbonization with the use of the comparative most cost-efficient technologies (Herrero et al., 2023).

References

BCG. (2024, April 29). *An evolving BRICS and the shifting world order*. https://www.bcg.com/publications/2024/brics-enlargement-and-shifting-world-order

Dams, T. (2024, February 27). *How China is pursuing a New World Order among the Geopolitical ruins*. Clingendael. https://www.clingendael.org/publication/how-china-pursuing-new-world-order-among-geopolitical-ruins

EP European Parliament. (2024, March). *EU-China relations: De-risking or de-coupling – The future of the EU-strategy towards China*. https://www.europarl.europa.eu/RegData/etudes/STUD/2024/754446/EXPO_STU(2024)754446_EN.pdf

Geeraerts, G. (2011, February). China, EU, and the new multipolarity. *European Review, 19*(1), 57–67. https://www.researchgate.net/publication/227391683_China_the_EU_and_the_New_Multipolarity

Gehrke, T., & Ringhof, J. (2023, May). *The power of control: How the EU can shape the new era of strategic export restrictions*. European Council on Foreign Relations. https://ecfr.eu/publication/the-power-of-control-how-the-eu-can-shape-the-new-era-of-strategic-export-restrictions/

Herrero, A. C., Grabbe, H., & Kaellenius, A. (2023, October). *De-risking and decarbonising: A green tech partnership to reduce reliance on China*. Policy brief issue Nr. 19/23, Breugel. https://www.bruegel.org/policy-brief/de-risking-and-decarbonising-green-tech-partnership-reduce-reliance-china

Letta, E. (2024, April). *Much more than a market: Speed, security, solidarity, empowering the single market to deliver a sustainable future and prosperity for all EU Citizens*. https://www.consilium.europa.eu/media/ny3j24sm/much-more-than-a-market-report-by-enrico-letta.pdf

Index[1]

[1] Note: Page numbers followed by 'n' refer to notes.

R. W.H. van der Linden, P. Łasak, *Sino-EU Economic Relations*, https://doi.org/10.1007/978-3-031-71814-4